The State of Sequoyah

The State of Sequoyah

Indigenous Sovereignty and the Quest for an Indian State

Donald L. Fixico

University of Oklahoma Press : Norman

Publication of this book is supported in part by the generous assistance of the Wallace C. Thompson Endowment Fund, University of Oklahoma Foundation.

Library of Congress Cataloging-in-Publication Data

Names: Fixico, Donald Lee, 1951– author.
Title: The State of Sequoyah : Indigenous sovereignty and the quest for an Indian state / Donald L. Fixico.
Description: Norman, Oklahoma : University of Oklahoma Press, [2024] | Includes bibliographical references and index. | Summary: "Relates how delegates from the Five Tribes of Indian Territory came to convene in 1905 to form their own, Indian-led state-to be named Sequoyah-why the U.S. Congress and president ultimately rejected their proposal and constitution, and the extent to which the idea remains alive today"—Provided by publisher.
Identifiers: LCCN 2024012352 | ISBN 978-0-8061-9463-9 (hardcover)
Subjects: LCSH: Five Civilized Tribes—History—20th century. | Indians of North America—Oklahoma—History—20th century. | Cherokee Indians—Oklahoma—History—20th century. | Chickasaw Indians—Oklahoma—History—20th century. | Choctaw Indians—Oklahoma—History—20th century. | Creek Indians—Oklahoma—History—20th century. | Seminole Indians—Oklahoma—History—20th century. | African Americans—Oklahoma—History—20th century. | BISAC: HISTORY / Indigenous Peoples in the Americas | HISTORY / African American & Black
Classification: LCC E78.I5 .F59 2024 | DDC 970.00497—dc23/eng/20240404
LC record available at https://lccn.loc.gov/2024012352

The paper in this book meets the guidelines for permanence and durability of the Committee on Production Guidelines for Book Longevity of the Council on Library Resources, Inc. ∞

To my Muscogee and Seminole relatives,

and to the principal chiefs

and all members of the

Cherokees, Chickasaws, Choctaws,

Muscogees, and Seminoles

Contents

Preface

At noontime on a cool mid-February day in 2023, my wife, Michelle, and I parked our small rental car in downtown Muskogee, Oklahoma, and began walking along the streets of the old historic district. Drawing from my research notes, we found the site of the old Turner Hotel and its annex, which were originally built by Charles Haskell at the corner of Court and North Third streets in early 1905. Several months later, the 143 then-modern rooms of the hotel housed the delegates who attended the Sequoyah Convention in the Hinton Theater across the street. Each light breeze that day evoked in my mind an excited delegate dashing across the street to argue for the founding of the state of Sequoyah. But today, the once magnificent five-story hotel and its annex are a parking lot, and the site where the impressive theater once stood is vacant. Although those two redbrick buildings are gone, the place is alive with history. Here was the climax of the once popular dream of the Indian state of Sequoyah.

Most people today have probably never heard of the state of Sequoyah movement. I spent my high school years in Muskogee and had never heard of it. The events that occurred at the empty spaces at Third and Court have nearly been forgotten, perhaps because the dream of an Indian state went unfulfilled. The stories we tell are usually about things that came to be, and the state of Sequoyah did not. Still, there is a story worth telling and remembering about the movement that led to the 1905 convention and how it inspired so many people to believe and work toward creating an Indian state.

This intriguing political movement began with the birth of Indian Territory, when the US government forcibly removed many Native nations to the

West, promising them self-governance through various treaties. Arguments for an Indian Territory independent of the United States soon followed, which eventually inspired a broader movement for an Indian state. The Five Tribes— the Muscogees (Creeks), Cherokees, Chickasaws, Choctaws, and Seminoles— were key players in this movement. After the Civil War, they worked toward common goals rather than just their own tribal interests. Politically stronger as a group, the Five Tribes worked together to organize a political alliance. American Indian nationalism, which depended on unity among the tribes, was forged from a rekindled struggle for Indigenous sovereignty, a fight that emanated from the ceremonial fires of each of the Five Nations.[1]

The following pages tell the story of extraordinary leaders, unexpected political alliances, and the cultural transformation of and transitions away from the Medicine Way tradition that formed a movement in support of a common cause. In the end, we learn how close we came to having a separate Indian state, and how the existence of that state is still possible today.

The first chapter explains why and where the Indian Territory was established. It describes how the Cherokees, Chickasaws, Choctaws, Muscogees, and Seminoles traditionally understood their sovereignties, culturally and politically. The enduring story of the removal of the Five Tribes from what is now the American Southeast is told through the process of rebuilding their nations in new reservation homelands.

Chapter 2 introduces the idea of an Indian state that began not with the Five Tribes but with the Delawares. This part of the book details how the idea for of an Indigenous state west of the Mississippi River came into being. It also explores the Confederacy's promise of statehood to the Five Tribes during the Civil War.

The third chapter describes how settlers pushed for opening Indian Territory to settlement and how several land-distribution schemes divided the original territory into Oklahoma Territory and Indian Territory. Eager white settlers called boomers wanted a state of their own. African Americans also settled in the Unappropriated Lands (also known as the Unassigned Lands) of Indian Territory after 1889 and started their own settlements.

Chapter 4 describes the days leading up to the Sequoyah Convention and the pageantry of the event itself, held in Muskogee on August 21, 1905. The chapter explains the inner activities of the convention and the contagious political excitement that it created. Nearly two hundred delegates gathered from the twenty-six districts in Indian Territory to vote overwhelmingly for the state of Sequoyah.

The fifth chapter details the congressional lobbying that sought to turn Oklahoma Territory into a state. The push for Oklahoma statehood detracted from and undermined the Sequoyah movement. The Enabling Act of 1906 merged Oklahoma and Indian territories into a single entity, which achieved statehood in 1907.

The last chapter begins with Edward McCabe, an African American, and his dream for a Black state in Indian Territory. These pages extend the story of how the idea of the state of Sequoyah continued well into the twentieth century. It describes how the Five Tribes continued to meet as the Intertribal Council of the Five Civilized Tribes.

The epilogue describes the 2020 Supreme Court decision *McGirt v. Oklahoma* and its relation to the proposed state of Sequoyah. The *McGirt* decision demonstrates how the issues and causes that drove the Sequoyah movement are as pressing today as they were in the early twentieth century.

Before detailing the Sequoyah movement further, it is important to know what constitutes a territory or state. Under the US Constitution, Congress can make a territory into a state by law at any time. Before that can occur, a territory votes in a referendum to have a constitutional convention, in which delegates work together to write a constitution for their proposed state to be presented to Congress for approval. Usually, Congress requests some changes to be made or rejects the constitution. For example, Utah requested statehood eight times before achieving its goal. The final step involves a memorial signed by the US president, which officially converts a territory into a state. One caveat is that a new state cannot be created from the territory of other states without their consent. All procedures are explained under Article IV, Section 3, of the US Constitution.

Indian Territory almost became a state, but it could have also been a commonwealth, republic, nation, or nation-state. These are western terms of governmental structures. *The Blackwell Dictionary of Political Science* offers useful definitions of these terms, and the following discussion draws its terminology from that reference work. Indian Territory likely could not have become a "commonwealth" because commonwealths are usually former territories of Great Britain like Australia and Canada.[2] Conceptually a "republic" is a purely democratic form of government. Indian Territory could have become

a republic like the United States, which is a confederation of state governments. According to the *Blackwell Dictionary,* "Today to say that a country is
a republic means that it is not a monarchy: its HEAD of STATE is a president
and not a hereditary monarch."[3] The same argument can be made for Indian
Territory becoming a "nation," defined as "a body of people who possess the
consciousness of a common identity, giving them a distinctiveness from other
peoples."[4] But this would have put it outside federal control, allowing it to
have its own sovereignty in a collective sense, which is what the Five Tribes
wanted. "Nation-state" was a possibility, but Indian Territory as a state would
have had to stand alone.

Some Indians wanted Indian Territory to have its own sovereignty, but
others wanted it to become a territory that eventually could turn into a state,
like other US territories had done. A state is "a complex concept used in at
least three contexts—philosophical, legal, and political. These areas are inter-
related, both historically and within the wider social framework."[5] Within
this framework, each of the Five Tribes possessed "sovereignty," which accords
"complete independence in the international context" and allowed each "to
maintain its integrity by ensuring that its frontiers and its nationals were
respected by other states."[6] The sixty-eight treaties the Five Nations agreed
upon with the United States demonstrates their sovereignty.

Beyond the legal issues, which became increasingly relevant to the Five
Tribes during the nineteenth century, individual leaders played a vital role.
These individuals imagined a need for change, while exercising leadership and
applied critical decision-making in dealing within the political, cultural, and
racial dynamics of the nineteenth century. In considering the process of territorial transition to statehood and the making of nation-states, we normally
think of territories that became official states, but according to whose government, which definition of a state, and what understanding of statehood? I
would argue here that local and regional areas manifest cultural and political
interests and form identities. For example, I once lived briefly in South Bend,
Indiana, and then for six years in a hamlet called Cassopolis in southwestern
Michigan, which was so tiny when I lived there it did not even have a McDon-
alds. By living in both places, I was able to experience firsthand how northern
Indiana and southwestern Michigan merged into a distinct region with common interests, friendships, and weather. Despite the lack of an official designa-
tion, I lived in "Michiana." This in-between place had an identity.

The populace of such areas develops distinct identities, and there are numerous examples of such communities that cross political boundaries and are not defined by them. These include rural areas like Appalachia, international border towns like El Paso–Ciudad Juárez, and the vast urban sprawl of Southern California. Each of these examples have "common ground." The communities develop over time; people live there for at least two or three generations, practicing common values, and their local worldview forms separately from the rest of the state or region. These common characteristics developed in the eastern half of the Indian Territory during the 1800s. They evolved through shared experiences, including Indian removal, the Civil War, and Dawes Act land allotments.

The Muscogees, Seminoles, Cherokees, Choctaws, and Chickasaws did not start out as nations or nation-states like those of Europe. Outsiders unfamiliar with the cultural infrastructures of the Five Tribes tend to view them vis-à-vis states that formed the United States. Within their Native realities, town communities originally clustered as alliances, or groups of towns, with their own distinct identities. Inherent sovereignty existed within each town group, and the town community was more important politically than the collective identity that became known as the Cherokee tribe, Muscogee tribe, and so forth. During the mid-nineteenth century, after removal to Indian Territory, all five groups made remarkable adaptations, reorienting themselves as political entities analogous to US states. They retained matrilineal infrastructures culturally, but politically they functioned as patriarchal political systems like US states. It is remarkable that the Five Tribes embodied matriarchal and patriarchal traits simultaneously. Ultimately, their collective desire was to become the state of Sequoyah, and they voted for statehood at their constitutional convention in 1905.

Even though the state of Sequoyah did not come to fruition, the movement surrounding it lived on. The story is complex and includes the Medicine Way, colonization, Manifest Destiny, Native identities and their reinvention, changing Indian worldviews, race relations, modernity, intertribal politics, and the power struggle in Indian-white relations. It is also about a dream, a vision, disappointment, and a renewal of hope.

Tempe, Arizona
January 2024

Acknowledgments

I am grateful to many people who have helped me with this book and have supported my work. I thank President Michael Crow and the Arizona Board of Regents for the Regents' Professorship that I hold at Arizona State University (ASU). I also appreciate the Distinguished Foundation Professorship that supports my research, and I am also grateful for the Distinguished Scholar title bestowed by the Wrigley School of Sustainability at ASU. I am appreciative of the support from ASU provost Nancy Gonzales, College of Liberal Arts and Sciences dean Patrick Kenney, Humanities dean Jeffrey Cohen, and School of Historical, Philosophical and Religious Studies (SHPRS) director Richard Amesbury. I also grateful for the work of the SHPRS staff who make my faculty duties much easier, including Becky Tsang, Marissa Timmerman, Yvonne Delgado, Teri Houston, and others as well as the school's student assistants. I am extremely grateful for my research assistant, Erica Price, who excels at tracking down research requests with prompt speed.

Traveling to Oklahoma for research has been a joyful way both to find new materials and to visit friends and relatives. I am grateful to the staff at the Oklahoma History Center in Oklahoma City and especially to Dr. Bob Blackburn, who retired in December 2020. At the Oklahoma Historical Society, I would like to thank Trait Thompson, the executive director; Chad Williams, director of the Research Division; Laura Martin, deputy director of the Research Division; Mallory Covington, manager of the Archival Collections; Sarah Biller; Carol Jasak; Melony Keeler; Rachel Mosman; Veronica Redding; Felicia Vaughan; and R. J. Wilkins. At the Okmulgee Public Library,

I appreciate the assistance of Amanda Hunt, who helped me with finding a source for the early history of the city. I am very grateful to the staff at the Western History Collections at the University of Oklahoma, especially Curator Todd Fuller and Assistant Curator Lina Ortega. I am grateful for the help from Blain McLain, archives assistant in Special Collections at the Vaughan Library at Northeastern State University in Tahlequah. I also appreciate the help of Jana Gowan, the reference and outreach librarian at the Helmerich Center for American Research at the Gilcrease Museum in Tulsa and also for the assistance that I received from Interim Director Melissa Kunz, Special Collections librarian Renee Harvey, Special Collections paraprofessional Milissa Burkart, and Abigail Dairagni at the McFarlin Library at Tulsa University.

In writing the last chapter, I sought the advice and suggestions from experts in other fields. I am grateful for recommendations and assistance from two friends in Melbourne, Australia, Claudia Haake (La Trobe University) and Bain Attwood (Monash University). Among my own colleagues at ASU, I appreciate the guidance from a pair of political scientists, Associate Dean Miki Kittilson and Jennett Kirkpatrick in the College of Global Futures. At the University of Oklahoma Press, I am grateful to Steven Baker, Alessandra Jacobi Tamulevich, and the rest of the staff, who made my manuscript pages into this book. I am also grateful for the comments and suggestions from the two outside readers who reviewed the manuscript with positive comments. In the last stages of the book, I appreciate the insightful suggestions, recommendations, and edits from Alice Stanton and Ryan Schumacher. Thanks also to Tom Jonas for making the maps.

I am appreciative to Frank and Linda Alexander. Frank is my oldest living relative, and I am grateful to my cousins, Angie Butler and Judy Proctor, as well as my late cousin, Barney Mitchell, who passed away just before Christmas Eve in 2019.

As always, I am grateful to Keytha Fixico, who wants to know more about our people, the Muscogees. I also appreciate the company of Josie the cat, who holds down the end of the sofa in my study and keeps it warm. Most importantly, I appreciate the help and support of the best researcher that I know, my wife, Dr. Michelle Martin, who is on the history faculty at Northeastern State University at Tahlequah. We have enjoyed many conversations about Indian Territory and the politics of the past in Oklahoma, which inspired me to keep working on this book. Last of all, I am grateful for my parents, John and Virginia Fixico, who are now gone, and to all my Muscogee and Seminole, Shawnee, and Sac and Fox ancestors, who lived in the Indian Territory when the dream of state of Sequoyah was alive, and to my grandparents, Lena Spencer Fixico, Jonas Fixico, Rachel Wakolee Mack, and Glade Wakolee.

Chronology

1862   Homestead Act. Surveyed areas of 160 acres are opened to settlers, who gained ownership after five years if improvements were made on the land.

1866   Four Treaties of 1866 affecting the Cherokees, Muscogees, Seminoles, Choctaws, and Chickasaws together, which redefined previous reservation boundaries to present boundaries.

1870   Congress fails to ratify Okmulgee Constitution, which would have formed a government for Indian Territory.

1887   Dawes Act starts allotment of tribal lands, except for Five Tribes.

1890   On May 2 the Organic Act creates Oklahoma Territory and Indian Territory.

1890   The Springer Amendment to the Indian Appropriations Act of 1890 places Unassigned Lands in Indian Territory to public domain for settlers.

1898   Curtis Act dissolves Five Tribes' governments and begins allotment for Five Tribes.

1898   On June 28 the Atoka Agreement calls for allotting Choctaw and Chickasaw lands, after the ending of their governments on March 4, 1906.

1905   On August 21 the state of Sequoyah Convention is held in Muskogee and delegates draft a constitution.

1906   On January 24 Congress rejects the bill that would have created the state of Sequoyah in favor of joint statehood with Oklahoma Territory.

On June 16, the Oklahoma Enabling Act merges Oklahoma Territory and Indian Territory into a single entity and allows for the drafting of a state constitution.

1907   November 16, Oklahoma becomes a state.

Prologue

The morning of August 21, 1905, finally arrived in Indian Territory. It was hot and humid, but the stifling air did not dampen the excitement in downtown Muskogee, where a large convention was about to take place. Monday was the busiest day of the week, when storekeepers eagerly opened their doors hoping for customers to buy their goods. With its growing population of more than 5,000 people, Muskogee was the largest and most prosperous town in Indian Territory. Established in January 1872 as a stop for fuel and water for the Missouri, Kansas and Texas Railroad (commonly called the Katy), downtown Muskogee survived and rebuilt after three fires, in 1887, 1894, and 1899. On the western edge of Muskogee, the Union Agency stood above the town on Agency Hill and oversaw the affairs of the Cherokees, Muscogees, Seminoles, Choctaws, and Chickasaws.

Most of the delegates had already checked into the new Turner Hotel at Third and Court streets. The day before, they had departed from their homes in all twenty-six districts of the territory. Jostling for seats in crowded train cars, they arrived in Muskogee, the seat of government for Indian Territory. Charles Haskell, a leading businessman and promoter of the state of Sequoyah movement, had recently completed building the Turner earlier in the year. Rumor had it that the convention was Haskell's idea. Haskell saw Muskogee for the first time in 1901, and he was thrilled with the opportunities that the bustling town offered. He named the ultramodern hotel after one of his best friends, Clarence Turner, a local businessman.

The delegates enjoyed the splendor of the five-story redbrick palace. The towering structure featured tall windows to maximize ventilation and boasted 143 rooms. Each room had its own telephone, which the delegates used to make sure that their part of Indian Territory was well represented. A magnificent entryway on the east side of the hotel was easily accessible to cable cars, which were extra busy for the next few days.

The present delegates gathered in bunches and walked across the street to gather at the Hinton Theater by 11:00 a.m. The theater, with its stylish architecture, was three stories tall. A gable roof made the theater look even taller as it welcomed guests to this historic event. The Hinton had opened with its first play only four months earlier.

Journalists eavesdropped on numerous conversations with pen and pad in hand. Newspapers near and far sent their reporters to bring back any news—scandalous or otherwise—about one of the most significant events yet in the history of the Indian Territory: the constitutional convention for the state of Sequoyah. Eager representatives of the territory's tribes rushed to complete their conversations before the opening of the convention. Nearly two-hundred Natives, along with whites, mixed bloods, and several freedmen, would meet for an entire week to strategize about the possibilities of an Indian state joining the United States of America.

ONE

The Birth of Indian Territory

He bent down to look into the soft brown eyes of his six-year-old daughter, Akoyen. He whispered to her to take the paper and pencil to the small group of Cherokees standing at a distance. The mixed-blood Cherokee stood up and leaned on his staff as he watched his daughter walk toward the group. The father was born with one leg just a bit shorter than the other. His limp always caught the attention of people who did not know him. But those who did know him called him Sequoyah. His name meant "hog or opossum within an enclosed space." He was also known as George Guess (or Gist), and he was of the Red Paint Clan, an affiliation inherited from his mother, Wut-teh. By blood Sequoyah was at least half Cherokee, but it was hard to know for sure due to his uncertain paternal lineage. His father was likely a German peddler from Georgia, although he may have been a half-blood Cherokee, as the *Cherokee Phoenix* reported in 1828.[1]

Akoyen walked back to her father with the paper, which she had written on. Handing it to him, she smiled, and a gleam sparkled in her brown eyes. The small gathering of Cherokees watched with curiosity. Then, Sequoyah proceeded to go down the list, reading aloud the things that each person said to Akoyen.[2] They were aghast! Was this magic? How had Sequoyah captured the white man's trickery and drawn spoken words?

Born about 1770, Sequoyah grew up in a Cherokee town called Tuskegee, in present-day Georgia, where his maternal family lived. His mother and her relatives raised her curious son, taught him how to farm, and introduced him to the trading business. As a young man, Sequoyah preferred the work of blacksmithing and silversmithing, and he created silver bracelets, rings, and other jewelry. After completing chores on his farm, he helped his mother run a small trade store. Sequoyah could not read or write English, but at the store he watched white men reading newspapers and sometimes books. The words on paper reminded him of talking leaves. In 1815, Sequoyah married Sally Waters, a Cherokee of the Bird Clan. Three or four years later, Sequoyah began an unfathomable task: translating the Cherokee language into a written form. At first Sequoyah drew a symbol for every Cherokee word. But after creating hundreds of signs and becoming frustrated, he tried something else.[3] Legend has it that his wife became so angry with him for abandoning his farm chores that she burned the pages of his experiment. After more than two years of tedious work, Sequoyah succeeded in 1821 in creating a Cherokee syllabary: talking leaves of eighty-six symbols, each of which represented a sound in the Cherokee language.

Like scattering quails, news about Sequoyah's feat spread throughout nearby towns. Some people spurned Sequoyah, believing he dealt with witchcraft. But others welcomed his visits. Sequoyah would travel to Cherokee towns to teach the written language, even trekking several hundred miles to the new homeland in the Indian Territory. He even ventured to Mexico, where some Cherokees had migrated, instructing his people there how to read and write their language. Within several years the Cherokee Nation, which included more than 20,000 people, became literate in their language.[4]

When Sequoyah was born, the Cherokees lived in the Old South, spread across present-day Alabama, Georgia, Tennessee, and North Carolina. Their culture was similar to four other peoples. The Indigenous nations of the Muscogees, Seminoles, Chickasaws, Choctaws, and Cherokees were called the "Five Civilized Tribes" by white settlers. Their local economies largely consisted of growing corn, beans, squash, melons, and other foods. These five sedentary groups, nowadays more commonly called the "Five Tribes," were not actually tribes, but consisted of town-like communities whose peoples spoke Choctaw, Chickasaw, Muscogee, or Cherokee, which were all part of the Muskogean language family, except for Cherokee. Cherokee was part of the Iroquoian family, which also included the languages spoken by the Mohawks, Oneidas, Cayugas, Onondagas, and Senecas.

Town-like communities formed the heart of the Five Tribes. Each one represented an autonomous nation-state allied with others in loose associations called the Choctaws, Chickasaws, Muscogees, Seminoles, and Cherokees. By custom every town-like community gathered once a year to take medicine to purify themselves. They danced at the annual Green Corn Ceremony in mid-summer to celebrate the harvesting of corn crops. This was the Medicine Way. Corn was believed to be a special gift from a much greater power than humans. The Cherokees told a legend of Selu, the first woman, who introduced corn to her people so that they would never starve.[5]

The Cherokees, with a population of about 24,000, called their towns *etowahs.* James Adair, an early traveler among the Cherokee, listed the number of their towns and villages as totaling sixty-four, which together hosted about 6,000 warriors.[6] Out of an original thirty-three, the Cherokees had seven clans, the Wolf, Deer, Bird, Red Paint, Blue (or Panther), Long Hair, and Wild Potato.[7] The Muscogees and Seminoles lived in town-like communities called *tvlofvs,* although these units encompassed a broader sense of belonging than the word "town" implies. They dwelled in either a red *tvlofv,* a war town, or a white *tvlofv,* a peace town. Each *tvlofv* had a ceremonial fire known as a *totkv etkv.* In common with the Cherokees, Choctaws, and Chickasaws, Muscogees and Seminoles were matrilineal societies. Everyone in the Five Tribes belonged to a clan inherited from their mother and an extended family that usually included grandparents or other relatives. Everyone had a place around the fire in the middle of their community.[8]

The Muscogees were divided into two subgroups. The *tvlofvs* of the Upper Muscogees rested along the Coosa, Tallapoosa, and Chattahoochee rivers. The Lower Muscogees lived in *tvlofvs* established along the Flint River. Altogether, both Muscogee groups resided in sixty to ninety riverine *tvlofvs* in present-day Alabama and Georgia.[9]

The Seminoles practiced the same Muscogee tradition of *tvlofv* communities in what became the Florida Panhandle and the central part of that state. During the mid-1700s, the number of Seminole towns rose to about two dozen. They consisted of a mixture of Muscogee Seminoles and Miccosukee Seminoles and were divided into nine major clans. These clans were called Panther, Otter, Wildcat, Wolf, Bear, Deer, Big Towns, Bird, Snake, and Wind.[10]

By 1730 the Choctaws had divided into eastern and western halves, which also consisted of red and white towns. In the east, the Choctaws lived in twenty-eight towns. To the west, the Choctaws resided in twenty-one towns.[11] The Choctaws had chiefdoms at three levels. A middle chiefdom of up to several towns exuded more authority than a lower one. The highest chiefdom consisted of many towns and possessed the most power among the Choctaw people.[12] The Choctaws clans included Wind, Bear, Deer, Wolf, Panther, Holly Leaf, Bird, Raccoon, and Crawfish.[13]

Like the Muscogees and Choctaws, the Chickasaws had red and white towns. The Chickasaws and Choctaws called each town an *iska*. The civil *iskas* produced the peace and medicine leaders.[14] The towns of the Chickasaws were located in one of three areas referred to as "old fields." As early as 1702, according to one report, seven towns were in one old field, a single town in another, and ten towns in the third. In total, the old fields contained eighteen Chickasaw towns.[15] The clans of the Chickasaws were Minko (chief clan), Spanish, Raccoon, Panther, Wildcat, Fish, Deer, Bird, Skunk, Squirrel, Alligator, Wolf, Blackbird, Fox (or Red Fox), and Haloba (meaning eagle or buffalo).[16]

Put together, the homelands of the Five Tribes covered roughly 325,000 square miles. After 1830 they would be forced to leave for new lands in the West. Since the mid-eighteenth century, an ever-increasing number of white settlers sought new homes west of the Appalachians and in the South, some within the homelands of the Five Tribes. Conflict followed, with settlers convinced that Indians stood in the way of progress. With the establishment of a new nation, the United States, after the Revolutionary War, came aggressive expansion. Starting with Delaware in 1787, new states from the North, South, and West joined the federation on a regular basis. Even though many Native groups adopted Euro American cultural practices, many white settlers and their leaders believed that the United States and Indigenous nations could not coexist in the same space, and the idea of an Indian territory somewhere west of the Mississippi River was born.

As early as 1796, President George Washington introduced a program meant to "civilize" the Cherokees.[17] Cherokee horticulture had impressed Washington, but he wanted them to become permanent farmers. Four years later, the Moravians established their first mission among the Cherokees. The Moravians believed there was no difference between race or gender, that everyone was spiritually equal. This did not mean that they considered traditional Cherokee religion to be equivalent to Christianity. In 1804 the Moravians opened a school to displace traditional Cherokee beliefs.

Realizing the increasing threat to their homelands, some Cherokees migrated westward in 1808 and 1810 to live along the Arkansas River. These people became the Old Settler or Arkansas Cherokees, and they fought the Osages, who asserted their claim to the region with military strength. Fighting between the Osages and newcomers compelled Secretary of War William Crawford to order the army to build a fort in the area. The fort, which also served as an outpost for fur trading, was named after General Thomas Adams Smith, and a town emerged nearby.[18]

The fort and a peace treaty in 1818 did not stop the fighting between the Cherokees and the Osages. Further bloodshed between Cherokees and Osages led to establishing a second outpost, Fort Gibson, in 1824 under the command of Colonel Matthew Arbuckle.[19] Starting as a cantonment named after Colonel George Gibson, whom Arbuckle admired, Fort Gibson became the oldest white settlement in what would become Indian Territory.

As more settlers pushed west, Congress formed Arkansas Territory on March 2, 1819. Indian attacks continued. New settlers survived raids by the Osages, Wichitas, and other Native groups. Among them was a thirty-year old Tennessee farmer and former US Navy ensign named Henry Wharton Conway, who arrived with ambitions to build a homestead and perhaps enter politics. Impressed by young Conway, the settlers of the new Arkansas Territory elected him in 1822 to be a territorial delegate to Congress. In 1824 Conway presented a resolution in Congress categorizing "the land west of Missouri, Arkansas, and Michigan" as Indian Territory. Whereas "Indian Country" had been loosely used up to this point to describe areas where Native peoples predominately lived, Conway introduced the term, "Indian Territory" to designate more specifically the location of Indian lands.[20]

The creation of Missouri Territory in 1812 and the development of Arkansas Territory established the eastern boundary of the vaguely marked Indian Territory. The southern boundary was not firmly marked until Texas joined the United States in 1845. The northern boundary was similarly sketchy, but it broadly included the western boundaries of Iowa and Minnesota. Everything seemed uncertain. But immense pressure from westward expansion forced some shape onto Indian Territory. Homesteaders poured onto the prairies and plains to grow wheat and corn, and they also hunted wild game.

More westward settlers meant more misunderstandings and violence between Indians and whites. Some Natives, such as the Old Settler Cherokees, had decided on their own to move westward. These Cherokee pioneers established a capital in 1813 at Tahlonteeskee, close to the source of the

Illinois River in what is now Arkansas, and within twenty years their population had grown to 5,800.[21] By 1828 the Old Settler Cherokees traded their lands in Arkansas for an area that would become northeast Indian Territory in present-day northeastern Oklahoma, which stretched fifty-seven-miles to the hundredth meridian.[22] The Old Settlers would not be the only Cherokees who felt compelled to move west.

After Georgia achieved statehood in 1788, officials there illegally asserted sovereignty over the Cherokee Nation. In 1819 the Cherokees ceded part of their territory in exchange for western lands. Not long before, Cherokees in North Carolina received reserves in treaties signed with the US government in 1817 and 1819.[23] Sequoyah was among those who signed the agreement in 1817, but he later changed his mind about moving west. He still lost his home, and moved to Willstown, also known as Fort Payne, in Alabama. Three years later, the Muscogees ceded their last lands in Georgia. Still, the Cherokees pushed back. The Cherokees established a supreme court in 1822. In 1827 the Cherokees wrote a constitution in Sequoyah's syllabary asserting their sovereignty and formalized legislative, executive, and judicial branches for a national government. With the success of Sequoyah's work, a year later the *Cherokee Phoenix* became the first American Indian newspaper when it was published in New Echota, Georgia. Intent on teaching his syllabary to as many Cherokees as possible, Sequoyah moved near a new settlement called Sallisaw in Indian Territory.

In 1828, white men cast 638,348 votes in favor of Andrew Jackson, a Democrat, electing him as president of the United States over John Quincy Adams, a National Republican. Advocating Indian removal, the president wrote a letter to the Muscogees arguing that their westward migration was to their well-being. He penned, "beyond the great river Mississippi . . . There your white brothers will not trouble you; they will have no claim to the land, and you can live upon it, you and all your children, as long as the grass grows or the waters run, in peace and plenty . . . In that country, your father the President, now promises to protect you, to feed you, and to shield you from all encroachment."[24] Jackson's promise would prove hollow; the tide of settlers could not be slowed down.

In October 1828, the Cherokees elected John Ross as their principal chief. The Cherokees found themselves in a web of tension as they moved toward a more centralized government. Ross had been born at Turkeytown, a Cherokee town in present-day Alabama, in 1790. His father was Scottish and his mother was a Cherokee-Scottish mixed blood. Ross was raised in the Cherokee tradition; yet, his parents' cabin home brimmed with books, and his mother and father also wanted him to be educated in the "white man's way." His given Cherokee name was Guwiguwi, translated as "mysterious little white bird." John Ross was one-eighth Cherokee, and although he spoke both Cherokee and English, his brown hair, blue eyes, and light skin made him look more white than Cherokee.[25]

Daniel and Mary McDonald Ross sent their beloved son away for formal education, and afterward, in 1811, he received an appointment as an Indian agent for the US Army. When the War of 1812 broke out, John Ross became an adjutant of a Cherokee regiment under General Andrew Jackson. After the war John Ross returned to Tennessee, where he obtained some land to build a tobacco plantation.[26] Within a couple of years, hard work yielded a warehouse, and Ross established a trading post on the Tennessee River with a ferry service. The fact that John Ross knew Andrew Jackson would help the mixed blood to represent his people in meetings with "Old Hickory," as the general was known, after the war hero became president. Although Ross seemed more white than Indian, Cherokee traditionalists put their full confidence in the "mysterious little white bird." Their new leader was bilingual and bicultural; yet, he always respected the Medicine Way of his people, and he was one of them. Ross would serve as the Cherokees' leader until he died at the age of seventy-five.

The year 1828 would prove memorable even beyond the elections of Jackson and Ross. A deer hunter on Cherokee lands near Dahlonega, Georgia, stumbled over a rock, revealing gold on the underside. News of the hunter's discovery spread quickly, and soon 4,000 to 5,000 miners, dubbed "Twenty-Niners," began swarming the area.[27] The gold rush increased the number of settlers encroaching on Cherokee homelands and brought new calls for removing Indians from the East to somewhere west of the Mississippi River. In response to the gold seekers and removal rhetoric, the Cherokee National Council passed a law in 1829 calling for the execution of any Cherokee who signed a treaty to cede tribal land.[28]

The question of how to remove the Cherokees led to lengthy debates in Congress. In 1830, both houses in Congress made the motions to vote on the Indian Removal Act, introduced by Senator Hugh White, a member of the

Committee on Indian Affairs. Often called "the Cato of the Senate" after the conservative senator of the Roman Republic, the fifty-seven-year-old White was a slave owner. He was also the chair of the Committee on Indian Affairs and initially supported Jackson's Indian removal plan, although he chastised the president for overstepping his authority.[29]

For several days in May 1830, members of the House of Representatives heavily debated the bill. A final vote tallied 102 to 97 in favor of the bill. Further Senate discussions added amendments to the measure. On May 26, the Senate voted 28 to 19 to pass. Two days later, President Jackson signed the Indian Removal Act into law. The Senate had added an amendment for a $500,000 appropriation. The money was intended to purchase new lands and pay expenses for the removal of Native groups to the Indian Territory. The landmark act stated:

> Be it enacted by the Senate and House of Representatives of the United States of America, in Congress assembled, That it shall and may be lawful for the President of the United States to cause so much of any territory belonging to the United States, west of the river Mississippi, not included in any state or organized territory, and to which the Indian title has been extinguished, as he may judge necessary, to be divided into a suitable number of districts, for the reception of such tribes or nations of Indians as may choose to exchange the lands where they now reside, and remove there.[30]

The passage of the Indian Removal Act came as the Cherokees were dealing with provocative actions by the state of Georgia. Georgia tried disempowering the Cherokees by passing state laws, which included a provision that they could not legally own land within the nearly 60,000 square miles that the state claimed. Governor George Gilmer privately confessed that the laws were intended to frustrate the Cherokees so much that they would stop their resistance and leave.[31]

In contrast to the aggressive approach of Georgia's governor and others, some members of Congress stood against the forced removal of the Cherokees and other tribes. In late spring 1830, near the time of the passage of the Indian Removal Act, Senators Daniel Webster of New Hampshire and Theodore Frelinghuysen of New Jersey convinced Cherokee leader John Ross to challenge Georgia in federal court and take his case to the US Supreme Court, if necessary. William Wirt, a gifted lawyer with a strong legal mind who had served as attorney general in the administrations of James Monroe and John Quincy Adams, represented the Cherokees. Tough as nails, Wirt's broad forehead, hawklike nose, and hunter's eyes gave him the look of a predator.

In the 1831 case *Cherokee Nation v. Georgia,* Wirt argued before the Supreme Court that the Cherokees were "a foreign nation in the sense of our constitution and law," which exempted them from Georgia's laws. Pointing to the fourteen treaties signed between the United States and the Cherokees by 1830, Wirt asserted that the state of Georgia had acted illegally. In a split decision of five to two, the Supreme Court ruled against Wirt and the Cherokees based on Article III, Section 2, of the US Constitution, which had been revised by the Eleventh Amendment on February 7, 1793: "The Judicial power of the United States shall not be construed to extend to any suit in law or equity, commenced or prosecuted against one of the United States by Citizens of another State or by Citizens or Subjects of any Foreign State."[32] In his majority opinion, Marshall claimed the Founding Fathers wrote the Constitution without taking into consideration the status of Indian tribes as nations equivalent to the United States. Marshall wrote that the Cherokees resembled a "domestic dependent nation," and therefore did not possess the authority to sue Georgia as a "foreign" nation. He also described the US relationship with the Cherokees as resembling that of a guardian to ward.[33]

The justices sided with Georgia in *Cherokee Nation v. Georgia* based on the majority's view of the governing infrastructure of the Cherokees. In their opinion, the Cherokees did not represent a national government, although the very name of the court case was *Cherokee Nation v. Georgia,* which indicated otherwise. Because Cherokee towns united in a loose system without a national government, one justice opined that the tribes were "nothing more than wandering hordes, held together only by ties of blood and habit, and having neither rules nor government beyond what is required in a savage state."[34]

During the following year, in 1832, a second case relating to the Cherokees and Georgia went to the Supreme Court. The case involved eleven missionaries working among the Cherokees. One of Georgia's laws covering the Cherokees called for all missionaries to obtain a license for permission to perform their work. The process included taking an oath that stated: "I . . . do solemnly swear . . . that I will support and defend the constitution and laws of the state of Georgia, and uprightly demean myself as a citizen thereof. So help me God."[35] The missionaries had refused to take the oath, but Georgia officials threatened to arrest and imprison the churchmen, who included Elizur Butler and Samuel Worcester. After the state's action, nine of the missionaries applied for their licenses. Worcester and Butler refused, and Georgia authorities promptly arrested them. After a jury found the two men guilty, Judge Augustin Clayton sentenced Worcester and Butler to four years of hard labor. Worcester and Butler questioned themselves and wondered if they had done the right thing.[36] Worcester and Butler served a year and four months of their sentences at Milledgeville Penitentiary.[37] On behalf of the two missionaries, William Wirt and a second attorney, John Sergeant, filed the court case officially known as *Samuel A. Worcester v. State of Georgia* in early 1832. The case would change everything when it came to American law and American Indians.

For three days, beginning on February 20, Wirt and Sergeant presented their argument before the Supreme Court. An anxious, extended period of deliberation followed. Finally, the court arrived at a decision on March 23. Georgia governor George Gilmer and other state officials believed the ruling would follow the precedent established by *Cherokee Nation v. Georgia*, but they were dismayed to learn otherwise. This time, John Marshall disagreed with the Georgia officials. The majority opinion, written by Marshall, read, "The Cherokee nation, then, is a distinct community, occupying its own territory in which the laws of Georgia can have no force, and which the citizens of Georgia have no right to enter, but with the assent of the Cherokees themselves, or in conformity with treaties, and with the acts of Congress."[38]

The *Worcester* case set a landmark precedent by asserting that the Cherokees possessed "sovereignty" equivalent to the sovereignty of foreign countries.[39] This comparison not only applied to the Cherokees, but to the other Five Nations and every Indian tribe. The Cherokees and other Indians could now be recognized as sovereign nations, putting them on a whole new legal standing.

Despite the court's ruling, Governor Gilmer refused to release Butler and Worcester from prison. Born near Lexington, Georgia, in 1790, Gilmer had long-standing resentments against Indians. He had fought alongside Jackson against the Muscogees in the Red Stick War of 1813–14. He recalled the Compact of 1802, when Georgia gave up claims to lands extending west to the Mississippi River with the understanding that the United States would remove all Cherokees from the state and dissolve their land rights. Butler and Worcester also proved to be short-term allies. The two missionaries compromised with Governor Gilmer's successor, Wilson Lumpkin, and agreed to stop missionary work with the Cherokees in Georgia. Like so many others, Butler and Worcester came to believe that the forced migration of the Cherokees to the West was inevitable.[40]

The Cherokees were not alone among the Five Tribes in facing difficult circumstances in the early 1830s. By the end of the first week of February 1832, concerned headmen and warriors of the Muscogee Nation sent a memorial to the US Congress. They described the pressure they felt "in various quarters to induce us to surrender the last remnant of the territories which were bestowed upon us by our God, to relinquish them to those who are desirous of becoming the proprietors of our possessions, and of seeking another home and another country beyond the Mississippi." They reminded Congress of the Treaty of Fort Jackson in 1814, which provided "no stipulations impairing our pre-existing rights and privileges, nor were we then told that our laws and customs were to be abrogated, and made to yield to the white man."[41] Knowing their old nemesis occupied the White House, the Muscogees hoped the anti-removal members in Congress would support them, and the Muscogee leaders were likely aware of the *Worcester* decision supporting Cherokee sovereignty. But the federal response was to send treaty negotiators to Cusseta *tvlofv* on the Chattahoochee River in Georgia to seek the Muscogees' removal.

The Muscogees had been facing pressure from white settlers since the early nineteenth century. In response, the Muscogees passed a national law calling for the death of any Muscogee who signed a treaty ceding tribal lands. Still, at least one Muscogee leader ignored this provision. This was William McIntosh, who was an opportunistic mixed blood from Coweta *tvlofv* and rose in status due to his being of the Wind Clan, from which *mekkos*, or town kings, came from. Also known as White Warrior and the leader of the Lower Muscogees, McIntosh held a council with US officials that resulted in the signing of the Treaty of Indian Springs in 1821. The treaty stipulated that the Muscogees surrender four million acres near the Flint River in Georgia. In exchange, the United States would pay $250,000 to the Muscogees over fourteen years, but this amount would also pay claims charged by Georgia settlers against the tribe. The agreement also called for McIntosh to receive $40,000 and 1,000 acres of choice land at Indian Springs, Georgia.[42]

Immediately a council under the leadership of Principal Chief Menawa protested the treaty. Menawa ordered two-hundred warriors called Law Menders to hunt down William McIntosh. They found him at home, stabbed him in the heart, and set his house on fire.[43] Anyone associated with McIntosh was deemed a traitor to the Muscogee people.

Tensions simmered for the next decade, but boiled over with removal. Some Muscogee leaders traveled to Washington in 1832 to meet with Secretary of War Lewis Cass, and during their visit he persuaded them to sign a treaty for removal to the West. Although Cass did not know much about Indians, he followed President Jackson's guidance to obtain Native lands. The Treaty of Washington in 1832, also called the Treaty of Cusseta, established the hundredth meridian as the western border of the Muscogee Nation in the newly formed Indian Territory. The removal agreement included a strong statement of Muscogee sovereignty: "Nor shall any State of Territory ever have the right to pass laws for the government of such Indians, but they shall be allowed to govern themselves."[44] The main part of the Muscogees moved to Indian Territory in 1836 and 1837.

While most Muscogees accepted the terms of the Treaty of Cusseta of 1832, many of the Red Stick Muscogees refused to go along with the removal agreement. War began in 1836 when Lower Muscogees of the *tvlofvs* of the Flint River decided to fight back against white intruders. No major battles occurred, but the Red Sticks continually attacked settlements. This was the last Muscogee stand to protect their homelands.[45]

Following the Muscogee War of 1836, soldiers put hostile warriors in chains and boarded them on a steamboat called the *Monmouth*. During a night of heavy rain at the end of October 1837 on the Mississippi River, the *Monmouth* collided with another steamboat and began to sink in the cold water. Of the roughly six-hundred Muscogees on board the *Monmouth,* 311 drowned, many of them still wearing chains.[46] They never had a chance in the murky waters of the Mississippi. The survivors endured a three months' harsh journey to the West.[47] To sustain themselves, the Muscogees sang this song, "Espoketis Omes Kerreskos" (This may be the last time, we do not know). Out of an estimated populations of 23,000 Muscogees, 3,500 perished along the Road of Suffering.[48] Upon arrival at Fort Gibson, the removal parties rested before moving on to their new claimed areas in the Muscogee Nation to "put down fire" for their new ceremonial stomp grounds.[49]

After resettling in their new *tvlofvs,* the Muscogees moved toward a national government, but they had an old issue to be resolved. The division of Upper and Lower Muscogee towns continued to sow discord. Both factions had their own national councils consisting of town leaders called *mekkos.* In 1840 representatives from each council met at High Springs, north of Hitchita, in the new Muscogee Nation. Over the following several years, the Muscogees transferred their main emphasis of authority from each *tvlofv* toward a central government. In 1859 delegates from Upper and Lower Muscogee *tvlofvs* met until they hammered out the first tribal constitution. The chiefs of towns were elected, a change from the tradition of *mekko* leadership from the Wind Clan. Now leadership was represented by a principal chief for both the Upper and Lower Muscogees. The first elected leaders were Motey Kinnard of the Lower Muscogees and Echo Harjo of the Upper Muscogees.[50] The Muscogees established at least three schools, Koweta, Tullahassee, and Asbury Manual Labor School, by the 1850s.[51]

The Seminoles also faced immense pressure to vacate the Southeast. Following the First Seminole War of 1817–18, the federal government tried to remove the Seminoles from Florida after two treaties had been signed, the Treaty of Payne's Landing in 1832 and the Fort Gibson agreement in 1833. But the Seminoles resisted. From 1835 to 1842, the Seminoles waged the longest Indian war against the United States in history. Red Stick Muscogees and escaped slaves from Georgia plantations joined them as allies, increasing the force of the Seminoles to about 3,000 fighters.[52] They were led by Osceola, the famed Seminole-Scottish mixed blood.

The Seminoles' superior knowledge of the terrain frustrated American hopes for victory. The main American strategy was to defeat the prominent war leader Osceola, believing the end of his leadership would bring the war to a close. Using peace talks deceptively in 1838, General Thomas Jessup ordered the capture of Osceola under a white flag of truce. Unexpectedly, the war leader soon died of pneumonia. It turned out, however, that the Seminoles were not solely dependent on Osceola's leadership. Jumper, Alligator, Tiger Tail, and Coe-Hadjo emerged, directing towns of warriors acting independently instead of operating as a single army. Over seven years, the United States sent a dozen generals to defeat the Seminoles and their allies.[53]

With each passing defeat, their reputations became tarnished. The hostilities diminished by 1840, but rather than seeking peace, the federal government continued the war for two more years, until 3,000 Seminoles agreed to remove, just as their Muscogee allies had already done.[54]

An 1845 treaty led to the Seminoles living in the Little River area of the new Muscogee homeland. Preferring their Medicine Way traditions, the Seminoles did not adopt a constitution but governed themselves as they always had, with representatives from the twenty-five *tvlofvs* at a national council. The Seminoles held annual meetings at Wewoka. In 1856 another treaty recognized Seminole independence from the Muscogees. Soon afterward, the Seminoles moved toward developing a national government and named John Jumper as their first chief.[55] Also known as *Heneha Mekko*, or "second chief," Jumper served twice as chief from 1849 to 1865 and from 1882 to 1885. He also became a Baptist preacher.

Removal of the eastern woodland tribes was both voluntary and forced. Tribal members were often pitted against each other and divided into at least two camps. Among the Cherokees, traditionalists led by John Ross opposed removal and wanted to remain in their homelands. The pro-removal side was led by the Ridge family, which included Elias Boudinot, Major Ridge, John Ridge, and Stand Watie.

The Treaty of New Echota of 1835 gave the Eastern Cherokees ownership of the new western homeland with the Old Settler Cherokees. The government agreed to pay for the complete removal of the Cherokees, and it purchased a strip of land in what is now southeastern Kansas for the Cherokees that became known as Cherokee Neutral Lands.[56] The treaty had a provision declaring the Cherokees would be paid five million dollars in exchange for seven million acres. John Ross and the majority of the Cherokees alleged that the treaty was a fraud and that only a portion of their leaders had signed it. Ross and about 2,000 Cherokee protested to President Andrew Jackson to no avail. On September 28, Chief Ross sent a petition to Congress, stating, "we are despoiled of our private possessions, the indefeasible property of individuals. We are stripped of every attribute of freedom and eligibility for legal self-defence [*sic*]." The petition also stated, "Our property may be plundered before our eyes; violence may be committed on our persons; even our lives may be taken away, and there is none to regard our complaints. We are denationalized; we are disfranchised."[57]

The treaty created political turmoil among the Cherokees, with three factions in tension with each other. Resentment turned to violence. The Eastern Cherokees could not forgive Major Ridge and his followers for signing the New Echota agreement. On June 22, 1839, a group of Cherokee men carried out the national law of death for those ceding tribal land, and they executed members of the Ridge family—Major Ridge, John Ridge, and Elias Boudinot. Boudinot was stabbed in the back with an eight-inch homemade knife and struck three or four times in the head with a war hatchet.[58]

Initially, John Ross, leader of the Eastern Cherokees, had refused to meet with Chief John Jolly, who argued that his Old Settler Cherokees should be in charge of forming a combined government. But less than a month after the killing of the Ridge family, the Ross faction of traditionalists met with the Old Settlers on July 12, 1839, with Sequoyah in charge. The factions agreed to an official "Act of Union," forming a unified Cherokee group. In September 1840, the Cherokees met and adopted a constitution similar to the one from 1827. In June 1841 the Cherokees met a third time and ratified the constitution and named Tahlequah their permanent capital.[59]

While the Cherokees, Muscogees, and Seminoles experienced fierce internal divisions and included at least some tribal members who resisted the move to Indian Territory, the Choctaws became the first of the Five Tribes to accept removal as a group. Negotiations initially occurred during the 1820s, but the leaders of the tribe refused the offer of removal at that time. Early in the next decade, at a place where rabbits jumped and played, roughly 6,000 Choctaws met with American officials during the muggiest days of early September. After much talk, the Choctaw leaders signed the Treaty of Dancing Rabbit Creek in late September 1830.[60]

Roughly 11,000 Choctaws moved west in three large parties in 1831, 1832, and 1833. They were carried by steamboats on the Arkansas, Ouachita, and Red rivers for part of the way, and then the Choctaws traveled over land to Fort Towson, Indian Territory. Each party suffered from the cold of traveling in winter and cholera.[61] About 2,500 Choctaws died along the way.

In spite of the difficulties faced by the removal parties, the Choctaws quickly adjusted to their new lives in Indian Territory. It was a matter of survival. The Choctaws gathered near Tuskahoma in present southeastern Oklahoma at Nanih Waiya, their mother mound, where legend says they emerged from the earth. Here, the Choctaws produced their second constitution on

June 3, 1834. Using the United States as a model, the new Choctaw government had an executive branch consisting of three elected chiefs, who served
four-year terms. A national council of ten representatives from three districts
met yearly. A judiciary had three appointed judges, who were supported by
eighteen elected lighthorse in carrying out the laws. The lighthorse were a
tribal police force. The constitution also contained a bill of rights and conferred the right to vote to all males over the age of sixteen but not to women.[62]

Missionaries continued working among the Choctaws in Indian Territory,
just as they had in Mississippi. Mission schools, which taught reading and
writing in English, convinced the Choctaws of the importance of education.
By 1842 the Choctaws operated a system of eight boarding schools. Funded
by treaty provisions and mission boards representing the American Board
Commissioners for Foreign Missions, schools opened their doors to students
at Spencer, Fort Coffee, Wheelock, and Armstrong.[63] In a letter dated June 17,
1845, Choctaw attorney George Harkins wrote his uncle in Mississippi,
Greenwood LeFlore, to tell him of the good conditions in Indian Territory:
"Peace and harmony reigns among the Choctaw people. Political strife that
was existing between the different leading men of the nation while in Mississippi, I am happy to say all hostile feelings are buried, and they are united
as a band of brothers in trying to promote the interest and happiness of their
people."[64]

Like the Choctaws, the Chickasaws realized their dire situation and
accepted the best terms they could obtain for being removed to the Indian
Territory. Their removal began in 1837 and would last until 1851. Federal
authorities contracted A. M. M. Upshaw of Pulaski, Tennessee, to super-
vise the Chickasaw removal. John M. Millard served as the conductor of the
removal with his assistant, William R. Guy.[65] Like other removal parties, the
Chickasaw groups stopped at the public house owned by Mrs. Mary Black, a
widow of "goodly proportions" who fed travelers with the help of her several
sons and daughters at her establishment "half way between Rock Roe and
Little Rock" in Arkansas.[66]

The Chickasaws negotiated an agreement with the Choctaws in 1855 that
separated the two peoples into two nations. In 1856, the Chickasaws named
Tishomingo as their new capital, and they drafted a constitution very similar to that of the Choctaws, except the chief executive was called a governor.
The first leader of the Chickasaws was Governor Cyrus Harris.[67] Like their

Choctaw brethren, the Chickasaws realized the importance of schools. By the 1850s, the Chickasaws operated boarding schools at Chickasaw Manual Labor Academy, Bloomfield, Colbert Institute, Wapanucka, and Burney Institute.[68]

Among the Five Tribes, the forced migration involved 16,542 Cherokees, 17,963 Choctaws, 21,762 Muscogees, 5,224 Chickasaws, and 4,883 Seminoles. An estimated 4,000 Cherokees died along the way, while the Choctaws lost 2,500 of their people, the Chickasaws and Muscogees both lost 3,500, and the Seminoles 1,500.[69] Of the total of 66,374 Five Nations people removed, an estimated 15,000 died along the way.

In addition to the Five Nations, more than twenty other groups, including the Shawnees, Potawatomis, and Osages, were removed to the Indian Territory. Between 1825 and 1836, out of a total of 374 ratified treaties between the United States and Native tribes, 229 involved ceding Indian lands.[70] Altogether, nearly 100,000 Native people were removed from their homelands to the Indian Territory.

An estimated 5,000 enslaved Blacks accompanied their Indian owners among the Five Nations to Indian Territory. Slavery among the Five Nations continued as it did in the Old South, although not all members of the Five Tribes owned slaves. Most owners were mixed bloods, and some were full bloods. The half bloods and quarter bloods emerged as the most prosperous slave owners. They became an Indian aristocracy similar to the white masters in the South, owning impressive plantation homes with large fields of cotton.[71]

Slaves in Indian Territory resisted their lot in similar ways to those in the Old South. One night in 1842, around 250 slaves ran away with the goal of crossing the Rio Grande to freedom in Mexico. Every escapee had "a pony or mule to ride," and they took some of their owner Joe Vann's "blooded race horses." A group of about forty Cherokees pursued and returned the slaves to their owners.[72] Slavery would remain a persistent dilemma for all Five Nations.

During the years of forced removal to the West, Indian Territory included what would become Kansas and Nebraska. The territory, otherwise known as Indian Country, was initially the enormous 828,000 square mile area designated by the Louisiana Purchase of 1803, but the pressures of territorial politics and westward expansion shrank its boundaries in the decades to come.[73]

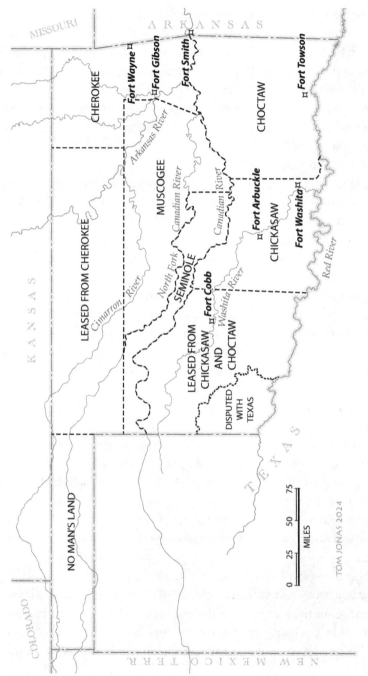

Post–Removal Indian Territory. Cartography by Tom Jonas.

The boundaries of Indian Territory took on more definitive shape between 1830 and 1848. As early as 1834, the House Committee on Indian Affairs referred to the area between the Platte and Red rivers as the Western Territory. Because the area was occupied by Indians, it was also called Indian Territory.[74] In a December 1835 message, President Jackson acknowledged Indian Territory was only for Native people: "A country west of Missouri and Arkansas has been assigned to them, into which the white settlements are not to be pushed. No political communities can be formed in that extensive region, except those which are established by the Indians themselves or by the United States for them and with their concurrence."[75] An 1848 congressional bill affirmed the southern border of Indian Territory at the Red River, the eastern border with Missouri and Arkansas, and the northern border at the Platte. The western boundary was a bit more complicated. It was at the 105th meridian to the middle of the future Colorado, but there was also an east–west line that cut through most of western Kansas to the one-hundredth meridian.[76]

During the 1850s, the US government enacted numerous policies that would affect Indian Territory and Native people on the Great Plains more generally. In 1851, Congress passed the Indian Appropriation Act, which established a policy of putting Indians in the West on reservations. Funds were authorized for superintendents, agents, sub-agents, and interpreters, plus the clerk of Indian Territory. A sum of $5,000 was marked for presents like farm tools and blankets, and $11,800 covered provisions for Native people.[77]

The purpose of this act was to settle nomadic plains and prairie tribes on reservations. At this time, though, the western tribes opted to maintain their traditional ways of living. As many as fifty million buffalo (or bison) roamed the Great Plains from northern Mexico to southern Canada, and at least twenty-eight different tribes pursued a hunting and raiding way of life. The buffalo symbolized the region, and they subsisted on grasses such as bluestem, big bluestem, little bluestem, switchgrass, Indiangrass, and at least twenty others. Bison, elk, pronghorn, and deer thrived in large populations. Wild game in flocks and herds easily outnumbered people.

Three years later, on February 20, 1854, Senator Robert W. Johnson of Arkansas introduced a bill for the organization of the country west of his home state. On July 28, the Senate Committee on Territories reported favorably on Johnson's bill, but offered a few changes. One recommendation called for three territories for three groups: Cherokee, with its capital at Tahlequah; Muscogee, with its capital at Creek Agency; and Chahta, with its capital at Doaksville. Together, the three proposed territories would constitute the state of Neosho. The bill died in committee the following December.[78]

Another bill that same year would go on to change the course of history for Indian Territory and the entire United States. On May 30, 1854, Senator Stephen Douglas of Illinois introduced the Kansas-Nebraska Act, which repealed the Missouri Compromise of 1820 and produced two territories, Kansas and Nebraska. The future Kansas area was the homeland of the Arapahos, Cheyennes, Comanches, Jiweres, Kaws (or Kansas), Kickapoos, and Kiowas. Others included the Ochethi Sakowins, Ogaxpas, Osages, Pawnees, and Wichitas. Some of the groups, such as the Arapahos, Cheyennes, Comanches, and Kiowas, were buffalo hunters and claimed hunting domains that were contested by other plains tribes and newcomer groups like the Sauks, Meskwakis, and Peorias, who arrived from the western Great Lakes.[79] Indigenous peoples of the future Nebraska included the Omahas, Otoes, Missouris, Pawnees, Arapahos, Poncas, and Cheyennes.

Meanwhile, the Five Nations asserted their sovereignty while also coordinating their efforts. For a week starting on November 8, 1859, the Five Tribes met at an International Council of Nations. The tribes met at North Fork in the Muscogee Nation. Each tribe had a small committee, which drafted laws to govern the convention and create "a code for international laws" for the "respective nations present." The convention approved of a total of fifteen resolutions to establish good relations among the present entities. Still, the delegates reiterated that they were acting independently and that their rights were conferred in the treaties that they had signed with the United States in the preceding decades.[80]

The Five Nations' efforts to assert themselves faced a serious challenge with the coming of the first transcontinental railroad in 1869. The railroad enabled settler populations to move farther west while westward expansion pushed Indigenous peoples on the plains into western Indian Territory.

Sequoyah was among the many Cherokees who went west. His syllabary produced almost immediate results, and within several years, his people were reading and writing their language. But Sequoyah was interested in much more than just teaching his people how to read and write their language. When Jeremiah Evarts, a missionary, asked Sequoyah why he created the syllabary, the Cherokee scholar paused, then replied that important ideas needed to be shared. He remarked that recording them on the talking leaves was similar to "catching a wild animal and taming it."[81]

In all of his travels to various Cherokee towns, Sequoyah kept a journal, which he used to record where he went, events he witnessed, people he met, and his ideas. Unfortunately, his journal was lost, and no one knows what happened to it. Perhaps it was buried with him when he died in San Fernando, Mexico, in August 1843.[82] What is certain is that Sequoyah wanted to advance the Cherokee people as a nation with the ability to read and write their language. His work and many sacrifices would not be forgotten.

During Sequoyah's seventy-three years, he had seen his people torn from their homeland, and he traveled with them on the trail westward to the new Cherokee Nation in the Indian Territory. He never forgot that day at his mother's store when he and three or four Cherokees talked about the white man's ability to write English. Sequoyah was carving a small horse from wood while listening to his friends. His friends concluded that writing Cherokee could not be done. Without looking up, Sequoyah replied, "It can be done." His skeptical friends shook their heads and laughed.

TWO

The Idea of an Indian State

On the second-to-last day of 1809, a baby boy was born in Boston. As the child grew, he learned to read at an early age, fancied books, loved poetry, and dreamed of becoming a writer. His uncle convinced him to attend Harvard; although he was accepted by the prestigious university, the poor lad lacked money for tuition and never attended. Forced to teach and tutor to support himself, he fell in love with an attractive student. The would-be scholar was Albert Pike.

Feeling like a failure because of his lack of wealth, Pike could not bring himself to ask the young woman to marry him. The New Englander wished to change his lot in life and decided to seek his fortune in the West, like so many other young men of his time. Pike's final stop was Fort Smith, Arkansas, where he drew upon his talent with words and became a newspaper editor.[1] Pike's intellect and imposing physical presence made a dramatic first impression on local residents. Six feet tall and weighing over 250 pounds, the learned gentleman wore his dark hair shoulder-length and had a full beard and mustache. Pike's robust physique was complemented by his understanding eyes and soft voice, which put those who met him at ease.

Pike found his quest for prominence rewarded after his move west. The New Englander had come to identify so fully with Arkansas that he joined the Confederate war effort after the state seceded. He even gained an audience with Confederate president Jefferson Davis, who found Pike to be delightful and in late February 1861 appointed the former New Englander to be commissioner of the Confederate States to the Indians west of Arkansas.[2] Pike used a surprising promise as a means to win the support of the tribes of Indian Territory for the Confederacy: statehood. But this was not the first time American Indians had been promised statehood in exchange for supporting a revolutionary war effort.

The idea for an Indian state had come up repeatedly in the early history of the United States. It began in the eighteenth century with the Delawares, also known as the Lenni Lenape. The Delawares commanded respect; at one time, they were the most powerful nation in what would become New England. Other Native nations called the Delawares the "Grandfathers" of Native nations due to their affluence and status as one of the earliest peoples in the region. Delaware leaders signed the first Indian treaty with the newly formed United States of America on September 17, 1778. The Treaty of Fort Pitt was the first of 374 ratified treaties, more than two dozen unratified treaties, and 94 legal agreements signed between the United States and Indian nations.[3]

Article 2 of the Treaty of Fort Pitt stipulated a "perpetual peace and friendship" between the Delawares and the United States. Both sovereigns agreed "if either of the parties are engaged in a just and necessary war . . . then each shall assist the other." This part of the treaty was more important to the United States than to the Delawares, as American leaders anticipated protracted war with the British and needed the support of the Indians. Article 6 of the treaty, added to keep the Delawares from signing a similar treaty with the British, extended an enticing offer to the tribe "to join the present confederation, and to form a state whereof the Delaware nation shall be the head, and have a representation in Congress."[4]

Perhaps it is no surprise that the United States failed to honor a promise made in its first treaty with a Native nation. The prospect of a state for the Delaware Indians lasted no longer than it took the ink to dry. Ironically, within a few months of the treaty, the non-Native state of Delaware became the American Union's first. Eventually, the Delawares signed a total of eleven treaties with the United States, and the government moved them nine times, more than any other tribe.

Each of the Five Nations had had their own, often-disappointing experiences in signing treaties with the United States. Perhaps, though, the secessionist rebellion offered the opportunity for a new start. On the eve of the Civil War, the Five Tribes met as the United Nations of Indian Territory.[5] The leaders of the Five Nations harbored mixed feelings about the Confederate cause and together faced the dilemma of whether to fight for the Union or the Confederacy. They had more common ground among one another than with either of those factions. They knew that the Confederacy consisted of the same settlers who had lusted for their homelands and driven them west. The Union, however, had not proven to be an attractive alternative. Contending with losses to the Confederacy in the East, Union leaders seem to have entirely forgotten about their treaty promises to the Five Nations.

The divisive task of choosing (or refusing) loyalties threatened to undo the results of painstaking efforts that had brought a degree of stability to Indian Territory. In the decades before the Civil War, the Five Nations and other Native groups had been undergoing political shifts that restructured their governments and brought about tentative intertribal alliances. Fort Gibson became a regular site for tribal meetings during the 1830s. A special commission created in 1832, consisting of Montfort Stokes of North Carolina, Reverend John Schermerhorn of New York, and Henry L. Ellsworth of Connecticut, represented an opportunity for holding the first councils created to address issues among the Five Nations.[6] An initial concern involved raiding by western tribes that targeted the Five Tribes' horses and mules. An 1833 meeting at Fort Gibson settled a boundary dispute between the Muscogees and Cherokees. The same council established Seminole independence from the Muscogees. In September 1834 General Henry Leavenworth and his soldiers held a council with the Kiowas, Comanches, and Wichitas. Leavenworth managed to persuade the leaders of the three groups to meet with the Osages and Five Nations to establish a peace with the western tribes.[7] Unfortunately, this agreement only established temporary peace, but it was a tentative step toward intertribal coordination. Another milestone occurred in 1842, when Muscogee chief Roley McIntosh invited the rest of the Five Nations and the Osages. They met at what became known as the Inter-Tribal Council of the Deep Fork River. The shared trauma of removal brought them together.

Although the tribes saw themselves as separate groups, they began reforming their traditional infrastructures by moving away from their customary system of autonomous towns. During the rebuilding years in the 1840s and 1850s, the Muscogees shifted power away from the *tvlofvs* toward a national government. Previously, from time immemorial, the *tvlofvs* had operated according to their own sovereignty, which the people called *boeafekcha* ("living spirit"). Now the same spiritual power began endowing a central, collective sovereignty. In 1859 the Muscogees adopted a new constitution and they revised it to alter the internal structure of their government.

Decades later, a Muscogee elder, Sam J. Haynes, recalled the election and council meetings held at High Springs, about fifteen miles east of Okmulgee: It "was the most peaceful election they had held. Motey Canard, who was nearly seven feet tall, was elected principal chief of the Lower Creeks. Echo Harjo became principal chief of the Upper Creeks, and Ok-tar-sars Harjo [was] named second chief. A constitution was adopted. It provided for the election by all the Creeks of one principal and one second chief for the Nation. There were no longer the Upper and Lower Creeks but henceforth the Muskogee Nation."[8] In addition, the Muscogees and Seminoles moved away from the official title of *mekko* (king) and adopted the term "chief." Tribal members elected candidates to the two positions. The Muscogee reservation was divided into four districts presided over by a judge appointed by the principal chief. A supreme court of five judges, also appointed by the principal chief, operated above the district judges.[9] The constitution established the Muscogee council house, and the town of Ocmulkee (Okmulgee) was founded in the same year of 1859.[10]

In the early 1860s with the Civil War looming, the weather was no one's ally. A severe drought plagued the land, punishing people, especially farmers praying for a decent harvest. An unrelenting summer scorched corn fields that yielded very little for home consumption, much less a cash crop. People went hungry while the rivers and creeks ran slowly and low, not anything like previous spring rains emitting swollen waters.[11] Hope began to dwindle until a stranger arrived, that very same Albert Pike who had made such an impression in Arkansas.

In June 1861, the new Indian commissioner of the Confederate States of America hoped to establish good relations with the Muscogees, Seminoles, Choctaws, and Chickasaws.[12] With an eloquence honed during his teaching days in New England, Pike's empathetic approach made him the right person to negotiate with Indian leaders. To the Confederacy's advantage, the Union had abandoned Fort Washita, Fort Arbuckle, and Fort Cobb in the Indian Territory.[13] Troops and supplies were badly needed east of the Mississippi. Through the first summer of the war, the South sensed victory over the Union.

In addition to the persuasive influence of Pike, the affluent McIntosh family convinced many Muscogees to side with the Confederacy. At least forty-five leaders signed a treaty with the Confederacy on July 10, 1861, at North Fork Town on the Canadian River. Article 5 of the treaty stipulated the Muscogees would own their land communally, "so long as the grass grows and the water run, if the said nation shall so please." Article 40 promised that the Muscogees and Seminoles "shall be jointly entitled to a delegate in the House or Representatives of the Confederate States of America," to serve two-year terms.[14] The Choctaws and Chickasaws agreed to a similar treaty with the Confederacy two days later. Article 28 of that agreement promised the Choctaws and Chickasaws that if they desired, they "shall be received and admitted into the Confederacy as one of the Confederate states."[15] At the conclusion of this meeting, Pike signed an eighty-seven-page treaty of friendship and allegiance with the Muscogees, Choctaws, and Chickasaws known as "An act for the protection of certain Indian Tribes."[16] On the first of August, Seminole leaders signed a similar document.[17]

Standing firmly against the two agreements, the Muscogee leader Opothleyahola tried his best to convince *tvlofv* leaders and important warriors to not sign the treaty, but to no avail.[18] Pike soon realized that his real opponent was not the Union army, but rather the noted Red Stick leader who preached to the people to avoid the white man's war. Also known as Old Gouge to the slaves who joined the neutral band of followers, Opothleyahola was in Pike's view "a crafty old man" who was a threat to the Confederacy.[19]

Pike's agreements echoed the 1832 Treaty of Cusseta between the United States and Muscogees. Even Opothleyahola, who opposed all treaty signing, made his mark on the Cusseta agreement. Why? Because article 14 acknowledged Muscogee sovereignty; they could form their own government and the federal government would recognize it: "The Creek country west of the Mississippi shall be solemnly guaranteed to the Creek Indians, nor shall any State or Territory ever have a right to pass laws for the government of such Indians, but they shall be allowed to govern themselves, so far as may be compatible with the general jurisdiction which Congress may think proper to exercise over them." The first part of the article specifically guaranteed that no state, such as nearby Arkansas or Missouri, or new territory had authority over the Muscogees.

Overall, Pike achieved notable success. After several meetings with Native leaders, he persuaded around twenty tribes, including separate bands, to accept the Confederate promises.[20] Pike invited the tribes to send a delegate to sit in the House of Representatives of the Confederate government.[21]

A young mixed-blood Cherokee opportunist surprised many by taking advantage of Pike's invitation. Twenty-seven-year-old Elias Cornelius Boudinot found his way to Richmond in September 1862 to claim a seat as the first American Indian to represent his people as a non-voting member of the Confederate Congress.[22] Born in 1802 at Oothcaloga in the Cherokee Nation, young Boudinot had studied law, became a newspaper editor, and revealed his entrepreneurial nature. He was the son of Elias Boudinot, who was killed with other members of the Ridge family for signing the Treaty of New Echota in 1835.

Opothleyahola and his neutral Indians, whom Confederate commander Douglas Cooper called "loyalists," continued to be a problem for the Confederacy. Several efforts to defeat them ensued, which culminating in three main battles. The first engagement occurred on November 19, 1861, and Opothleyahola's warriors surprisingly outwitted Cooper's scouts and then held off a Confederate force at the Battle of Round Mountain (also called the Battle of Red Fork).[23]

The number of neutralists under Opothleyahola included about 1,500 Indians from the Five Nations and others, as well as Black slaves, and consisted mostly of women and children. On the morning of December 9, Cooper ordered his men to attack the weary refugees, who had taken shelter in shallow caves at Bird Creek. When the smoke cleared, Opothleyahola had won again. Although the neutralists managed to defeat Cooper, the cold proved too formidable.[24]

In the third and last engagement, victory went to the harsh winter and to troops under Confederate colonel Daniel McIntosh, a Muscogee, in defeating Opothleyahola's starving caravan. Known as the Battle of Chustenahlah, it was really a fight for survival. The Confederates captured many slaves, and only about 250 men, women, and children survived the battle, fleeing to Fort Row in Kansas.[25] The eighty-five-year-old Opothleyahola managed to make it to Kansas, but he caught pneumonia and died. His friends buried him next to his daughter near present-day Belmont, Kansas.[26] With the ground frozen, fires were made to thaw the earth enough to dig a grave.

The greatest battle of the Civil War in Indian Territory involved about 9,000 troops at Honey Springs, also known as the Battle of Elk Creek, on July 17, 1863. Since April, the Union had been invading Indian Territory, with Colonel William A. Phillips leading an Indian force from Baxter Springs, Kansas. They met little resistance and seized Fort Gibson without a fight.[27] But both sides understood that control of Indian Territory depended on who possessed Fort Gibson, and the Confederates sought to retake it.[28] At Honey Springs, an estimated 3,000 fought for the Union side and 6,000 fought for Confederacy on that fateful rainy day in summer. James G. Blunt commanded the Union army and won. The prize was Honey Springs, a busy stagecoach stop along the Texas Road with direct access to Fort Gibson on the south bank of the Arkansas River.[29]

East of the Mississippi, the tide of the war had turned. On February 20, 1865, with the end of the war in sight, a Republican senator from Illinois, James Harlan, introduced a bill to establish a civil government in the Indian Territory. The bill received Senate approval on March 2, but members of the House proved less receptive. This session of Congress ended just a couple of days later, thus ending Harlan's bill for making Indian Territory into a formal territory within the United States.[30]

The news of General Robert E. Lee's surrender to General Ulysses Grant in early April 1865 at Appomattox Court House, Virginia, arrived late in Indian Territory. Like falling dominos, every Confederate commander surrendered save one. General Stand Watie, a mixed-blood Cherokee who had signed the Treaty of New Echota in 1835, stood alone. Watie and his men raided and attacked US military posts and homesteads, stores, and wagon trains. They even burned down Cherokee chief John Ross's house while he was in Washington trying to negotiate a new treaty at the end of the war. Only Choctaw leader Peter Pitchlynn could convince Watie and his men to surrender. At Doaksville, located near Fort Towson and close to the Texas border, Stand Watie signed a ceasefire agreement on June 23, 1865, making him the last general of the Confederate States of America to officially surrender.[31]

As it did to many places and people east of the Mississippi, the Civil War devastated Indian Territory and the Five Tribes. The war divided each of the Five Nations, and factionalism played the most destructive role among the Cherokees and Muscogees. Still, the US government was in no mood to make distinctions at war's end. The four treaties of 1866 imposed on the

Cherokees, Muscogees, Seminoles, and Chickasaws and Choctaws punished them for siding with the Confederacy. Federal officials overlooked the fact that leaders like Isparhechar, Ward Coachman, and Joseph Perryman had changed sides and ended up fighting for the Union.[32] Each of the Five Tribes had to abolish slavery and grant tribal citizenship and property rights to their former slaves, now known as freedmen. The four treaties permitted a north–south and east–west railroad to cross their lands. Worst of all, they had to surrender more than half of their reservations.[33]

Contending with the harsh terms of the 1866 agreements, the Five Nations entered the Reconstruction years with unstable governments. In a message to the Choctaw General Council during 1867, Chief Allen Wright, recently elected principal tribe, described the prevailing conditions throughout the Indian Territory. Generally, things were "brighter" than the year before; yet, "in many counties there were no lawful officers to execute the laws, hence there were many outlaws still roaming through the country." He stressed the creation of lighthorse police and starting schools as positive developments, but he noted that drunkenness and smallpox plagued the Choctaws.[34] In a letter to Chickasaw governor Cyrus Harris in the following year, Wright addressed still another urgent problem, western Indians like the Comanches and Kiowas raiding Chickasaws and Choctaws.[35]

With the reduction of their reservations during the post–Civil War era, many families of the Five Tribes had to remove again. In evacuating the western parts of their lands to make room for up to 15,000 newly displaced Indians from elsewhere, the Five Nations experienced much upheaval. In 1872 the Osages of Kansas, numbering about 1,500 people, agreed to accept a reservation in northeastern Indian Territory. The Shawnees and Delawares, also from Kansas, were forced to live on former Cherokee land. The Otoes and Missouris moved from a reservation on the Kansas–Nebraska border to Indian Territory. Other tribes moved from Kansas included the Sacs and Foxes and the Potawatomis. The Kickapoos in Mexico, who believed they were safe there, were induced to return to Indian Territory. The Miamis, Cayugas, Senecas, and Quapaws were removed from their homelands from east of the Mississippi.[36]

By the 1870s the government had created thirteen new reservations for new tribes in Indian Territory with eight Indian agencies. These included the Quapaw agency for the Quapaws, Senecas of Sandusky, Eastern Shawnees,

Wyandots, Confederate Peorias, Miamis, Ottawas, and Modocs, while the Osage Agency supervised the Osages and the Kaws. The Pawnee Agency supervised the Poncas, Pawnees, Otoes and Missouris, Tonkawas, and the Nez Perce. The Sac and Fox Agency watched over the Sacs and Foxes, Citizen Potawatomis, Absentee Shawnees, Iowas, and Kickapoos. The Cheyenne-Arapaho Agency held responsibility for the Cheyennes and Arapahos. The Wichita Agency represented the federal government to the Wichitas and Affiliated Tribes as well as the Caddoes. The Kiowa-Comanche Agency covered the Comanches, Kiowas, Kiowa Apaches, and Apaches. Finally, the Union Agency covered the Five Nations, plus the Delawares and Shawnees.[37]

In 1868 the federal government forced the Cherokees, Choctaws, Chickasaws, Muscogees, and Seminoles to write a constitution that unified all Five Nations into one. On September 27, 1870, with Indian Affairs superintendent Enoch Hoag in charge, the delegates of the Five Nations were to gather at Okmulgee, but the delegates for the Choctaws and Chickasaws did not attend. The meeting reconvened two months later, and after three days, on December 6, 1870, they produced what became known as the Okmulgee Constitution. The delegates presented the constitution to Congress, but congressmen criticized the document for retaining too much sovereignty for the tribes and rejected it.[38]

The *New York Sun* newspaper commented at length on the bill, which was introduced by Guilford Wiley Wells of Mississippi to organize the territory of Oklahoma. The term "Oklahoma," meaning "red people," was first used four years earlier by Reverend Allen Wright, the principal chief of the Choctaws. The article reported that "the Okmulgee Constitution proposed the formation of a Territorial Government, the officers of which should be chosen by the Indians from their own race, practically independent of the United States Government but operating under its sanction, without any modification of the tribal relations already existing among them." The proposed Indian state would be "subdivided into nearly twenty different nations, all speaking different languages, and each under its individual chiefs [sic]."[39]

While tribal representatives attempted to negotiate new terms with Congress, members of the Five Tribes continued practicing their Medicine Way traditions during the Reconstruction years. To honor the gift of corn to the people, the Five Nations held stomp dances leading up to the Green Corn Ceremony in mid-summer to give thanks for a bountiful harvest. This

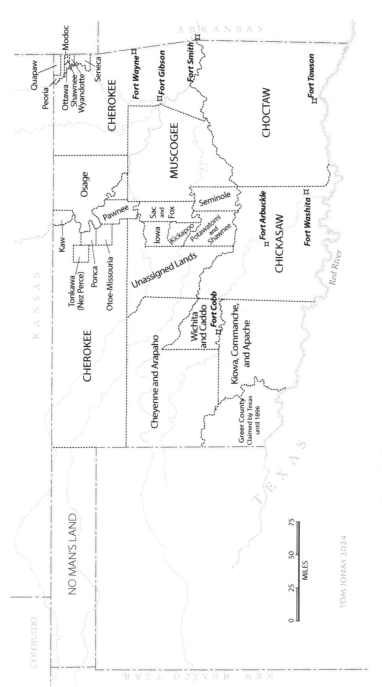

Post–Civil War Indian Territory. Cartography by Tom Jonas.

was their new year's celebration, which included putting things right and dealing with serious crimes. An integral part of the ceremony was cleansing the body internally and externally. Although the Five Tribes welcomed outsiders to join their ceremonies, the Medicine Way sometimes conflicted with the efforts of Christian missionaries. Nevertheless, many Native people practiced both Christianity and the stomp-dance tradition of the Green Corn Ceremony.

Missionaries achieved significant success in Indian Territory, as demonstrated by the growing number of churches. While the full bloods preferred traditional ways, the increasing populations of mixed bloods among the Cherokees, Muscogees, Seminoles, Choctaws, and Chickasaws adopted many "white" ways. Reverend Cyrus Byington played an instrumental role in spreading the Christian religion among the Choctaws. Byington committed himself to learning to speak Choctaw. He was convinced that for children to learn English, "the easiest and quickest way was, to teach them to read their own language first."[40] In 1825 the first book in the Choctaw language was a speller that not only helped Native children to learn to read, but also offered a means of instruction to non-Choctaws. Another missionary, Alfred Wright, also learned to speak Choctaw and worked with Byington in translating the Bible into the Choctaw language.[41] In 1835 Reverend John Fleming, who worked among the Muscogees, published *The Child's Book* or *Istutsi in Naktsoku* in the Muscogee language at Union Mission in the Cherokee Nation. It was the first book to be published in the Indian Territory. Thanks in part to the work of missionaries, each of the Five Nations made significant strides in learning to read, write, and speak English.[42]

After initially rejecting Christianity during the post-removal years, the Seminoles began to change their minds. Two years after the Civil War, the Seminoles built the Thomas Town Church south of Wewoka and constructed another church near Maud.[43] This warming attitude toward Christianity did not mean that the Seminoles turned their backs on tradition. Many Seminoles practiced both the stomp dances of the Green Corn Ceremony and Christianity, although some converted members criticized the old Medicine Way, deeming them dying traditions. In the following years, however, churches were built near the stomp grounds of Arbeka, Eufaula, Green Leaf, and Mekusukey. Compared to the other denominations, the Baptists exercised the largest influence over the Seminoles.[44]

During the Civil War, a Baptist missionary named Joseph Samuel Murrow worked to convert the Seminoles to Christianity. In 1867 Murrow left the Seminole Reservation to do missionary work among the Choctaws. With a mere six members, Murrow started the Baptist Church of Atoka during the first week of May 1869. Three years later, Murrow founded the Choctaw-Chickasaw Baptist Association, which lasted for many years. A man of boundless energy, Joseph Murrow founded and reorganized at least a hundred Indian and white churches.[45] With the help of missionaries, the Choctaws started four churches in 1870 and the Chickasaws had established two churches in the 1870s.[46]

Although the Baptists surged ahead of the Presbyterians and Methodists in making inroads in Indian Territory, the other denominations also had some success in converting Native and even African American souls. For example, the Southern Methodist Church was instrumental in establishing the African Methodist Episcopal Church, including the Colored Methodist Episcopal Church.[47]

Cultural borrowing was a means of survival and adaptation for the Muscogees, Seminoles, Choctaws, and Chickasaws. Reading, writing, and speaking English, converting to Christianity, and forming national governments, the Five Nations began to operate like the surrounding states. But not all went smoothly. In September 1871, excitement filled the air among the Muscogees when they reelected principal chief Samuel Checote; yet, change provoked resistance. The new 1867 constitution called for paper ballots, but many of the voters wanted to continue the custom of standing in a line behind the candidate of their choice at the council house in Okmulgee, as called for by tradition. Soon, however, voting by paper ballot became the custom among Muscogees.[48]

One enormous cultural change among the Native nations during the Reconstruction years was a shift from a matrilineal to a patrilineal social structure. For centuries, clan membership and other privileges and customs were passed down by one's mother side of a family. The power Native societies vested in women was very different from Euro American cultures, in which women had few rights. As in other areas, the Five Nations sought a path that could accommodate tradition and their new realities. They retained matrilineal customs but legally adopted patrilineal aspects, such as passing down the surname of the father to his children, to appease government officials.

Like Texas, Arkansas, Missouri, and Kansas, the Five Nations of the Indian Territory operated schools, justice systems of courts, and proceeded to adopt capitalism as a main part of their values. From 1866 to 1906 the tribes operated at least fifty-seven schools.[49] In early June 1875, one Choctaw citizen, Tuskahoma, suggested that the National Council create an education committee to plan to establish boarding schools. He suggested developing coal mines on the reservation to pay for the cost and operation of the schools.[50] To that end, men from Italy and Eastern Europe arrived to work in the mines.[51] Some Chickasaws and the Choctaws complained about these newcomers. On September 1, 1875, Choctaw governor Coleman Cole wrote to the editor of the *Vindicator* that "when we bought this land or soil from the United States Government, we never bought the white people with it, and they must know as well as I do, that if they reside here they must pay for that privilege—and if they do not they are intruders. We cannot have our timber, grass, etc., destroyed by white intruders."[52] In the last week of September, Governor Cole issued a proclamation. It stated for all white persons "claiming Choctaw citizenship by birth, or marriage" to appear before the council "on the first Monday in October, 1875, and prove their right of citizenship."[53] The Choctaw constitution permitted any white man who married a Choctaw woman to be "entitled to all the rights and privileges of a citizen by blood" after paying a license fee of $100.[54] Two years later, the *Cherokee Advocate* reported that Governor Cole intended to drive out the intruders and seize their land.[55] Cole's extreme views upset some Choctaws, and the tribal congress began proceedings to impeach Governor Cole. But the Choctaw Senate entered a *nolle prosequi* "wish to not prosecute" decision that led to the dismissal of the governor's impeachment.[56]

The Muscogees also saw one of their leaders impeached during the 1870s. On December 6, 1875, newly elected Principal Chief Lochar Harjo gave a few words that would prove ironic: "I would first congratulate you upon the present unity and harmony of the Muskogee people, who for many years have had their peace and harmony disturbed by divisions among them but at present I am happy to say they seem more united than for many years before."[57] Within a year, the Houses of Kings and Warriors, which also served as a court, voted by two-thirds majority to impeach Harjo. He was charged with breaking his oath of office and for associating with certain troublemakers, including one J. B. G. Dixon, "an obnoxious white man" who had obtained the "rights of Creek citizenship" illegally.[58]

Newcomers to Indian Territory would be a persistent cause of concern for the Five Nations in the later years of the nineteenth century. In May 1880 Chickasaw governor B. C. Burney wrote, "Surrounded as we are by a people who can only be kept out of our Nation by the armed forces of the United States government, it seems to me eminently desirable that the relations of the Indian Tribes with each other should be closer and more binding than they are at present."[59] But within two weeks, Burney was replaced by the newly elected Benjamin Overton, his brother-in-law. In his final message to the Chickasaw legislature, Burney warned that the people had "been but too willing to listen to the seductive inducements of the stock owners who were prohibited by our laws from bringing their cattle here, and the result for several years past has been that many hundreds of cattle have been pastured here, claimed by citizens but really owned by non-citizens."[60]

The Cherokees had their troubles, too. In early August 1882, Chief Dennis Wolf Bushyhead headed a delegation to protest the continual intrusion of whites on their reservation to Interior Secretary Henry M. Teller in Washington. The intruders included all types—farmers, cattlemen, and woodsmen. The delegation's letter to Teller complained "the United States officials encourage the designs of covetous and lawless persons." The intruders caused "great damage," and the tribes wanted to be reimbursed for their destroyed property. The letter also stated that the white intruders were "answerable to no law. They cut and sell our timber. . . . They buy or pretend to buy. They carry on merchandizing and stock business in violation of the law. Some of them have even laid off towns and sold, or pretended to sell lots to citizens of the United States in violating of all law." The Cherokees wrote that the whites had driven people off the land. They further complained, "They steal stock. They alarm and irritate our citizens, and the evil has reached such magnitude that it will be necessary for the Cherokee Nation to protect her own people by expelling them if the United States is unable to fulfill her treaty obligations."[61]

These problems continued for the next three years. On November 3, 1885, Bushyhead wrote to the Cherokee Senate that he disagreed with the current tribal law and wanted stronger restrictions to limit the outside workers coming to the reservation.[62] Many non-Cherokees hoped to become citizens of the Cherokee Nation by moving there. In early December, the Cherokee

Senate considered a bill "to create a joint Commission on Citizenship to try and settle claims to Cherokee Citizenship."[63]

One of the most significant agents of change in Indian Territory after the Civil War came on hoof. Cattle drives led by white ranchers and cowboys—viewed today as a part of the romance of the Old West—transformed the daily reality for the Chickasaws, Choctaws, Seminoles, Cherokees, Muscogees, and other Natives in Indian Territory. The territory fell between Texas and Kansas, the former where cattle were raised or captured, and the latter where cattle were shipped by train to packing plants in Kansas City, St. Louis, or Chicago. Cattle drives through Indian Territory started before the Civil War, but the true cowboy era emerged after 1865 and lasted for about the next twenty-five years.

Cowboys driving herds had a chance to see Indian Territory and what it had to offer—vast grazing lands. Foremen negotiated agreements with tribal leaders, bribed them, or tried to graze their cattle for free–if they could get away with it. The most famous trail was the Chisholm, which started as far south as Kingsville, Texas, and passed through the heart of Indian Territory to reach bustling cow towns of Wichita, Newton, Abilene, or Dodge City, the so-called queen of the cow towns. Another route, the Western Trail, passed through the homelands of the Plains Indian nations in the territory, and the Sedalia Trail cut through the southeastern part of the Choctaw Nation as well parts of the Muscogee Nation and Cherokee Nation.[64]

Although they were basically sedentary people who cultivated corn and supplemented their agricultural efforts with hunting and fishing, the Five Nations learned about cattle and how to raise them after removal to Indian Territory. Cattle became a part of the changing economies of most of the tribes in the territory. Receiving grazing money from cattlemen and raising cattle, sometimes even in large herds, became a part of life for some Native ranchers. Cowboys traveling north also saw the opportunity to make Indian Territory their new home. One daring Texas cattleman approached a Chickasaw woman and blurted out a marriage proposal: "You have the land. I have the cattle."[65] After obtaining an official license, Texas men who married Chickasaw women believed they had the right to develop all of the land they wanted.[66] The non-Chickasaw husbands then rented or leased as many acres of land as they could to white farmers and ranchers. Such exploitation compelled the Chickasaw leadership to restrict the "intermarried whites by temporarily disfranchising them."[67] After marrying Native women, some men then brought their previous families to the reservations, a practice that affected not just the Chickasaws, but the other Five Tribes as well.

The amount land controlled by cattlemen became a serious issue for the Five Nations. A government investigation in 1885 reported that the Cherokees had been induced to leasing six million acres in the Cherokee Outlet to the Cherokee Strip Live Stock Association for $100,000 per year, which amounted to less than two cents per acre. In six different leases, the Osages leased 380,000 acres at six cents per acre. The Kaws leased 52,000 acres at four cents per acre and another lease of 300 acres at fifty cents per acre. The Nez Perces, Poncas, Pawnees, Otoes and Missouris, Iowas, and Sacs and Foxes leased about half of their lands.[68] To protect themselves against outsiders controlling large areas of their lands, the Cherokees passed an "act to prevent monopoly," which stated that "inclosure [sic] of large bodies of land for whatever purpose is violative of the paramount ownership of the people in the common property of the Nation."[69]

The cattle business also brought outlaws, toughs, rustlers, and criminals of all sorts to the Indian Territory. The heyday of outlaws in the territory occurred from about the end of the Civil War to the mid-1890s, as stealing cattle, altering their brands, and then selling them was a profitable enterprise. Even unreliable lawmen became outlaws. Considering this state of affairs, who was supposed to enforce the lawmen in Indian Territory?

The tribes already had their own justice systems consisting of courts and lighthorse police. But these were not sufficient in the eyes of the federal government. In 1875 President Ulysses Grant appointed thirty-seven-year-old Isaac Parker as the new judge of the Western District of Arkansas to exercise jurisdiction over the 74,000 square miles of Indian Territory. Parker did this by hiring two-hundred deputy marshals to go into the territory and arrest criminals of all races to be presented before his court at Fort Smith. But arresting outlaws was dangerous, and over half of the marshals simply quit. Parker's deputy marshals almost always fought with the tribal lighthorse. Both deputy marshals and the lighthorse represented different worldviews and different ideas about the law. For example, Native courts had their own way of dealing with capital offenses. Based on honor, if a criminal was sentenced to be executed, the person was given a certain amount of time to put his affairs in order before his execution. While crime was a serious concern in the territory, the invasion of outsiders living on and using Indian lands caused much more trouble.

Throughout these years, the Five Nations and others in Indian Territory remained frustrated by outside influence over their legal and political affairs. As early as 1874, leaders of the Five Nations protested to President Grant, "We agreed to a General Indian Council, or a confederation of Indian tribes and nations, then in and to come into the Indian country, *for the purposes specified in the treaties of 1866; and for no other purposes, and with the distinct understanding that no territorial government should be placed over the Indians, without their express consent* [emphasis in original]."[70] More than a decade later, Principal Chief Dennis Wolf Bushyhead of the Cherokees warned his national council about "many dangerous bills of a judicial character" then under consideration. He also noted that "the federal government wanted to purchase a portion of the territory for white settlement."[71] There were also judicial matters that impinged on the sovereignty of the Five Nations and their Native neighbors, such as the Osages. For example, a federal district court in Texas presumed to adjudicate civil matters for a part of Indian Territory and the Western District Court at Fort Smith, Arkansas, extended its authority over the border portion of the territory.[72] Although the Five Tribes had their own governments and courts, the federal government created the first federal district court in Indian Territory in 1889 and located it in Muskogee, which usurped the sovereignty of the Muscogee Nation. Other federal district courts followed in Ardmore and in McAlester, which impinged upon the Chickasaws and Choctaws.[73]

The struggle over these jurisdictional overlaps found at least one unlikely supporter for the statehood of Indian Territory. In a lengthy letter to Cherokee delegate W. A. Duncan on March 16, 1894, Judge Isaac Parker of the Western District Court of Arkansas concluded that Congress should recognize that "your rights should be protected and that you should be let alone to develop that civilization that the Government said sixty years ago you were capable of developing, when it recognized your autonomy and considered that your local laws were sufficient to promote intelligence and finally bring you to that state of civilization that, in my judgment, you have arrived at now, you will believe me, as ever, most truly."[74] Despite the support of Judge Parker and others for the cause of Indian statehood, Muscogee principal chief Pleasant Porter had given up hope. "The exclusive right of our people to self-government under our own laws, while guaranteed by treaty, has long since ceased to exist," he said. And "for the operation of our laws to maintain the right of person and property is to [be] prevented by the gradual assumption of authority in one question and another by the government of the United States as to give us self-government in name only."[75]

During these decades, the Five Nations took steps toward acting in a more coordinated manner. The treaties of 1866 directed the Five Nations to form an intertribal council to meet annually.[76] The idea was for the general council to become a part of the process in becoming a single territory. After they learned that Congress was entertaining bills to abolish their separate governments, a meeting of delegates took place in Okmulgee every year from 1870 to 1876.[77] In his first annual address in 1879 to the Cherokees, Principal Chief Dennis Bushyhead supported what he called the General Council of the Tribes, which met twice at Eufaula on May 27 and on July 1. Some tribes from the West joined the Five Nations at these meetings to discuss common concerns such as outside intruders, especially cattlemen driving their herds through tribal lands. Bushyhead said, "In my judgement such conventions afforded a needed opportunity for interchange of thought and ideas, that must tend to unite all in a common band of sympathy for mutual protection."[78]

Along with cowboys and outlaws, the railroad arrived in Indian Territory after the Civil War and brought major changes with them. A provision in each of the four treaties of 1866 signed jointly by the Cherokees, Muscogees, Seminoles, and Choctaws and Chickasaws held that one railroad was allowed to travel north and south, and another railroad could travel east and west.[79] Newspapers and gossip promoted the race to build the first line. In 1870, the Missouri, Kansas, and Texas Railroad, commonly known as the Katy, extended its tracks to the northern border of Indian Territory, which was also the border of the Cherokee Nation. While settlers were still barred by law from entering Indian Territory at this time, the railroad was now the primary connection of the Five Nations to the outside world.[80]

In 1870 and for the next two years, railroad companies in addition to the Katy laid tracks from Kansas through Indian Territory to Texas. Originally called Muskogee Station because it was a stop for the Katy, Muskogee became the most prosperous urban area in Indian Territory. After the opening of the Unappropriated Lands to settlement in 1889, Muskogee grew even more quickly in population. Vinita in the Cherokee Nation, Checotah in the

Muscogee Nation, McAlester in the Choctaw Nation, and other settlements felt the impact of the railroads even before the first land run in 1889.

The cattle trails and railroads into Indian Territory ushered in increasing numbers of white and Black settlers. Many Black migrants were boomers and Exodusters from the Deep South, although many freedmen were former slaves of masters from the Five Nations. Some evidence suggests that slavery in Indian Territory was not as harsh as in other areas. For example, Seminole slaves had their own cabins and gardens to support themselves.[81] One former slave of a Cherokee master remembered:

> Everybody had a good time on old Jim Vann's plantation. After supper the colored folks would get together and talk, and sing, and dance. Someone maybe would be playing a fiddle or a banjo. Everybody was happy. Master never whipped no one. No fusses, no bad words, no nothing like that. The slaves who worked in the big house was the first class. Next, came the carpenters, yard men, blacksmiths, race-horse men, steamboat men, and like that. The low[est] class [of slaves] worked in the fields.[82]

Among the Choctaws and Chickasaws, about 4,000 freedmen began developing settlements of their own in the Leased District previously under Choctaw and Chickasaw control that was turned over to the United States in the 1866 treaty.[83] Not everyone was pleased with this development. As early as November 6, 1866, the Chickasaw Nation requested that the federal government remove freedmen from their reservations. Unfortunately, this was not the only instance of anti-Black racism among the Five Tribes. Cherokees forbade intermarriage with African Americans by law.[84]

Whether Black, white or Indian, everyone realized the power of the press. Although the weekly *Cherokee Phoenix* began publishing in the old Cherokee homeland in 1828, the first newspaper published in Indian Territory was the *Cherokee Advocate* of Park Hill on September 26, 1834.[85] Surely watching the Cherokees, the Choctaws started their first newspaper in 1848, the *Choctaw Telegraph*, published in Doaksville. The mixed-blood entrepreneur Elias C. Boudinot started a newspaper in 1875 in Muskogee called the *Indian Progress*, but the Muscogees chased him out of town, and he had only enough time to load his press onto a wagon to escape to Vinita. Like many traditionalists in the Five Nations, Muscogee leaders feared that the newspapers would bring radical change at the expense of their people forgetting the old Medicine Way. Soon, however, they realized the advantage of expressing their legal rights and started a tribal newspaper in Eufaula called the *Indian Journal* in May 1876.[86] The Chickasaws did not launch their first newspaper, the *Pauls Valley Enterprise*, until 1887. Supplementing age-old oral tradition, the Five Nations newspaper boom lasted beyond the first land run in 1889. Until Oklahoma statehood, at least seventy-five newspapers operated in the Choctaw Nation alone.[87] There were nine Black newspapers by 1900, and twenty-six more by the time Oklahoma became a state in 1907.[88]

By the end of the century, the white population of Indian Territory had ballooned to 109,400, while the Black population increased to 18,000. The Indian population remained about the same as it was in 1865. The new white residents were "tenant farmers, coal miners, railroad workers, cowboys, and merchants" as well as preachers and teachers.[89] While the newcomers filled important roles in Indian Territory, their presence contributed to a general anxiety about Indigenous sovereignty and land rights.

In 1887, the US government passed the Dawes Act. Although the Five Tribes and four other tribes were exempt from this law, it still affected them significantly. On October 3, 1893, Muscogee leader L. C. Perryman recommended to the National Council "that you take some action in the premises, to the end that we may be able to treat with said [Dawes] commission in an honorable and intelligent manner whenever they may visit this Nation."[90] As delegates representing the Muscogees in Washington, Pleasant Porter and A. P. McKellop stated the tribe's cause for becoming citizens in order to form their own territory. They stated, "the day is rapidly approaching when the Indians now constituting these independent governments must be absorbed and become a part of the United States." The two statesmen added, "To-day they are surrounded by settled states and territories; white citizens, by the permission of the Indians themselves, have been admitted into their territory, until now the white people domiciled within the borders of the Five Civilized Tribes outnumber the members of the tribes and are rapidly increasing."[91]

In general, more traditionally oriented members of the Five Nations strongly opposed allotment. In early December 1896, Choctaw full bloods decided to meet with the Dawes Commission at the Antlers Convention held at Fort Smith. Although they opposed allotment, the full bloods decided in their own council to negotiate with the commission. In the first of two major points, the full bloods stated, "We favor the continuation and preservation of our government as it now exists, and was handed down to us by our forefathers; and while it may be that a change is inevitable, we do not believe that our people are prepared for such change and we know that at least three-fourths of the Indians by blood do not desire it, as is shown by their votes in the late election."[92] However, allotment was not universally opposed in Indian Territory.

The land allotment issue dominated the Cherokee election in 1892, compelling Principal Chief Bushyhead and the other candidates, George Benge and Joel B. Mayes, to state their positions of whether to accept or reject allotment. At first Bushyhead hesitated, but then he expressed his support for allotment if it proved to be in line with the tribe's constitution.[93] The *Cherokee Telephone* reported, "Bushyhead, who was apparently trying to maintain his equilibrium on the allotment fence [*sic*] has been dropped with an ominous thud into the ranks of the allotters and the eagles of victory will perch upon his banner next August."[94] Bushyhead won reelection largely due to his constant speech stumping.[95]

Still, the specter of allotment remained cause for vigilance. In an eighteen-page ultimatum to the Dawes Commission on October 28, 1897, the Cherokees reminded the commissioners of the promise in the Treaty of New Echota in 1835. The Cherokee leadership stated, "the immemorial right of self government was recognized by the United States as belonging to the Cherokee Nation in the fifth article of the treaty of 1835, and the recognition was bought and paid for among other things held to be valuable, if not invaluable, by the Cherokees—by their original homes east of the Mississippi."[96]

One of the major concerns for the Cherokees and other tribes was the Dawes Act's requirement that tribal members accept allotments to receive individual ownership of surveyed tribal lands. Many mixed-blood Indians accepted this change while full bloods were reluctant, especially among the Keetoowah Cherokees. The Keetoowahs were the most traditional of the Cherokees and met regularly to oppose the idea of allotment.[97] It became apparent to the Keetoowahs that accepting allotments and ownership of them meant mimicking the practices of white settlers, tilling the soil to develop farms and raise livestock. By August 1901, the *Chelsea Reporter* noted that "about 1400 full blood Cherokees had not enrolled with the Dawes commission" and that soldiers from Fort Gibson might be deployed to assist in their enrollment to receive land allotments.[98] In late November, Frank J. Boudinot, the secretary of the Keetoowahs, and his family appeared before the Dawes Commission to enroll and receive their land allotment certificates. Supporters of allotment believed that many other traditional holdouts would follow Boudinot's example.[99]

With the Curtis Act, passed in 1898, calling for the end of tribal governments on March 4, 1906, the Muscogees tried to prepare themselves. They passed an act in early November 1905 to create a delegation consisting of Principle Chief Pleasant Porter, Roley McIntosh, and G. W. Grayson. The delegation had the full authority "to agree with the government upon a plan that will give a legal basis of all landed interests conveyed through the Creek Nation after March 4th, 1906, and arrange with the government for the final payment of all the assets due the Nation from the United States."[100] Congress denied this request by taking no action.[101] To help prepare the Muscogees for what was to come, Principal Chief Porter had the tribe pay George W. Grayson $225 "for translating and printing in Creek, 2500 copies of the Curtis and [five] Statehood Bills."[102] In an assertion of sovereignty, Porter argued that the Native people of Indian Territory "are now transformed into industrial, civilized and self-maintaining communities; that they have evolved systems of governments and laws similar to those of the states of the Union; that in fact they have ceased to be an uncivilized people requiring the paternal care of the United States government, and on the contrary both their interest and common justice demand that they be clothed with citizenship and be accorded all the rights, privileges and immunities belonging to the citizens of the United States."[103]

Around this time, in 1905, the Kinta Separate Statehood Club published a thirty-two-page booklet entitled *Addresses and Arguments by Prominent Men in Favor of Separate Statehood for Indian Territory*. It made three arguments for an Indian state to become the forty-sixth in the American Union. The arguments focused on treaties, federal laws, and statements by individuals. For example, article 4 of the Choctaw Treaty of 1830 stated, "that no Territory or State shall ever have a right to pass laws for the government of the Choctaw Nation of Red People and their descendants, and that no part of the land granted them shall ever be embraced in any Territory or State."[104]

In another case, article 5 of the treaty with the Cherokees in 1835 stated, "nor shall either or any part of either ever be erected into a Territory without the free and full consent, or without the legislative authority of the tribe owning the same."[105] Article 4 of the treaty with the Creeks and Seminoles of 1845 stated that "no State or Territory should ever pass laws for the government of the Creek or Seminole Tribes of Indians, and that no portion of [their lands] shall either or any part of either ever be erected into a Territory without the free and full consent, or without the legislative authority of the tribes owning the same."[106] Muskogee-based lawyer and businessman Charles Haskell, a steadfast friend of the Muscogees, summed up the case succinctly: "The fact is, the Indian is as ready for statehood now as he will ever be."[107]

Perhaps no nation better exemplified the changing nature of tribal governance in the post–Civil War era than the Muscogees. The Muscogee Council House on Sixth Street in downtown Okmulgee symbolized this transition from a loose association of autonomous *tvlofvs* to a national government. After the Civil War, the Muscogees formed two governing councils, North and the South, similar to the Upper and Lower towns in the Old South. In 1868 the two divisions of government merged into one, headquartered in a national council house constructed of logs. Ten years later, in a sign of this change becoming permanent, a two-story limestone council house was built.[108]

One can imagine the conversation when Albert Pike reported his progress of negotiations with the Indian nations to Confederate president Jefferson Davis. Undoubtedly, Davis was elated with the final results: over twenty different tribes, bands, and communities had agreed to fight for the South. But to convince the leaders and headmen of the Five Nations to permit their warriors to fight against the Union, Pike had promised the tribes that they could form a state and join the Confederate States of America. Surely Jefferson Davis, a haughty southerner, had some difficulty accepting the possibility of Indian Territory becoming a Confederate state. In his own words, Davis remarked, "giving to certain tribes the unqualified right of admission as a State in to the compact of the Confederacy, and in the meantime allowing each of the tribes to have a delegate in Congress. These provisions are regarded not only impolite but unconstitutional, it not being within the limits of the treaty-making power to admit a State."[109] Despite his reservations, the South needed Indian Territory on its side to win, so the promise endured. Of course, Indian Territory would not become a Confederate state because the Confederacy ceased to exist after 1865. But the prospect of statehood for Indian Territory gained new traction in the decades that followed.

THREE

Boomers and Land Runs

Some people shy away from attention, but other people crave it. "Colonel" Charles C. Carpenter fell into the latter group. Born in Ohio, young Charles joined the US Navy at the age of sixteen. As an adult, he longed for fame and fortune, but, given the choice, he would have opted for poverty over riches if it meant being famous. Prior to the Civil War, Carpenter ventured west to Kansas and later became a Jayhawk on the Union side during the Civil War. In the same year of Custer's defeat at Little Bighorn, 1876, Carpenter boldly led a small settler party to stake homesteads in the Black Hills of the Dakotas.[1]

When Colonel Carpenter swaggered into a room with his flashy smile and wide eyes, he made an immediate impression and inspired two distinct reactions: love or hate. He wore his hair shoulder-length, which he complemented by a long mustache and short beard. His attire accentuated his frontiersman appearance. He wore a waist-length buckskin coat with fringe, and he preferred knee-high black boots. To top it off, he donned a wide-brimmed hat turned up like a crown. Undoubtedly, in his style of clothes and hair, Carpenter was imitating the flamboyant George Armstrong Custer, the martyred hero of the Little Bighorn.

Officially, Carpenter was not really a colonel, although he loved the title, but he liked "general" even more, another title some people gave him.[2] Perhaps a huckster, pitch man, con man, and idealist, he was for certain an opportunist. Charles Carpenter saw the Unappropriated Lands, the area in the middle of Indian Territory left over from the treaties of 1866 that had not been promised to any of the tribes, as prime real estate waiting to be seized by someone with courage. He believed that he was the right man to lead others onto the promised lands. The so-called colonel was guided by the lust for land that courses through the veins of American history.

Yet Carpenter would not be known as the most famous boomer in Indian Territory. (The term "boomer" derived from the people who joined the gold and silver booms in nineteenth-century America and those who believed the rumors of free land to be opened to settlers). Born on December 30, 1836, the most well-known boomer, David Lewis Payne, grew up on a poor farm in Indiana. Like many young men of his day, Payne heard the clarion call, "Go West, young man, go West and grow up with the country." This encouraging slogan made famous by newspaper editor Horace Greeley was borrowed from a newspaper article published in the *Terre Haute Daily Express* in 1851.[3]

In 1860, prior to the start of the Civil War, Congress debated a homestead bill that was fiercely opposed by southern Democrats, who wanted western territories to become slave states. Still, the bill passed both houses, but President James Buchanan, a Democrat, vetoed the bill. After the southern states seceded from the Union, the bill came up again, with Congress once again voting in its favor. President Abraham Lincoln signed the bill into law on May 20, 1862.[4]

The Homestead Act was crafted with the image of Thomas Jefferson's yeoman-farmer democracy in mind. Instead of large chunks of land owned by the wealthy, the bill aimed to make land-owning accessible to the common person. In a speech at Cincinnati, President Lincoln said encouragingly, "In regard to the Homestead Law, I have to say that in so far as the Government lands can be disposed of, I am in favor of cutting up the wild lands into parcels, so that every poor man may have a home."[5] Inspired by the Civil War context, it stipulated that land recipients must not have not joined the current rebellion against the US government. Beyond that requirement, any man or woman who was at least twenty-years old or a head of household if younger could file for 160 acres of land. If the grantee demonstrated occupancy by making improvements on it for five years, the person could file for a fee patent of ownership of the land.

But Indian Territory was exempted from the Homestead Act. The government rejected all requests from boomers and freedmen to open up the Unappropriated Lands, or any part of the territory, to settlement. The government argued the Unappropriated Lands had never been intended for public domain.[6] But the boomers promoted a kind of "racialized agrarianism" that was built on the Jeffersonian ideal of yeoman democracy.[7]

In the late 1870s, David Payne reached his early forties and stood in the prime of his life. Sturdy as an oak, he stood six feet, four inches tall. His broad shoulders seemed massive, and he possessed a square jaw and inviting gray eyes. Flashing a charismatic grin, Payne loved the outdoors and was a free spirit at heart. Earlier, he and his brother Jack had left the family farm in Indiana and headed west to Kansas to pursue their fortune. Instead of seeking riches, David Payne joined the Civil War on the Union side and enlisted in the Fourth Kansas Volunteer Infantry.[8]

Years later, Payne's future and those of many others, especially the Native people of Indian Territory, were changed by a newspaper article. Printed on one sheet, "The Indian Question: The Logic of Events," appeared in the *Chicago Times* on February 17, 1879. In it, Elias C. Boudinot, the mixed-blood Cherokee lawyer, responded to a letter from Augustus Albert of Baltimore, Maryland. Boudinot explained how an area of almost three million square miles was not promised to any tribe, and he provided a map of these Unappropriated Lands. In Boudinot's opinion, this vast acreage in the middle of Indian Territory did not belong to anyone.[9] Reportedly, the *Times* received numerous letters wanting to know more.

The land Boudinot referred to as the Unappropriated Lands were also known as the "Unassigned Lands," a term that appeared on a map in 1885. The map showed the reduced land sizes for the Five Nations following the four treaties of 1866 and which lands were left after other Indian nations had been removed to the territory in the years since.[10] The key signatures on the four treaties belonged to Elijah Sells, the superintendent of Indian Affairs, and Dennis N. Cooley, the commissioner of Indian Affairs and the man most intent on punishing the tribes for fighting for the Confederacy. Among the Five Tribes, the federal government forced the Muscogees to sell the western half of their land, 3,250,560 acres, for which the United States paid thirty cents per acre, amounting to a total of $975,168. The Muscogees were allowed to keep the eastern half of their assigned territory, about 3,000,000 acres.[11] Possessing 2,169,080 acres, the Seminoles had to sell their land to the government and had to buy back a portion of their former land. The Seminoles had to pay an increased price of fifty cents per acre and could only afford to buy back about a quarter of the land.[12] The government treated the Choctaws and Chickasaws in the same fashion and compelled the two tribes to part with the southwestern corner of Indian Territory, which was called the Leased District and amounted to about seven million acres, for a price of $300,000.[13] Government pressure led to the Cherokees to sell the Cherokee Outlet, a strip of their land west of their reservation that stretched to Texas and consisted of 12,500 square miles.[14] The government planned to make room in the western half of the territory for a second wave of removed Indians.

At the same time, settlers cast covetous eyes on lands in Indian Territory. As the *Kansas City Times* described, "there are fourteen millions of acres within the Territory from which the Indian title has been extinguished by Government purchase. The largest portion of these Government lands lie next to the five civilized tribes, so-called, and the northern boundary is about ninety miles south of the Kansas line."[15] In 1872 "a large number of whites from Kansas" arrived unannounced on the Cherokee reservation. Commanding General John Pope of the Department of the Missouri ordered Captain J. J. Upham to lead the Sixth Cavalry to remove about 1,500 squatters.[16] The settlers put up a fight, and Pope needed reinforcements. Help came from Interior Secretary Carl Schurz, who asked Secretary of War Alexander Ramsey to send soldiers to the boomer hotspots in Coffeyville, Wichita, and Arkansas City in Kansas.[17] Despite government efforts to keep them off Indian lands, more boomers arrived.

One of them was a dashing man often addressed as "colonel." During April 1879, Charles Carpenter and his new bride, Mary, arrived in Independence, Kansas, to set up shop. Carpenter began to do what he did best, persuade people to follow his vision. He dreamed of setting up settler colonies in the part of Indian Territory referred to as the "Unappropriated Lands," which he promised would be a new Canaan. Most settlers dreamed of having a homestead for their families with a small farm raising wheat and corn. Not only did Colonel Carpenter sign boomers up for a small fee to join his colonies, but he also convinced store merchants in Independence to help his enterprise by stocking up on goods that settlers would need for their expeditions to the forbidden Indian Territory.[18] During the first week of

May 1879, most everyone expected Carpenter to lead potential homesteaders into Indian Territory, but the colonel stayed behind in Independence after Inspector John McNeil of the US Indian Office arrived on the scene. McNeil warned Carpenter that if he did not stop that he would be arrested and put in prison. Carpenter rode away, and thereafter David Payne became the popular leader of the boomer movement.

While white settlers believe that Unappropriated Lands were meant for them based on their understanding of the Homestead Act, African Americans, especially freedmen, desired the same opportunity to possess a home and a farm. This was especially true for those who had been enslaved by Indian masters.[19] The end of the Civil War witnessed thousands of African American "Exodusters" migrating from the Deep South to the West. The most active years of this migration were between 1879 and 1881, when many freed slaves as many as 40,000 left with hope for the promised lands in the West. Most went to Kansas, while others set out for Colorado, Nebraska, Ohio, Montana, the Dakotas, and the Southwest.[20] Like the white boomers, many Black migrants keep their eyes on the lands in Indian Territory.

Both white and Black settlers were now pushing to invade the Unappropriated Lands, compelling the Interior Department to send a request for help to President Rutherford B. Hayes. The president hastily issued a proclamation on April 26, 1879, against illegal settling on any Native lands in the Indian Territory. Two days later, on April 28, 1879, a boomer colonization party staked out a new settlement and named it the city of Oklahoma. Also called Boomer Creek, the camp rested on the Deep Fork of the Canadian River. Newspapers argued that "these were public lands." The settlers arrived mostly from Missouri, Kansas, and Texas, "carrying their household goods and farming implements." Trying to enforce the president's proclamation, the military patrolled along the lengthy borders of Indian Territory.[21]

The growing influx of illegal settlers gravely concerned the Five Nations and other tribes of the territory. Commissioner of Indian Affairs Ezra A. Hayt soon learned that "thousands of persons of white and some of colored blood claim citizenship, which is stoutly disputed by the Indian authorities."[22] Outsiders desired to become insiders, but they also wanted control over the land. Lewis N. Hornbeck, a newspaper editor, claimed before Congress that "I have met men since I came here, who said they were Indian who did not look any more like an Indian than you do. Imagine my surprise when he told me that he was an Indian, being an eighth blood, and a member of the Chickasaw legislature."[23] Livestock and natural resources like timber were stolen by intruders at will. Commissioner of Indian Affairs Hiram Price reported, "spoliation of valuable walnut timber has been and is still being constantly carried on, and unless some stringent and effective measures are devised to stop it, that whole section of country will be completely denuded of timber."[24]

The press worked against government efforts to keep settlers out of Indian Territory. The *Kansas City Times* printed a representative article, "On to Oklahoma," on May 4, 1870: "This territory, comprising the vast region extending from Kansas to Texas and westward from Arkansas, is almost unsurpassed in fertility of soil, climate and natural resources. It is well watered, and the rainfall is abundant; the climate is mild and equable, and in agricultural resources the territory ranks foremost in the Southwest." The paper lamented that this region "destined to develop into one of the largest, most populous and flourishing States of the Union, is given over to the exclusive occupancy of the Indian tribes, removed thither during the past forty years, negroes who were their slaves, half-breeds, and whites who by marriage are held to have joined the tribes."[25]

Editorials and articles kept appearing, questioning how long could the government deny settlers from homesteading in Indian Territory.[26] Ezra A. Hayt was a former businessman and tried to run the Indian Bureau in a businesslike manner, but he drew sharp criticism from the *New York Times* and others who believed the federal agency could be more effective.[27] After a couple of years as commissioner, Hayt resigned from his position, thereby putting the boomer problems in the hands of E. M. Marbel. The new acting commissioner was appalled by how boomers persistently misrepresented the words of President Hayes, citing Manifest Destiny as justification.[28] The boomers were convinced that President Hayes had changed his view since his proclamation of April 26, 1879. Marbel wrote the boomers believed "in his last annual message he had admitted that said lands were public and should be settled upon, and hence that they were violating neither the President's proclamation nor any law of the United States in emigrating to and locating upon such lands."[29]

The boomers more than frustrated Commissioner Marbel, and Secretary of the Interior Carl Schurz contacted Alexander Ramsey, the secretary of the War Department, about sending more soldiers to Kansas's southern border.

During the summer of 1879, troops from Fort Riley patrolled towns to demonstrate to the boomers and other opportunists to keep out of the Indian Territory.[30] At the request of Schurz, Hayes issued a second proclamation on February 12, 1880:

> I, Rutherford B. Hayes, President of the United States, do admonish and warn all such persons so intending or preparing to remove upon said lands, or into said Territory, without permission of the proper agent of the Indian Department, against any attempt to so remove or settle upon any of the lands of said Territory; and I do further want and notify any and all such persons who may so offend that they will be speedily and immediately removed therefrom by the agent, according to the laws made and provided, and that no efforts will be spared to prevent the invasion of said Territory."[31]

The proclamation had no effect on the boomers. Their unyielding stubbornness compelled Schurz to contact the War Department for even more soldiers "along the line between the Indian Territory and Kansas, to prevent unauthorized persons from entering the Territory." Furthermore, "details were made for the arrest and removal of such intruders as might be found within its borders." But it seemed neither presidential proclamations nor federal law would stop the boomers.

One of these boomers, David Payne, continued planning with "Oklahoma Harry" L. Lee, a wealthy Wichita resident, to lead a colony of twenty-five sodbusters into Indian Territory in April 1880.[32] Eventually, a unit of soldiers found Payne and his party encamped about two miles south of the North Fork of the Canadian River. The soldiers immediately arrested Payne and eleven boomers and then escorted "the intruders . . . outside the Territory and there discharged, with a warning not to return."[33]

In mid-July soldiers caught Payne and twenty-two of his associates in Indian Territory, and on August 10, they "were again arrested by the United States forces, and, in pursuance of the order of the President, turned over to the United States marshal for the western district of Arkansas, to be held for prosecution under the United States laws relating to intruders in the Indian country." Judge Isaac Parker released Payne and his boomers "on bail to appear for trial at the November term of the United States district court."[34] Payne missed his court appearance on November 3. His lawyer, Elias C. Boudinot, tried to get the case dismissed according to wrongful jurisdiction, but Judge Parker denied his motion.[35] Following several delays, Judge Parker ruled on May 21, 1881, that Payne broke the law in trying to settle in Indian Territory. Parker charged Payne with a $1,000 fine for trespassing on the Unappropriated Lands.[36]

Answering criticisms by the *Indian Journal* newspaper in Muskogee, Payne fired off a letter to the editor, which was published in early August 1880. "There is a determination on the part of the people to settle these lands which your people ceded to the government," said Payne. "And on which there is not an Indian or an acre of land cultivated. We will settle the country and hope in ninety days to have a town of 10,000 people. We want industrious and solemn people and the rules of our colony prohibit the sale of intoxicating liquors." Payne went on to boast, "We will have churches and schools and hope to be good neighbors of yor [sic] people and that friendly relations may exist between our cities. We do not propose to interfere with anyone's rights but we propose to claim and maintain our own."[37]

Payne only intensified his efforts in the following months. On November 3, 1880, David L. Payne, now president of the newly named Oklahoma Colony, issued a proclamation in the *Wichita Beacon*:

> This is, therefore, to give notice that all persons desiring to join the third expedition to the Indian Territory under the auspices of the Oklahoma colony should hold themselves prepared to move at five days [sic] notice. We shall carry heavy freights, and rally in such force as shall insure the success of the expedition. The date of the movement can not [sic] be announced at this time. Every colonist should take assorted hardware and implements essential to pioneer settlement, and should also provide himself with subsistence for at least thirty days. We shall do [intend] to stay.[38]

In 1881 and for the next three years, the prince of the boomers led at least eight expeditions into the Indian Territory. He was not alone in his efforts. William Couch led his share of intrusions during the mid-1880s.[39] From North Carolina, Couch had made his way to the West to become a boomer in 1879. Now that Payne was not the only one leading these expeditions, he decided to travel to Washington in early 1882. He lobbied Secretary of the Interior Henry Teller to designate land in Indian Territory for settlement by the boomers. As an opportunist, Payne likely saw the assassination of President James Garfield only a few months earlier as a chance to seek a change in policy while the nation mourned and Washington was in shock.

Against expectations, Secretary Teller told Payne to stop the expeditions, but his warning did no good. In early May 1884. Payne collected a group of eager boomers and they traveled south. The small group camped at a place called Rock Falls on the Chikaskia River. The small river branched off the Arkansas River and nourished a small, fertile area surrounding it. Rock Falls held much potential. But once again, Payne and his boomers faced official rebuke. President Chester A. Arthur responded and declared a third presidential proclamation against boomers settling in Indian Territory. President Arthur's ultimatum read:

> I, Chester A. Arthur, President of the United States, do admonish and warn all such persons so intending or preparing to remove upon said lands or into said Territory against any attempt to so remove or settle upon any of the lands of said Territory; and I do further warn and notify any and all such persons who do so offend that they will be speedily and immediately removed therefrom by the proper officers of the Interior Department, and, if necessary, the aid and assistance of the military forces of the United States will be involved in removing all such intruders from the said Indian Territory.[40]

The boomers ignored the third presidential proclamation just as they had the others. Deputy Marshal W. B. Williams arrived at the boomer camp on August 13, 1884, and arrested Payne and those with him. The lawman informed Payne that he and his group would be escorted to Wichita, Kansas, to face trial.[41] Fearing this punishment was not strict enough, a military commander arrived with a unit of soldiers and instead took Payne and the boomers to the federal court at Fort Smith, Arkansas, to face Judge Isaac Parker, who was very familiar with the Payne and his intruding tactics.

The trip to Fort Smith proved arduous for David Payne. His knees ached badly from rheumatism. His bland diet of bacon, bread, and coffee deprived him of essential vitamins. In late August the soldiers, Payne, and his boomers arrived at Fort Smith. Appearing before the familiar face of the "hanging judge" on September 8, 1884, Payne was charged with trespassing again along with the crime of selling whiskey in Indian Territory.[42] In pain from rheumatism and unable to pay the $1,000 bond, Payne languished in jail for almost a month. Passing the hat around, fellow boomers finally raised enough money to post bail for him. While Payne's release was being processed by the court, Judge Parker warned him to never again step into Indian Territory.

The beleaguered boomer traveled back to Kansas, skirting Indian Territory. He arrived at Wichita on September 12 to face yet another criminal charge. Payne's crime called for a grand jury to be appointed by the US district court in Wichita. The charge alleged that Payne and his boomers had intruded illegally into the Cherokee Outlet, a northern part of the Indian Territory. Payne's lawyers filed an appeal. Judge C. G. Foster announced Payne's next court date for November 11, 1884.[43] On that day, Judge Foster issued his ruling in the case known as *United States v. Payne.* Ignoring the fact that Payne trespassed into the Cherokee Outlet, Judge Foster ruled "the colonists are vindicated in their claim to peaceable possession of Oklahoma."[44] Foster's unexpected ruling was a spectacular turnaround for the boomer movement and a disheartening blow to the Five Tribes in Indian Territory.

Elated, Payne arrived at the courthouse in Wellington, Kansas, a boomer beehive, and delivered a two-hour speech to a large crowd. He elaborated about the court's decision, his rights, and the rights of boomers to have their day of settlement in Indian Territory. After much cheering, congratulations, handshaking, and backslapping, the boomer prince returned to his room at the De Barnard Hotel.[45] Early the next morning, November 28, 1884, David Payne and his common-law wife, Rachel Anna Haines, rendezvoused with *Oklahoma War Chief* editor, J. B. Cooper. After giving their orders for breakfast, they waited, but Payne was unusually quiet. While waiting for a glass of milk, Payne closed his eyes. The editor lightly shook Payne's shoulder and said, "Wake up, Cap and eat your breakfast before it gets cold." Rachel Haines and J. B. Cooper realized the prince of the boomers was gone at age forty-seven.[46] He had died of heart failure. The boomer prince was buried in the Wellington cemetery. (Family members had Payne reburied in 1995 at Stillwater in Payne County, Oklahoma, which carries his name.)

Boomers hoped that Payne's death might soften the federal response to their activities. A memorial presented by Senator Preston B. Plumb of Kansas to Congress in January 1885 read: "Petition of residents of Stillwater, in Oklahoma, urging Congress to order the withdrawal of Federal troops from their midst, and to as early as [the] day is possible organize Oklahoma as a territory, and provide for the appointment of a Governor, and the election of necessary officers."[47] The memorial was referred to the Senate Committee on Indian Affairs, but went nowhere.

Black migrants continued their efforts to settle in Indian Territory into the 1880s. African Americans in Illinois and other northern states formed the Freedmen's Oklahoma Immigration Association. The organization focused on an area that would become Guthrie. Near there, African American settlers succeeded in establishing a few smaller settlements.[48] Many African Americans were seeking to escape discrimination in the South, where their legal rights were limited by Jim Crow laws.[49] The possibility of free land in the Indian Territory was worth taking a risk despite federal opposition.

Later in the decade, it appeared the tide might finally turn in favor of the boomers and other settlers. In 1888, Congressman William Springer, a Democrat from Indiana, chaired the Committee on Territories and he introduced a HR 1277 and this measure became the "Oklahoma Bill." His bill proposed to carve a new Oklahoma Territory out of Indian Territory.[50] The measure, which the boomers supported, divided Indian Territory in half to create two territories. On February 1, the House approved the bill, and it moved from there to the Senate Committee on Territories. Unfortunately for the boomers, the measure was tabled. The boomers found themselves strenuously opposed by Texas cattlemen who drove their cattle through the various Indian reservations to the Kansas cow towns. For the moment, the cowboys had won.[51]

One year later, Congressman William Springer strategically attached the Oklahoma Bill as a rider amendment to the Indian Appropriations Act of 1890. Congress usually passed Indian appropriation bills to fund the Bureau of Indian Affairs in order to fulfill its treaty promises to tribes and operate its agencies throughout Indian Country. As Congress reached the end of its session, former General James Weaver pushed for Springer's bill. At first, the bill failed to pass the House by a few votes. The next day the bill was reintroduced and passed with the required majority.[52] All seemed well until the day before Congress adjourned. The Senate debated the bill, but the only consensus was for it not to be voted on.

Congress met again during the first week in December. Boomer lobbyists William Couch and Samuel Crocker worked hard to get "their" bill passed. Born in Devonshire, England, Crocker was raised in Michigan before he brought his newspaper editing skills to the boomers. Two weeks went by with little action. In an effort to end this stalemate, Congressman Springer proposed a rider, section 13, to be attached to the Indian appropriations bill. The amendment called for the Unappropriated Lands to become public domain and open for settlement. This time, the Senate voted to pass the bill. On March 2, 1889, at the end of his term, President Grover Cleveland signed the bill into law. The boomer dream had come true.

Forty-eight hours later, newly elected President Benjamin Harrison issued a proclamation to open the Unappropriated Lands to settlement at high noon on April 22, 1889.[53] Land offices were to be opened at Kingfisher and Guthrie.[54] Soldiers nervously guarded the starting lines on all four sides of the Unappropriated Lands.

Cheaters who sneaked across the starting line and hid from the army patrols until after the race started were originally called "moonshiners" for their habit of trespassing at night. Five or six months later, moonshiners also became known as "sooners" because they were the first ones to file land claims. There were also "legal sooners" who worked in government positions such as deputy marshal or in a job that required a special permit, as was the case for railroad employees. The military allowed these legal sooners to be in the Unassigned Lands before April 22.[55]

April 22, 1889, was a crisp Monday morning with a cloudless blue sky. The hours dragged on slowly. One young claimant, James Hastings, described the scene: "there was an immense gathering of the land hungry from every state in the Union, that flocked to the towns like Arkansas City for weeks before the opening date. Here the cavalry attempted the hopeless task of holding back the overly zealous ones and keeping all men out until the legal date for entering."[56] At one official site of the run, at precisely high noon, an officer commanded a bugle to be blown while a flag was dropped to commence the run. At other sites, an officer fired a gun or ordered a cannon shot. The mad race of 50,000 crazed people was on. By wagon, horseback, and on foot, they rushed. Some crowded onto the five trains that hauled people into the Unassigned Lands, and many jumped off to run for a claim.[57]

Some settlers believed that all you had to do was to drive a stake into the ground with your name on it. But military officials and others supervising the land run instructed settlers that they had to find a marker on their chosen land and write down the number on the marker and file it at the land office in Guthrie or Kingfisher.[58] Right at noon on the day of the run, special deputy

Orion Eli Mohler opened the double doors of the land office at Guthrie. The first person to file a land claim was Mark A. Cohn, who paid his $14 filing fee, plus filing claims for two special deputies and legal sooners, Benton J. Turner and James H. Huckleberry.[59] Within six hours Guthrie became a city of 15,000 people, and Oklahoma (later Oklahoma City) had 10,000 by nightfall.[60] Boomer leader W. L. Couch was named the temporary mayor of the city of Oklahoma.[61] The new settlement of Guthrie became the territorial capital. One hundred days later, Guthrie would boast four thousand houses, several hundred tents, five banks, fifteen hotels, three music halls, fifty grocery stores, and three daily newspapers.[62] By the end of July 1889, a total of 5,764 people had filed claims on 903,962 acres. Before the end of the following year, 7,033 more settlers filed on an additional million acres. Claimants had five years to improve their homesteads, but a severe drought in the early 1890s challenged settlers' efforts to follow through.[63]

Among the estimated land rushers were nearly 3,000 African Americans, according to one report.[64] Mostly they staked claims to lands that white settlers did not want. Besides the small number of Blacks who filed land claims, most of them obtained land from "land speculators, boosters, and individuals who sold them abandoned or unworked parcels, known as relinquishments."[65] Immediately with the emergence of Guthrie and Oklahoma City, segregation occurred. But rural areas were exceptions; neighbors lived farther apart from each and depended on each for help. In general, recent European immigrants, many of whom had experienced discrimination in the homelands, were more welcoming toward Black settlers. These new immigrants had little knowledge of slavery.[66]

Among Black settlers were freedmen who had been enslaved to Native masters in Indian Territory. In fact, these former slaves were sometimes called Native freedmen, and they did not initially welcome Black newcomers, who were called "state Negroes."[67] The way that Black newcomers imitated white boomers created tension with Native freedmen. Black editor J. E. Toombs explained the political importance of Black landownership in the *Muskogee Comet*.[68] Toombs insisted that townships and counties "can be controlled and officered by colored men, for they own the land and have the votes which if properly handled will land in office whosoever they will."[69] These differences between Native freedmen and "state Negroes" eventually were overcome when both groups realized that they needed to stand together against Jim Crow and white supremacy.

As early as 1892, whites ran Black settlers out of the town of Lexington in Cleveland County in Oklahoma Territory and out of Blackwell toward the end of 1893. Whites had tried to run Blacks out of Ponca City the year before on December 19, but they failed.[70] Racist farmers known as white cappers drove African Americans out of Norman three years later, according to the *Kingfisher Press* on September 24. More examples of racial violence occurred throughout the next several decades.

New settlers, white and Black, made home dwellings called dugouts or sod houses ("soddies"). Tough roots and prairie grass were cut with a special plow to produce bricks that were "four to eight inches thick and twelve to eighteen inches wide." The typical soddie was about sixteen by twenty feet. Cracks in the sod bricks let in wind and flies, so they had to be filled. The inside walls could be worked and smoothed enough to be "plastered with a mixture of clay and ashes" or white-washed. Some people papered the walls with any kind of paper they could find. If wood could not be found, the roof often leaked after a rain and had to be repaired. Wood floors were rare, but packed earth produced a floor that became "hard as oak" and could be swept and mopped.[71]

The Five Tribes watched the land run with concern. Chickasaw governor William L. Byrd warned "that no white man shall remain in his domain under any circumstance."[72] In addition to white squatters, African Americans tried to settle on Chickasaw lands.[73] A part of the problem was due to some Chickasaws hiring outsiders to work on their farms and in other capacities requiring labor. In 1892 Governor Byrd proposed a law to "force the Citizens of the Chickasaw Nation to see that their employees get permits and . . . their having to leave the nation would be . . . because of their refusal to get permits."[74] The sense that their lands were being overrun would get worse for the Five Tribes and other Native people in Indian Territory in the years to come.

The second land run occurred on September 22, 1891. This time, the area opened for settlement covered six counties of 1,120,000 acres of the surplus lands of the Iowas, Sacs and Foxes, Shawnees, and Potawatomis. The Cimarron River formed the northern boundary. George W. Stiles was a teenager at the time and later described the day of the race: "At the river I saw a sight never to be forgotten. Hundreds of anxious home seekers had gathered at the vantage point. Among the eager throng were many covered wagons, vehicles of all descriptions, sulkeys, rigs, spring wagons, anything with wheels, men on foot and on horseback. This was merely a sample of what was taking place at many other strategic points along the boundary lines of the Sac and Fox Indian Reservation. At the sound of the guns sharply at 12 o'clock, the race was on."[75] On April 19, 1892, the third run was carried out for former Cheyenne and Arapaho lands of 4,300,000 acres. Roughly 25,000 people participated. Officials charged each settler $1 to $2.50 per acre.[76]

Even more people migrated west and joined the land runs when the entire country fell into a financial panic. By the end of 1893, 500 banks and 1,600 businesses closed, causing 20 percent of American workers to lose their jobs. These hard times would endure for four years.[77]

On September 16, 1893, the biggest land run in American history, the Cherokee Outlet Run, took place with 100,000 people participating despite truly unfavorable conditions. One young man said the weather for the entire week was "the hottest weather of anytime this summer. Ther. 104 and 106 deg. The first 3 days; no wind, and a burning hot sun, and the dust choking everybody; night so cold, people that had overcoats wore them—the last 2 days we had strong winds and Pa said he saw the cloud of dust that hovered over Kiowa for 25 miles. It couldn't be dryer than now, and dust is very deep in the roads, and if you could see the crowds of people—6000 registered here."[78] The young settler wrote, "It was amusing to watch the people—every kind vehicle imaginable—horse back and mule back—all had their name on a board to drive in the ground when they got a claim. Some were carrying spades. Some wagons loaded with their little all. One old man went by singing, 'Uncle Sam has room enough to give us all a farm.'"[79]

After making their claims to land or town lots that had been surveyed, people had ninety days to file their claims at the land office in Enid, Perry, Woodward, or Alva. Filing a claim meant a whole day of standing in line. People "fainted by the dozens and some died." Clerks from the land booths sold water for ten cents.[80] Some people sent in their claim by mail to be processed.[81] Much had happened after the first land run in 1889, the next year and a half followed with a severe drought that seemed to curse homesteaders. Rain hardly fell.[82] The final land run took place on May 23, 1895, when about 10,000 settlers raced for around 200,000 acres of Kickapoo surplus lands.[83]

Natives responded to the land rushes in ways that were sometimes inconsistent. Chickasaw governor William Byrd, who had once pushed through a tribal law that disenfranchised all intermarried white men from voting in Chickasaw elections, was by 1894 "turning to the white men who he deprived of the right to vote and is asking [for] their support. How can they support him if they are not allowed to vote?"[84] Another tribe responded with racial prejudice. The flood of Black outsiders provoked opposition from the Osages. The Osage leadership requested US marshals to carry out the Osage attorney general's proclamation "notifying all negroes on the Osage Indian reservation to leave the premises before July 1, 1895."[85]

After several chaotic land runs involving thousands of people, the federal government tried another method that it hoped would be more orderly: a land lottery. A land lottery had only been conducted once before in American history, in Georgia, coincidentally for Cherokee land. The lottery was to be operated by Secretary Ethan Allan Hitchcock and the Department of the Interior.

The land to be distributed had once belonged to Plains Indian nations. In 1891 the Wichitas ceded their land from where the Washita River flowed north into the Canadian River. This area included territory from the ninety-eighth meridian and west for forty miles. In 1892 the Kiowas surrendered their land from the ninety-eighth meridian west to the North Fork of the Red River. The Red River bordered both areas on the south and the Washita River on the north. A law passed on January 4, set August 6, 1901 as the deadline for completing land surveys and the opening 2.1 million acres.[86] The vast land desired consisted of five counties and parts of seven other counties.[87]

Individuals wishing to participate in the lottery could register at El Reno and Fort Sill throughout July 1901. By July 24 over 16,000 people had registered. Early in the morning of July 29, thousands of eager people showed up at the offices in El Reno and Fort Sill to see if they were among the fortunate recipients of a quarter section of land. As many as 30,000 people watched and applauded after each drawing. Two thousand ballots were drawn each day until a total of 6,500 was reached. A group of clerks processed the winners' documents for their new land sites.[88]

On August 1, 1901, the second land lottery took place in Oklahoma Territory. After the 957 members of the Wichita and Caddo tribes were allotted land, a surplus of 152,714 acres was left. A three-million-acre reservation had been granted to the Comanches, Kiowas, and Kiowa Apaches according to a treaty they signed with the US government in 1867. Now only 235,000 acres remained in Native hands, creating a surplus of 2,765,000 acres. On August 6, another land lottery sought to distribute 3.5 million acres of Kiowa, Comanche, and Apache lands.[89]

Ultimately, officials would experiment with yet another means of disposing of ceded lands. The last means of opening former Indian Territory lands to settlers was by auction, also called sealed bid. The highest bidders vied for tracts of up to 160 acres out of a half million acres of the Big Pasture lands on the Kiowa and Comanche reservations. The auction took place in December 1906 and the average price per acre was ten dollars.[90]

At this point, no surplus Indian lands were left. In all, seven land runs, three land lotteries, and one auction made this land available to settlers in Oklahoma Territory from 1889 to 1906. Participants had a variety of motives. Some people participated for "mere curiosity or from love of adventure."[91] For the most land hungry of all, the boomers, excitement fueled the anticipation of each land run, leading to chaotic scenes. As *Outlook* magazine described, "In Oklahoma a mobocracy was established with the guiding principle, 'to each according to his speed.'"[92] One can only imagine that Native people observed the land runs with grave concern. The *Oklahoma Democrat,* a newspaper in the newly founded town of El Reno, compared the Ghost Dance phenomenon spreading among Natives on the plains in 1890 to the crazed land grabs: "Talk about messiah crazes and the foolish antics of the aboriginees [*sic*], they in comparison stand as nothing to the wild and dangerous excitement incident to lot [land claims] jumping in Oklahoma."[93]

The cast of history is full of larger-than-life characters, including the full-of-beans Charles C. Carpenter, who basked in the excitement surrounding the early days of the boomer movement. The "colonel" was there at the beginning but disappeared when things got difficult. Once David Payne inherited the movement, Colonel Carpenter fell into obscurity. But he still inspired strong words. The *Cheyenne Daily Leader* in Wyoming derided him as a "constitutional deadbeat" and a "drunken braggart." The *Arkansas City Traveler* called the colonel a "sore back, crooked legged, cross-eyed cuss." The *Kansas City Times* ridiculed Charles Carpenter as a failed Moses leading the boomers to the land of milk and honey in the old Indian Territory with a cartoon of him carrying a rock tablet with the words, "Onto Oklahoma." At some point, though, Charles Carpenter became lost to history, and we can only imagine what his thoughts were on the land rushes that came after he left the picture. Perhaps he watched from Kansas while reading the local newspaper about President Harrison's proclamation to open the Unassigned Lands and triumphantly exclaimed, "Onto Oklahoma!"[94]

Line drawing of Sequoyah teaching Akoyen the alphabet. General Personalities Collection No. 134, Cherokee Tribe No. 2 Binder, Western History Collections, University of Oklahoma.

SE-QUO-YAH TEACHING AH-YO-KEH THE ALPHABET.

Pleasant Porter, who served as principal chief of the Muscogees (Creeks). Ferguson (Walter) Collection No. 70, Creek Tribe No. 6 Binder, Western History Collections, University of Oklahoma.

Alexander Posey, Muscogee poet.
Ferguson (Walter) Collection
No. 323, Creek Tribe No. 6 Binder,
Western History Collections,
University of Oklahoma.

Autographed portrait of
William H. "Alfalfa Bill" Murray
in younger years. William Murray
Collection, Folder/Envelope 4,
Western History Collections,
University of Oklahoma.

Sequoyah, by Charles Banks Wilson. Accession No. 28, Oklahoma Historical Society Photograph Collection, Oklahoma History Center.

Seal of the state of Sequoyah. Accession No. 30061.003, Oklahoma Historical Society Photograph Collection, Oklahoma History Center.

Charles Haskell. Helen Holmes Collection No. 1101, Western History Collections, University of Oklahoma.

Edward McCabe. Norman Crockett Collection No. 58, Western History Collections, University of Oklahoma.

James Norman. William Murray Collection No. 36, Western History Collections, University of Oklahoma.

Sequoyah Convention at the Hinton Theater in Muskogee, Indian Territory, 1905. Haskell (C. N.) Collection No. 32, Cherokee Tribe No. 2 Binder, Western History Collections, University of Oklahoma.

Confederate general Albert Pike.
Accession No. 2302, Mrs. O. A. Cox
Collection, Oklahoma History
Center.

Hinton Theater, Muskogee. Accession No. 19274.6, Shiloh Museum Collection, Oklahoma History Center.

Turner Hotel, Muskogee. Accession No. 19274.9, Oklahoma Historical Society Photograph Collection, Oklahoma History Center.

FOUR

The State of Sequoyah Convention

Fate seems to walk hand in hand with certain individuals to fulfill a destiny; some people think of this as having a guardian angel. Pleasant Porter was that kind of individual. On September 22, 1840, Pleasant Porter was born in the Muscogee Nation, and his Native name, Talof Harjo, meant "Crazy Bear." His mother was Phoebe Perryman, a mixed-blood Muscogee, and his father was Benjamin Edward Porter. Phoebe and Benjamin chose another name for their son that became more popular for baby boys later in the nineteenth century. Pleasant was a favorite of his grandfather John Porter, who wanted his grandson to be educated like white boys and girls.

Pleasant Porter's mother was of the Bird Clan; therefore, he was too. An active child, Pleasant enjoyed playing outdoors, going fishing, and swimming during the humid days of summer. Some people claimed to have heard him talking to the North Canadian River. Young Pleasant probably should have died two or three times during his childhood, but he possessed an unyielding spirit. He was bitten by a water moccasin, broke one of his legs in three places when he fell from a wagon, and, with a cousin, he ate poison *Datura stramonium*, also known as thorn apple or Jimson weed. His cousin died. While fighting in the Civil War, Porter was wounded in the head twice and shot in the thigh, which caused him to limp for the rest of his life.[1] After hearing all of these near-death experiences, Muscogee elders agreed that Pleasant Porter possessed strong medicine from his Bird Clan, and *owallas*, or "prophets," sensed he would do many things during his life's journey.

Well before the Sequoyah convention of 1905, preparations were made to transfer Indian Territory to US territorial status. An organic act passed by Congress was needed to officially bestow territorial status on Indian Territory as a part of the process of becoming a state. On March 17, 1870, Senator Benjamin F. Rice, a Republican from Arkansas, introduced a measure to his colleagues "to create the Territory of Ok-la-ho-ma out of the Indian Territory." The bill found a favorable reception, especially from Alexander McDonald of the Committee on Territories. Initially, the committee members favored Rice's bill "as a matter of economy to the government and the Indian Nations, as a simple act of justice and fair-play to the Indian, and to carry out in good faith the stipulations of the treaties of 1866."[2] But then the bill languished. A report from the House Committee on Territories featured criticism from George C. McKee of Mississippi. McKee claimed that the bill proposed to separate the tribes from roughly 23 million acres of land.[3]

Rice's bill did not find widespread favor in Indian Territory. For example, Pleasant Porter supported the idea for territorial status, but his main concerns were for the Muscogee Nation. Delegates for the Cherokees, Choctaws, and Muscogees issued several memorials against the bill for territorial status.[4] In his third and fourth annual messages to Congress, President Ulysses Grant disagreed and "recommended creating a territorial form of government over Indian Territory." Over Indian objections, Grant sided with the railroads to open Indian Territory to settlers to help rebuild the country's economy after the Civil War.[5]

The railroads were of particular concern for the Five Nations. In January 1875, the Cherokees and Chickasaws issued memorials opposing the recommendation of a federal commission to create a US territory in Indian Territory. The two nations could see that J. D. Land, the chair of the commission and the treasurer of the Atlantic and Pacific Railroad, had ulterior motives. As an alternative, the Cherokees issued a memorial requesting the creation of a territory under US authority that consisted exclusively of the Five Tribes. More than 4,000 Cherokees signed the document.[6] To help protect Cherokee identity, the National Council established a citizenship court to verify members and to protect the reservation from illegal outsiders.[7]

Even more newcomers would arrive in the years to come. In 1880 Indian Agent John Q. Tufts estimated that 6,000 white people lived on the reservations of the Five Nations, and that number did not include railroad employees.[8]

Eight years later, attorney Robert Owen, a Cherokee mixed blood, asserted that the number had risen to 38,500 outsiders. External laborers with permits from the tribes made up an additional 22,000 workers.[9]

With the influx of new people came pressure to confer official territorial status on Indian Territory, although the proposals were spread out over several decades. There were also proposals that sought to deal with perceived lawlessness in the region. In his first annual message to Congress on December 6, 1881, President Chester Arthur proposed "extending the laws of Arkansas over all Indian Territory not occupied by the Five Civilized Tribes." As a caveat, he added that "this did not in any way mean immediate territorial status for the Five Civilized Tribes." Almost ten years later, on October 1, 1891, Commissioner of Indian Affairs T. J. Morgan "suggested the early passage of an enabling act for the creation of either a territory or a state from Indian Territory."[10]

Morgan's idea was indicative of a new trend, especially after the creation of Oklahoma Territory in 1890. In the early 1890s, there was renewed discussion in Congress about a sovereign Indian state. In 1892 Congressman Samuel W. Peel of Arkansas introduced a bill "for the admission of Indian Territory as a separate state." In another bill, Senator Bishop W. Perkins of Kansas proposed a bill "for a single state formed of Oklahoma [Territory] and Indian Territory."[11] A new bill based on Peel's proposal was made into law on March 3, 1893. The measure not only created a commission to negotiate land allotment with the Five Tribes, but section 16 ended with a promise "to enable the ultimate creation of a Territory of the United States with a view to the admission of the same as a State in the Union."[12] After learning about this opportunity, the Quapaws, who numbered about seventy-one people, told their Indian agent, T. J. Moore, that they wanted to be a part of Indian Territory because of the prospect of statehood.[13] Agent Dew M. Wisdom reported from the Union Agency in Muskogee that "the Indians would prefer first statehood, with their system of land tenure to remain undisturbed, and that the complicated question of allotment be worked out as the exigencies of the future may demand."[14]

Proposals for statehood for Indian Territory could also be heard in the US Senate. In 1894, Arkansas senator James Henderson Berry introduced a bill that aimed to prepare Indian Territory for statehood. A Democrat, Berry wanted Indian Territory to become the Territory of Indianola. Thereafter, statehood would follow. The Arkansan's motives may have been somewhat cynical. Most likely Senator Berry envisioned the proposed Territory of Indianola becoming a Democratic state.[15] Oklahoma Territory was heavily Republican.

Berry's proposal ran into opposition from Senator Charles Faulkner of West Virginia, who chaired the Senate Committee on Territories, and the bill died in committee. One would have thought that Senator Faulkner, also a Democrat, would have supported Berry's bill. West Virginia had its own distinctive history, having seceded from Virginia during the Civil War and becoming a Union state in 1863 by presidential proclamation.[16] Faulkner's opposition to the bill stemmed from a major political consideration. He understood that the people of recently created Oklahoma Territory also desired statehood, and he did not support the idea of two new western states.[17]

Another proposal arose from the allotment process. After negotiations with the Choctaws and Chickasaws, the Dawes Commission reached an understanding known as the Atoka Agreement on June 28, 1898. Although the agreement called for allotting Choctaw and Chickasaw lands after the termination of their governments on March 4, 1906 (as called for by the Curtis Act, passed a few months earlier), one of the provisions proved to be intriguing. The agreement stated that "the land now occupied by the Five Civilized Tribes shall, in the opinion of Congress be prepared for admission as a State to the Union."[18] Several months later, the Dawes Commission negotiated another agreement with the Cherokees. On January 14, 1899, the commission promised that the Cherokees "would never be made a part of any state of territory without their consent; or that if made a part of a state without such consent the state or territory would include only the lands of the Five Civilized Tribes."[19]

Fearing that they would lose control of their homelands if they left the political maneuvering to others, leaders of the Five Nations decided they had to act. Among the most influential was Pleasant Porter. On September 5, 1899, the Muscogees elected Pleasant Porter as their new chief. In his annual message to the Muscogee National Council in early October 1900, Chief Porter called for "the upward tendency of Indian civilization and progress that is bringing the Indian citizen into a full enjoyment of all the rights and privileges of American citizenship."[20] Porter saw the transition toward American citizenship as a natural process and he supported the idea of assimilation, which meant learning to read, write, and speak English and other aspects of "the white man's ways." Yet the leader envisioned that his people would retain their Muscogee identity. In the coming years, Porter supported another means of adapting to the American mainstream while preserving Indigenous rights: the movement to create an Indian state, which would be dubbed Sequoyah.

On September 26, 1902, the leaders of the Five Nations met at the Commercial Hotel on East Choctaw Avenue in McAlester. Muscogee chief Pleasant Porter took charge. Seminole chief Hulbutta Micco (meaning "Alligator King") and Cherokee chief Thomas Buffington attended, although Chickasaw governor Palmer Mosley sent a representative in his place.[21] It is unknown if Choctaw chief Greenwood McCurtain attended. The second chiefs of each of the Five Nations attended the meeting, as did prominent individuals like J. R. Goat, A. P. McKellop, Cheesie McIntosh, Roley McIntosh, Alex Davis, W. L. Joseph, Thomas Little, James H. Johnson, and Douglas Johnston. These leaders agreed "to unite on a plan for the future of the territory and then make a vigorous fight until the victory [of statehood] is won."[22] In fact, Seminole leader Hulbutta Micco had already expressed his opinion through an interpreter to the *South McAlester News* that he wanted "an Indian state."[23] Although the Choctaws and Chickasaws felt that the meeting focused too much on the Muscogees, the meeting at McAlester convinced them to give full support to the statehood movement.

The next meeting of the leaders of the Five Nations took place on November 28, 1902, at the courtroom in Eufaula in the Muscogee Nation. Pleasant Porter chaired the meeting and Henry Ainsley served as secretary.[24] After much discussion, the delegates proposed a resolution against any combination with Oklahoma Territory: "We are opposed to and protest against any legislation by congress that contemplates the annexation of the Indian Territory or any part thereof to the Territory of Oklahoma, or any state." The leaders insisted "upon our tribal governments continuing intact and our tribal conditions remaining unchanged until March 4, 1906, at which time should Congress deem it wise to change the present form of government in the Indian Territory."[25] The delegates at Eufaula also requested "that a state be formed out of the territory composing Indian Territory without the preliminary steps of a territorial form of government."[26] The delegates were well aware the Curtis Act of 1898 called for the end of the governments of the Five Tribes on March 6, 1906. They also saw the approaching end of their tribal governments and schools as a means for the United States to assert more control over them, usurping treaty guarantees to their sovereignty.

Racial and political differences between Oklahoma and Indian territories were exacerbated by violence. A particularly gruesome example occurred when a white mob hanged and burned alive two Seminole teenage boys, Palmer Sampson and Lincoln McGeisey, near Maud for allegedly killing a white woman.[27]

Just as Five Nations leaders gathered at Eufaula, other meetings in Indian Territory threatened to splinter the statehood movement—and any political action undertaken by Native people—into many ineffectual directions. Attempting to keep things under control, the Eufaula delegates wanted an accounting of other people "assembling in convention at different places in the Indian Territory, purporting to represent the wishes of the people of the Indian Territory as we do know that they represent no part of the Indian population and a very small part of the white population of Indian Territory."[28] Before they adjourned, the delegates agreed to meet again the following year.[29]

Political concerns mandated a meeting sooner rather than later. Choctaw principal chief Green McCurtain called for a meeting of the leaders of the Five Tribes in late May. With a receding hairline and walrus mustache, the Republican Choctaw came from a prominent political family. His parents named him after noted Choctaw leader Greenwood LeFlore, hence his unusual first name. Once again the leaders met at Eufaula, on May 21 and 22, 1903. Their discussions called for a constitutional convention to be held no later than February 1, 1904. They wanted to draft a constitution that would cover their combined reservations when the abolition of the governments of the Five Nations occurred in early 1906.[30] As the Curtis Act stated, "This stipulation is made in the belief that the tribal governments so modified will prove so satisfactory that there will be no need or desire for further change till the lands now occupied by the Five Civilized Tribes shall, in the opinion of Congress, be prepared for admission as a State to the Union."[31]

Arrangements were made for the next meeting, which would be held in September 1903, again at Eufaula. To start the meeting officially, the delegates voted Henry Ainsley, who represented the Choctaws, to serve as chairman. Alexander Posey, a mixed-blood Muscogee, served as the secretary. To represent the Chickasaws, Governor Palmer S. Mosley appointed a white lawyer, William "Alfalfa Bill" Murray, to attend in his place.[32] A native of Toadsuck (now Collinsville), Texas, Murray had earned his nickname, "Alfalfa Bill," while stumping in western Oklahoma Territory during 1902. After he encouraged farmers to grow alfalfa, the editor of the *Tishomingo Capital-Democrat* dubbed Murray "Alfalfa Bill," and the name stuck.[33] "Back in 1889, Murray had married Mary Alice Hearrell, who was the niece of the prominent Chickasaw, Douglas H. Johnston.[34] Having married into the tribe, Murray was embraced by the Chickasaws, but he faced criticism for marrying an Indian woman and favoring the interests of Indians over white concerns.[35] Murray recalled later that, "I was the only white man participating [at the September 1903 meeting]. All our work was, as it were, laying ground wires, with which to charge future batteries."[36] After the meeting, Murray surmised the Indian leaders wanted to prepare their communities for statehood, but they did not think it would happen for at least several years. Recalling a meeting with the Choctaw legislature meeting at Tuskahoma in 1904, Murray thought the idea of the Indian state seemed "as yet, premature" to them.[37] Choctaw enthusiasm for statehood seemed to have cooled somewhat since the September 1902 meeting in McAlester.

Even if the prospect of statehood seemed distant, the impending Curtis Act added urgency to tribal elections. The August 10, 1904, election in the Chickasaw Nation is representative of the turbulence. Indian police had to patrol the polling sites. The campaign was brutal, and trouble resulted from the buying of votes with "large quantities of whisky" and cash.[38] Schools were a particular concern. The federal government had authorized $100,000 for operating sixty new schools for Indians and whites in Indian Territory, but the Chickasaws viewed this as paternalism. Despite knowing their government was going to be dissolved, the Chickasaws continued to operate about twenty schools of their own.[39] Rather than surrender to the full authority of the United States, the Chickasaws exercised their rights. This kind of bold assertion of sovereignty was on display at an intertribal gathering the next month. In October 1904 tribal leaders gathered in Muskogee during one of coldest autumns in the history of Indian Territory. At this meeting, Muscogee chief Pleasant Porter and Cherokee chief William Rogers issued a proclamation that stated "a majority of the Five Civilized Tribes" favored and wanted "separate and independent statehood." In the proclamation, they proposed for the Five Nations to meet again in October of the following year to pass a resolution. They asked for "President Roosevelt to insert a few lines in his annual message to Congress" that fall recommending legislation to provide "for a commonwealth for the Indian Territory and the Osage Nation to be inaugurated March 4, 1906."[40]

Cold weather also marked a gathering of Seminoles in Vinita the following winter. Here, though, statehood was not the dominant topic of conversation. On February 12, 1905, Vinita recorded the coldest day in Indian Territory since record-keeping began in Fort Gibson in January 1824. Vinita reported an incredible temperature of twenty-seven degrees below zero! Undoubtedly the severe cold made the idea of moving elsewhere seem more attractive. Fed up with their current situation, the Seminoles planned to start a colony "in one of the wilder sections of Old Mexico, where they hope the pale face will not come."[41]

Seminole leader Hulbutta Micco, also known as the "Alligator King," accompanied Isaac Jones, Parjuck Harjochee, and Alice B. Davis, an interpreter, to Mexico in search of a new homeland. The journey took its toll on the elderly Alligator King, who died on March 25, 1905. Because second chief Thomas Little had died the previous November, the Seminole council appointed freedman Jacob Harrison, who had been Hulbutta Micco's former secretary, as acting chief.[42] Harrison's tenure proved to be short after the council held a special meeting to impeach him based on little evidence. The council removed him from office, and replaced him with former chief, John Brown, a Seminole and Scots mixed blood, who was a wealthy businessman.[43]

The idea of moving to Mexico did not just appeal to the Seminoles. It spread like a prairie wind among the Muscogees and Cherokees, and they gossiped about it during their stomp dances throughout the summer. One Cherokee citizen, S. S. Stephens, "believed that, as soon as some provision was made for the selling of the lands, Cherokee and Creek full-bloods would go to Mexico, where they could buy land at a low price . . . [like] Indian life that the Territory once had, but are now destroyed by the advance of civilization."[44] An elderly Muscogee, D. L. Berryhill from Okmulgee, known as "the old war horse of the Muskogee Nation," was said to have prepared to lead "5000 full-blood creeks" to Mexico.[45]

Along with the idea of moving to Mexico, the statehood remained an important topic of discussion for Native people in Indian Territory throughout 1905. Some people of the Chickasaw Nation were supportive, but the western half of the nation grew skeptical. Charles N. Haskell, a white friend of the Muscogees, went to the office of Chief Pleasant Porter to urge a meeting of the Five Nations leaders, including Green McCurtain of the Choctaws and William C. Rogers and of the Cherokees.[46]

Haskell was laying the groundwork for the most significant convention on the Indian statehood movement to ever occur, which would take place in his adopted hometown of Muskogee. Charles N. Haskell was the kind of person that got things done. He was described as "a man of tireless energy, doing, and resourceful to the Nth degree."[47] Initially he came to Indian Territory as a railroad builder seeking new opportunity.[48] In April 1901, Haskell, who had become a lawyer and businessman, saw Muskogee for the first time. The possibilities of the bustling town impressed Haskell so much that he decided to move his family away from their twenty-three-room house in Ottawa, Ohio, to points west. Charles's wife, Lillian, and his six children lived in Fayetteville, Arkansas, which Haskell commuted to from Muskogee on weekends to see his loved ones.[49] Perhaps not coincidentally, he expanded the Ozark & Cherokee Central Railroad to connect Fayetteville and Muskogee. In Muskogee, Haskell built the Turner Hotel at the corner of Court and North Third streets, which was named after a close friend, C. W. Turner, who owned a local hardware store. The Haskell family lived on the third floor of the hotel for a part of the year.[50]

Like so most American communities of the day, Muskogee was divided along social and racial lines. Upper-class whites divided the community by building schools for the privileged on the west side. Those less fortunate lived on the east side of the Katy tracks, and Blacks were relegated to the north side. Indians and whites preferred segregation, with the Black townsmen having to accept "no mixing or social equality." Regarding desegregating schools, one white said, "The whites won't have it, and the Negroes don't want it."[51]

After moving to Indian Territory, Charles Haskell became good friends with Muscogee chief Pleasant Porter. One morning Haskell showed Porter a copy of the *Muskogee Phoenix* that reported "a call for a convention of the Five Civilized tribes for the purpose of asking Congress to admit Indian Territory as a state." As he had in the past, Porter once again expressed skepticism. "Well, it won't amount to anything. You know the white people will pay no attention to anything the Indians do. Our wishes would have no weight with Congress." Haskell remarked such a request "might amount to something, [if] it was handled properly, and could be of great value to the Indians by letting the world know how they stand on the question of statehood."[52]

The statehood movement seemed to be gaining momentum during the summer of 1905. On July 5, James Norman, a mixed-blood Cherokee and boarding house owner, called for a meeting on August 7 of anyone who wanted an American Indian state to become reality. Norman envisioned seven delegates from "each of the twenty-six recording districts" of Indian Territory, which now contained 1,411,000 people.[53] Of Norman's meeting, Pleasant Porter believed "it is not worth bothering about." But Porter's good friend, Charles Haskell replied, "It is worth bothering about General. You tribal leaders must grasp control of the situation before it gets into improper hands."[54] Although the August 7 meeting did not happen, Alfalfa Bill Murray later remarked that Norman had "lighted [a] match [to] set the prairies on fire" for all over the Five Tribes.[55]

July 5 was a busy day for the Indian statehood movement. That day, the Democratic national committeeman from Indian Territory, Robert L. Williams, a white lawyer from Alabama, arrived in Muskogee to solicit support for statehood. Williams, who would become Oklahoma's third governor, met with James A. Norman, Choctaw leader Green McCurtain, and Cherokee leader William C. Rogers. A gathering of twenty-two "prominent Indians" met in Pleasant Porter's office in Muskogee about a week later, on July 11.[56] They decided to follow up on Norman's initial call for a meeting to formally schedule a constitutional convention to begin on August 21 and to be held in Muskogee.[57]

While Pleasant Porter remained skeptical, other Five Nations leaders lent their support to the statehood movement. Green McCurtain told Porter that he had "submitted the question of separate statehood to my people who had endorsed it overwhelmingly by popular vote" and had worked with the other tribal leaders "to make a success of this plan" for the state of Sequoyah.[58] Twenty-six districts in Indian Territory began selecting their delegates to the Muskogee convention. The *Cherokee Advocate* predicted a successful meeting, "by the time the constitution convention is pulled off, interest in it will be at fever heat in all parts of Indian Territory." Addressing another possible political future, the *Advocate* added, "it is well known by congressional leaders that joint statehood is not the choice of the majority in Oklahoma."[59] On July 14, 1905, twenty-three Muscogee leaders instructed Pleasant Porter to oppose any form of government forging Indian Territory with the Oklahoma Territory.[60] Still, even the idea of joint statehood had some supporters in Indian Country. William Murray observed that the editor of the *Ardmoreite* newspaper worked hard to convince the western half of the Chickasaw Nation to join with Oklahoma.[61]

The prospect of statehood for Oklahoma Territory added urgency to the planning for the August meeting in Muskogee. In the *Tishomingo News,* Pleasant Porter remarked that "Oklahoma is endeavoring to dominate the new state and is seeking admission for joint statehood with Indian Territory. The Indians resent this which explains the calling of the constitution convention, which meets here in August. We want statehood, and if Oklahoma must be admitted as a part in our state, it is our purpose to let that Territory come in under a constitution framed by Indian Territory Representative [*sic*]."[62] Toward the end of July, Porter spoke "strongly in favor of statehood for Indian Territory alone and told of the continual pledges made by the United States government through treaties, and promises with the Indians whereby the Indians should have a state of their own when they so requested."[63]

On July 18 Haskell, Porter, and other representatives of the Five Nations met in room 511 of the new Turner Hotel. Choctaw national treasurer George W. Scott (a Chickasaw) represented Chief Green McCurtain, and Alfalfa Bill Murray, who had traveled from his home in Tishomingo, represented Chickasaw governor Douglas J. Johnston. Haskell expressed his doubts about separate statehood, but wanted to know the thinking of other leaders about the idea. Murray commented, "Personally, I cared little whether we had single or double statehood. The point was the Great United States had made the Indians a solemn promise that if they would abandon their homes and establish themselves in the western wilderness, never should Territorial or State Government include their domain without their consent."[64]

Much was anticipated for the convention in downtown Muskogee due to start on August 21. The Turner Hotel quickly filled its rooms, as did nearby rooming houses. A total of 176 delegates arrived, of which 104 were Democrats and 72 were Republicans.[65] The delegates consisted of Indians, whites, mixed bloods, and a few freedmen like Dennis Cyrus, a Seminole freedman who was a renowned lighthorse and had served as a US deputy marshal.[66]

An hour before the convention began, Choctaw chief Green McCurtain and Seminole chief John F. Brown asked to meet privately with Charles Haskell.

They wanted Haskell to be the chairman of the convention. Although flattered, Haskell replied that an Indian should preside over this important meeting, and he thought this individual should be Pleasant Porter. Although feeling a bit under the weather, Porter accepted, but on the condition that Haskell serve as vice chair and relieve him of some of the expected mundane duties.[67]

Meanwhile, the delegates gathered at the Hinton Theater at 11:00 on a torrid Monday morning. It was a rainless 92 degrees. After the formal appointment of select members to the Committee on Permanent Organization, Rules and Order of Business, they broke for lunch. The first order of business in the afternoon session was the selection of officers. The delegates confirmed the selection of Pleasant Porter as president and chose five vice presidents to represent the Five Tribes: William C. Rogers for the Cherokees, William H. Murray for the Chickasaws, Green McCurtain for the Choctaws, John Brown for the Seminoles, and Charles N. Haskell for the Muscogees.[68]

For the first couple of days, the delegates met in committees and listened to speeches. The Cherokee mixed-blood politician, Robert L. Owen, argued for separate statehood. He said, "Neither territory really desires joint statehood, Indian Territory earnestly desires prohibition, Oklahoma Territory does not. The United States is bound to maintain prohibition in the Indian Territory and we must have independent statehood to carry out this pledge. . . . There are no sympathetic relations existing between the Twin Territories."[69] Robert Owen also spoke of the need for an Indian name for the proposed state, and he suggested Sequoyah.[70] Other delegates agreed because the late Sequoyah was widely respected for inventing the Cherokee syllabary and helping to spread literacy among his people.

Perhaps the most important order of business for the delegates involved naming a committee to draft a constitution for the proposed state of Sequoyah. Fort Gibson was selected to be the capital for at least the first six years. Although Muskogee seemed the likely choice, Fort Gibson was just inside the Cherokee Nation and next to the Muscogee Nation. The delegates selected William Hirt Hastings, a Cherokee, to chair the Constitution Committee. Fifty-five members were eventually named to the committee to demonstrate equal representation from various parts of Indian Territory.

After all the official delegates for the constitutional convention had been counted, the final number was 182, including those who arrived late. About thirty elected delegates did not attend the meeting held at the Hinton Theater.[71] During the meeting, the editor of the *Muskogee Phoenix* noticed the absence of the Chickasaws, "We sincerely trust Mr. Murr[a]y will succeed in getting someone here to assist him in representing the Chickasaw Nation. . . . It would be less embarrassing on the roll call if districts 16, 18, 19, 20, 21, 22, and 26 had some one [*sic*] to answer present."[72] The delegates decided that four candidates would represent Sequoyah. In a show of fairness, two would be Democrats and the other two would be Republicans.[73] At about 5:00 p.m. on Tuesday, August 22, Charles Haskell suggested that the convention adjourn for two weeks to give the Constitution Committee enough time to write the constitution.[74] The others agreed, and the delegates voted to meet again at 9:00 a.m. on September 6.

Early the next morning on August 23, Chairman Hastings began naming his appointments to the eleven subcommittees.[75] For six days, they toiled day and night to draft their parts of the constitution, working late into the nights and consuming much coffee wherever they could find office space in Muskogee. The subcommittees had their portions ready on the morning of August 29.[76] As the secretary of the convention, Alexander Posey had to hurry to finish drafting the constitution.[77] The subcommittees also produced a map by creating new counties for the proposed state of Sequoyah. Every day the delegates made changes until a cartographic masterpiece lay on the table.[78] The combined 31,069 square miles of the Muscogee, Seminole, Cherokee, Choctaw, and Chickasaw reservations that made up Indian Territory were almost the size of Indiana and nearly equal to the average size of 32,884 square miles for the twenty-six states located east of the Mississippi. In fact, Indian Territory was larger than Delaware, Connecticut, New Jersey, Massachusetts, and New Hampshire put together. By the beginning of the twentieth century, the proposed state of Sequoyah boasted a larger population than sixteen eastern states.[79]

By noon on August 29, the delegates were ready to finalize the constitution. The delegates voted Cherokee chief William C. Rogers to be the temporary chairman because Pleasant Porter was not available. A well respected Cherokee mixed blood, Rogers had a bushy mustache, thick eyebrows, and a receding hairline, but his strongest feature was his penetrating brown eyes.[80] Chairman Rogers called the convention to order. The first order of business called for reviewing the preamble: "Invoking the blessing of Almighty God and reposing faith in the Constitution and Treaty obligations of the United States, we, the people of the State of Sequoyah, do ordain and establish this Constitution."[81] Someone made a motion to accept the preamble, but heated discussion followed.

The proposed name, the state of Sequoyah, caused considerable differences of opinion. In another version, Alexander Posey had suggested the "Native State of Sequoyah," but later it was shortened to the "State of Sequoyah."[82] The delegates offered several alternative names. Masterson Peyton wanted the proposed state to be called Indianola. George W. Grayson argued loudly for Tecumseh. Other suggested names included Seminola, which was offered in a resolution by Alexander Richmond of Wewoka, and Jefferson.[83] Robert L. Owen who had suggested the name Sequoyah, argued against Jefferson "as it might enlist the opposition of some republicans who did not revere the name of Jefferson and who might consider the name too suggestive of political affiliations."[84] Charles Haskell and others argued passionately for the "State of Sequoyah," and this name won the support of the majority of the delegates. Around this time, the *Muskogee Phoenix* reprinted a poem written by J. S. Holden in 1898, "Sequoyah," which had been previously published in the *Fort Gibson Post*.[85] The poem had proven prescient, as it envisioned a future state name after the great Cherokee statesman.

SEQUOYAH

The Cadmus of his race
A man without a peer;
He stood alone—his genius shone
Throughout a Hemisphere.
Untutored, yet so great;
Grand and alone his fame—
Yes, grand and great—the future state
Should bear Sequoyah's name.
In ages yet to come,
When his Nation has a place,
His name shall live in history's page,
The grandest of his race.

The next day, Wednesday, August 30, another heated argument occurred when Charles Haskell and S. M. Rutherford disagreed over how to proceed with Sequoyah's political representation, and the dispute continued after the convention met again in September. Should there be four elected congressmen or one delegate to represent the state of Sequoyah? Rutherford pushed for one territorial delegate. Haskell argued for four elected congressmen: "statehood for Indian Territory; territorial form of government; go straight to the devil; or be joined with Oklahoma." Haskell won the day.[86]

By late afternoon, the delegates decided to adjourn. Before they left, they agreed to meet again in two weeks. The Constitution Committee met on September 5 to review the final draft of its work. Some boundaries of the proposed counties were changed, but the most important point of discussion came from some citizens of Eufaula who wanted their town to be the capital of the proposed state instead of Fort Gibson.[87] Their petition claimed that Eufaula was a mere three miles from the geographic center of the state of Sequoyah. To make their case more persuasive, the citizens also promised they would provide all of the buildings and land for the new capital.[88] A resolution was approved, but not without opposition, that Fort Gibson would be "a temporary capital for six years" and then a vote would be held to "allow the people to select a permanent capital."[89]

Until the next meeting scheduled for September 6, observers expressed numerous opinions on the convention's work, not all of them positive. Some critics complained about the prominent role of white men such as Charles Haskell, Alfalfa Bill Murray, and Judge John R. Thomas. Jeering anti-Sequoyah crowds twice closed public halls reserved for speeches promoting statehood. Despite the opposition, usually from supporters of statehood for Oklahoma, Haskell, Murray, and Thomas spoke anywhere a meeting could be held, even though their detractors followed. Their stop in the small town of Davis in the Arbuckle Mountains in the Chickasaw Nation was indicative of the high interest in the Sequoyah statehood movement, pro and con, where between three hundred and four hundred people showed up. For Alfalfa Bill, the Sequoyah movement was a matter of justice. For Murray, the Sequoyah movement was a matter of justice. It did not matter whether there would be one state or two. The United States, he argued, had promised the Cherokees, Muscogees, Choctaws, Chickasaws, and Seminoles that their reservations would never be governed by a state or territorial government "without their consent."[90]

On Wednesday, September 6, Pleasant Porter officially called the Sequoyah Convention back to order at 9:20 a.m. In the Hinton Theater, decorated with flowers and ferns, a large picture of Theodore Roosevelt hung above the speakers' area, which was adorned with American flags and pictures of Indian chiefs on both sides. A seal for the state of Sequoyah also appeared on the wall.[91] The most notable discussions to follow would come the next day. In the evening session of Thursday, September 7, the delegates again argued over the site of the capital. Vehement arguments for Fort Gibson, Eufaula, or South McAlester followed.[92] After the speechmaking died down, the delegates voted to accept the constitution, which covered forty pages.

Just before the convention ended at last, the delegates made a resolution of appreciation to thank the people of Muskogee for their hospitality. They also recognized Pleasant Porter for his fairness as the convention chairman Charles Haskell for his hard work, and W.W. Hastings for his efforts as chair of the Constitution Committee. The delegates also expressed their gratitude to the press of Muskogee, the Katy Railroad, and the Muskogee Commercial Club. The meeting adjourned with a reading of a poem by James A. Norman, a benediction by Reverend A. Grant Evans, and the singing of the Christian hymn, "God Be with You Till We Meet Again."[93]

In the wake of the convention, Pleasant Porter called a meeting of the chiefs and governors of the Five Tribes on September 26 at South McAlester. Chief Porter wanted to formulate "a general plan for bringing the Indian territory into statehood at the expiration of tribal government[s] in 1906."[94] Making sure the momentum remained steady, the Cherokee National Council met on September 29 and enacted Joint Resolution No. 11. The resolution opposed merging Indian Territory with Oklahoma Territory. The resolution expressed support for single statehood for the combined reservations of the Five Tribes along with the Quapaw Reservation. Lastly, the resolution endorsed the constitution of the proposed state of Sequoyah.[95] Following the lead of the Cherokees, the national councils of the Choctaws and Chickasaws passed resolutions to support statehood for Sequoyah.

But not everyone in Indian Territory supported the Sequoyah movement. Not long after the constitutional convention, an estimated three hundred people met in Checotah on September 23 to oppose the idea of an Indian state.[96] Colonel Roy Hoffman of Chandler, a former law officer, called the meeting, "a most unfortunate affair for single statehood" and was not "a representative, deliberative body."[97] The *Miami Record-Herald* also reported that Chickasaw governor Douglas Johnston "stamped the movement with his disapproval," although a delegation from Paul's Valley in the Chickasaw went to the convention "merely . . . to have a representation and 'shape' county seat lines."[98] A handful of lawyers from Chickasaw argued there was no authority from Congress for creating the state of Sequoyah. But Alfalfa Bill Murray pointed out that "North and South Dakotas [*sic*] and three other States had held voluntary Conventions, framed a Constitution, and were admitted by Congress upon their Constitutions without an Enabling Act at all." He criticized the lawyers for not knowing their history, adding that Arkansas was admitted "with a voluntary Convention—No Enabling Act—and with a population of only 51,509, including 9,838 slaves."[99]

The Muscogee Nation was of two minds. One group of traditionalists like Chitto Harjo and Eufaula Harjo wanted an independent nation-state, as was promised in the Cusseta Treaty of 1832. The other view, represented by Pleasant Porter, wanted Indian Territory to become a state of the United States. The Muscogee National Council met on October 28, and voted overwhelmingly, forty-six to twenty-six, against the state of Sequoyah. In their resolution, the council reiterated that Muscogee "consent" was required to form any state or territory from their land, based on the treaty of 1832.[100]

The statehood efforts for both Sequoyah and Oklahoma became national news. In early October 1905, the *New York Times* reported, "Many conventions have been held and resolutions adopted; committees and delegations have been selected and sent to Washington, but in no instance have they represented more than individual groups of opinion." Confusion abounded. The *Times* went on to observe, "'separate' Statehood advocates have gotten together and voiced their sentiments. 'Single' Statehood advocates have done likewise, but never have the citizens as a whole held a real constitution convention nor taken any other regular steps to show that they are deeply interested in the matter. The territorial press and politicians declare that Oklahoma and Indian Territory are in need of Statehood, but they do not seem to have any clear idea or positive and unalterable conviction as to the form or time in which it should be granted."[101]

Despite the naysayers, state of Sequoyah advocates continued their work. Pleasant Porter called for a meeting to convene in South McAlester in the Chickasaw Nation. He probably chose this location to ensure the support of the Chickasaws, who had been the most skeptical of the Five Tribes about the state of Sequoyah. At 10:30 a.m. on October 14, the delegates met and approved the constitution, signed by Chairman Pleasant Porter and Secretary Alexander Posey.[102] Later that day, the delegates created a committee of twenty and another committee consisting of the four congressional nominees along with Charles Haskell and William Murray. Their task was to present the request for statehood for the state of Sequoyah to the president of the United States in early December.

On November 7, 1905, the constitution of the proposed state of Sequoyah was submitted in the first general election of Indian Territory. According to one observer, the Sequoyah movement "furnished a powerful argument in demonstrating the fitness of the people of Indian Territory for Statehood; whether it be separate or joint Statehood . . . and if these people must go into a Constitution Convention with Oklahoma, they have demonstrated their right to demand equal terms with her."[103] Support for separate statehood came from many churches in Indian Territory because of their prohibitionist outlook. They said, "the basis of their opposition is that Oklahoma is saloon territory, and, as they claim, 'whisky soaked.'"[104] There were many newspapers opposed to idea of Native statehood, and in the words of one contemporary observer, they "reproduced numerous interviews and letters of Senators and Congressmen committing themselves, in advance of the meeting of Congress, to joint Statehood and discouraging the separate Statehood ideas; and it employed every possible argument to persuade the voters to stay away from the polls on November 7."[105] Still, voters approved of the state of Sequoyah by a landslide.[106] In the final tally, 56,279 residents of Indian Territory voted to adopt the constitution, while 9,073 disagreed.[107] On December 3, 1905, the Muscogee group left for Washington, DC, to meet with President Roosevelt. The president briefly met with the group around December 8. He informed the group that it was against Republican Party policy to form two states from Indian Territory and Oklahoma Territory. This was a devastating blow from the former pugilist. David Hodge, a full-blood Muscogee Republican, was shocked by Roosevelt's words. Showing his disgust, he walked out of the room, although the president tried to smooth things over. "Come back, Mr. Hodges [*sic*]; we'll talk of this more."[108] But it was too late. Hodge caught the next train to Indian Territory and became a Democrat for the rest of his life.

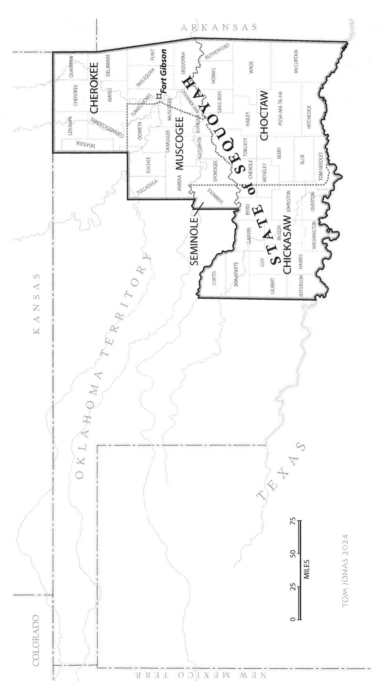

State of Sequoyah. Cartography by Tom Jonas.

At this crossroads in history, effective leadership was needed. As the Sequoyah statehood movement both gained momentum and suffered set-backs, Muscogee principal chief Pleasant Porter proved himself more than equal to the task. President William McKinley had called him "the greatest living Indian."[109] The *St. Louis Dispatch* admiringly wrote, "Gen. Porter has great mental capacity. He is a grand statesman, a warrior, a philanthropist and a man in every meaning of the word. He is magnificent to look at. He is now in the prime of his life, as hale and strong as when he hunted on the prairies of the Creek country in his youthful days. He is above 6 feet in height and weighs close to 200 pounds. He was shot in the leg and through the mouth during the civil war, but he does not show any effect from either wound."[110]

FIVE

Becoming Oklahoma

A big decision had to be made, but first some careful steps had to be taken. Each of two contiguous territories wanted statehood. The president stood at a window of the Oval Office and peered westward. He reached for his pince-nez glasses and cleaned them, but he stopped to ponder the complex possibilities of two new states in the West. That might mean four new senators and several congressmen for the rival Democratic Party. Since the end of Reconstruction in 1877, the Republicans had remained in control of both houses of Congress and the president wanted that streak to continue.[1] As he looked out the window, he fitted his glasses, and muttered out loud to himself, "an Indian state?"

As a child, "Teedie" Roosevelt suffered from asthma and had to wear glasses to correct his extreme near-sightedness. As he grew older, he always felt he had to prove his toughness and became fiercely competitive. Born in New York, Roosevelt enjoyed the West and had even cowboyed on his Elkhorn Ranch in Montana and his Maltese Cross Ranch a few miles away in North Dakota. He learned about Indians, was curious about them, and had even traveled to Indian Territory by train to go wolf hunting. Even though he was an old-stock American, he thought of himself a self-made man, and he believed everyone in the country should earn their own way. A driven individual, he wore many titles before becoming president: governor, secretary of the navy, cowboy, war hero, and even deputy sheriff of Billings County, Montana. But even as the youngest US president to date at age forty-two, he felt compelled to do more.

The decision weighing on Roosevelt and other officials in Washington concerned but the latest step in a process that had become commonplace. In the last two decades of the nineteenth century, Dakota Territory, Montana Territory, Washington Territory, Idaho Territory, Wyoming Territory, and Utah Territory had become states. The growing population of Indian Territory suggested it could be next.

Following the first land run in 1889, a large flood of white settlers and African Americans had arrived in the new Oklahoma Territory and in Indian Territory. The Indian population was becoming heavily outnumbered. The US Bureau of Census reported for 1890 the population for both Oklahoma Territory and Indian Territory had reached 258,657 people: "(172,554 White 54.2 percent; 21,609 Negro 8.4 percent; and 64,456 Indian 24.9 percent)." In Indian Territory there were 109,393 whites out of a total population of 180,182.[2] By 1900 the population had quadrupled for both territories, which had a combined 790,391 residents "(670,204 White 84.8 percent; 55,684 Negro 7.0 percent; and 64,445 Indian 8.2 percent)." For 1890 and 1900, the Asian American population registered less than 2 percent and the number of Hispanic Americans was unknown. Newcomers entered Oklahoma Territory at the rate of 50,000 per year.[3]

Plans for organizing Oklahoma Territory date to the early 1870s. In 1872 and 1873, Elias C. Boudinot drafted a bill for the creation of Oklahoma Territory, which ultimately failed. Conditions seemed to have changed by late February 1877, when W. P. Boudinot, the older brother of E. C. Boudinot, received a letter that stated that a couple of lobbyists favored a bill founding the territory. Yet again, politicians in Washington did not favor the legislative measure.[4] Congress was already occupied with seven other territories vying for statehood.

Conditions seemed a little more promising more than a decade later. On January 17, 1890, Republicans gathered in the young city called Oklahoma (renamed Oklahoma City in 1923) to discuss territorial organization. The Democrats held their own meeting in that city on March 11 for the same purpose.[5] Guthrie emerged as the leading candidate for the territorial capital, followed by Oklahoma and Shawnee.[6] Later the seat of Logan County, Guthrie brimmed with Republicans who had migrated from the north, and African Americans and European-born immigrants accounted for almost 80 percent of the population. Like the city called Oklahoma, Guthrie helped to anchor the Santa Fe Railroad line.[7]

This time, Washington politicians proved more receptive. On February 4, 1890, Republican Senator Orville H. Platt of Connecticut introduced what became known as the Platt Bill.[8] This measure met the approval of the House on April 21, and two days later, the Senate gave its approval. On May 2, President Benjamin Harrison signed Senate Bill 895, which became an organic act that created the twin territories of Oklahoma Territory and Indian Territory. Oklahoma Territory received a panhandle that had been known as Old Beaver County. Once known as Cimarron Territory, the area of 3,051 people formed a perfect rectangle of 166 miles long and 34 miles wide. It had governed itself since 1850, when it was created, and was called "No Man's Land," although it was also known as the Public Land Strip and the Neutral Strip.[9]

The new Oklahoma Panhandle already had had an interesting history. In 1850 Texas surrendered its claim to the area. Residents of the rectangle petitioned Congress in February 1887 to become a territory of the United States, but this request was denied. Ten months later the politicians of Cimarron made a second unsuccessful request. Taking a somewhat different approach in the late 1880s, Indiana senator Daniel W. Voorhees, a Democrat, introduced a bill for the Cimarron Territory to become a part of Kansas. The bill passed in both the Senate and House of Representatives, but President Grover Cleveland vetoed the measure.[10] The outspoken senator had had a history of disagreement with Cleveland, especially on tariffs. Taller than most and sometimes called "the Tall Sycamore of the Wabash," Voorhees had once joked, "Why, the cow and the goose are the greatest fools in the world, except the man who thinks that a tariff can be laid without protection."[11] No doubt Cleveland would not sign any bill into law introduced by the Tall Sycamore. Three years later, "Old Beaver County" became part of Oklahoma Territory.

According to the organic act, the twin territories organized as incorporated territories of the United States.[12] The act also called for a territorial governor and secretary to be appointed by the president, as well as a bicameral legislature with a house of twenty members and a senate consisting of thirteen members. All the members were to be elected by voters from their districts. Three judges named by the president were to head the judiciary system.[13]

President Benjamin Harrison appointed George Washington Steele as the first territorial governor of Oklahoma. Born in 1839 in Indiana, Steele had studied law, like so many young men of his time. He was also a military man.

During the Civil War, he served as a lieutenant colonel under General William Tecumseh Sherman and earned promotion to major in the Union army. At the end of the war, he returned to Indiana to enter the banking business and hang out a shingle for his law practice. His close friendship with President Harrison led to his appointment as the first governor.[14] Harrison appointed Edward B. Green to be the first chief justice of the territory and John G. Clark and Abraham J. Seay as associate justices.[15] David Archibald Harvey won election in 1890 to serve as the first delegate to represent Oklahoma Territory in Congress.

The first territorial legislature for Oklahoma Territory convened in 1890, and it included a number of dubious characters, one being Representative Ira Terrill. Originally from Illinois, he migrated to Kansas, became a boomer, and accompanied William Couch on his last visit to Indian Territory in 1883. Terrill called himself a lawyer even though he did not hold a law degree, and when Speaker of the House Arthur N. Daniels would not recognize him, the former boomer got his attention by drawing a gun.[16]

Unfortunately, racial prejudice won the day with the passing of Council Bill 2. Both Republicans and Democrats voted for segregation, although three of the four Populist representatives voted against it. Green I. Currin, the only African American representative in the first legislature, spoke for integration, but his was a losing cause.[17] Born in Tennessee in 1842 or 1844, Currin was an Exoduster who joined the Black migration to Kansas, and there he earned widespread respect as a lawman. He moved to the newly created Oklahoma Territory during the land-rush era. In his forties and neatly dressed, Currin towered over six feet tall and wore a beard. Representing Kingfisher, Currin introduced Oklahoma's first civil rights bill, House Bill 119, which was designed to punish individuals for racial violence. It failed by one vote.[18]

The territory would also evince anti-Indian racism in its law code. On March 12, 1897, the legislature passed a bill entitled "Indians Must Marry According to Law," which stated, "Indians and their descendants, shall procure marriage licenses in the same county and have their marriages solemnized by the same persons and returns thereof made in the manner as is provided by the laws of this State for the making of marriage contracts by other persons."[19] Ostensibly, the law aimed to outlaw polygamy. This presumption failed to consider the cultural norm among some tribes, such as the Muscogees and

Comanches, that obliged men to take more than one wife to care for widows. In that same year, Oklahoma Territory passed an anti-miscegenation law that prohibited whites from marrying individuals from other races.[20]

It did not take long for Oklahomans to agitate for statehood. The city of Oklahoma was the site selected for a statehood convention held on December 15, 1891. The convention produced an Oklahoma statehood memorial, which stated, "That in the interest of good government all of the old Indian Territory should be included in the future state of Oklahoma, and that by so doing there will be no conflict with treaty stipulations and no infringement upon the rights of property of the Indian tribes."[21] The memorial argued that because of "the aggressive and enterprising character of our people, the time has come for Congress to pass an enabling act as herein indicated, and that at an early day we should be permitted to throw off our territorial pupilage and assume the dignity and responsibility of a sovereign state."[22] In February 1892 Congressman Sidney Clarke of Kansas and other members of the Statehood Executive Committee presented their case in support of HR 4629 before the Committee on Territories, but the initiative failed.

After learning about the statehood push for Oklahoma Territory, some individuals from Indian Territory, including Elias C. Boudinot of the Cherokees, made appointments to meet with the Committee on Territories. Boudinot, who was a lawyer, pointed out the legal implications for the Five Tribes. Contrary to the delegates of the Oklahoma convention, he argued joint statehood of Oklahoma Territory and Indian Territory would cause legal problems due to the nearly seventy ratified treaties that the Five Nations had made with the United States. He also claimed that the Cherokees, Muscogees, Seminoles, Choctaws, and Chickasaws were not ready for statehood.[23]

Hoping to maintain momentum, on September 30, 1893, Oklahoma statehood promoters organized a statehood meeting held at the Methodist Episcopal Church in Purcell. Roughly three hundred delegates attended. This meeting again produced a memorial; the delegates wanted allotment of tribal lands, the dissolution of the Five Nations, and the disestablishment of reservations.[24] The statehood promoters organized another meeting at Kingfisher in late November. The purpose of this meeting was to lobby support for a bill known as HR 4857, which would promote dual statehood for both Oklahoma and Indian territories.

With much to do, the second session of the Fifty-Third Congress reconvened in December. The House Committee on Territories, which, was chaired
by Representative Joseph "Fighting Joe" Wheeler of Alabama, considered HR
4857. After the committee studied the bill, Congressman Wheeler submitted a report that supported the addition of Oklahoma Territory as a state.
There were several reasons why the territory, which contained 36,353 square
miles and about 250,000 residents, deserved the honor. Oklahoma Territory
had thirty banks and already had a territorial university at Norman, an agricultural and mechanical college at Stillwater, and a territorial normal school
at Edmond. Each school had about one hundred students, and Oklahomans
planned to "make a complete system of education from the lowest to the highest." The territory boasted a total of 323 churches, with the Methodist Episcopal
Church having the most at 165. Considering these signs of progress, Fighting
Joe's committee noted that "the people who settled Oklahoma brought with
them little more than energy, pluck, endurance, and more than the average
of the progressive spirit which characterizes the best American citizens." Near
the conclusion, the report stated that "the committee are [sic] convinced that
there is a very enviable future for this Territory, and that its progress would
be much enhanced by its being admitted to statehood."[25] For the next two
months, a subcommittee in the Senate debated the bill, focusing mainly on
joint statehood for the two territories.[26] Republican senators proved reluctant
to admit another state, and the bill died before receiving serious consideration.

There was yet another potentially unwelcome political development in
store for Indian Territory. A rider attached to the Indian appropriation bill in
1893 enabled President Cleveland to appoint a commission to negotiate the
allotment of tribal lands belonging to the Five Tribes.[27] The act permitted the
commission to assign allotments to the members of the Five Nations with or
without their consent.[28] The purpose of this body, known as the Dawes Commission, challenged the validity of all 256 ratified treaties signed with the 39
Indian nations of Indian Territory.

One nation shows how steadfast the opposition to allotment was in Indian
Territory. In February 1894 the Dawes Commission met with the Muscogees
at Checotah, the "gem of the prairie," to begin negotiations with tribal leaders. In April, Chief Legus Perryman called for a vote of the people at the
council house in Okmulgee. Standing on the front steps of the council house,
Perryman called for everyone against allotment to stand on the west side

and for those for it to stand on the east side. Legend has it that about 4,000 people moved to the west side to show their opposition to allotment. After a brief silence, one person, Moty Tiger, walked to the east side and stood alone. When asked for an explanation, he replied, "the wave of settlers would soon ruin Indian nations as independents," forcing allotment to happen anyway.[29] Interestingly, Moty's name in Muscogee meant "the first to cross over."

Around this time, though, the Oklahoma statehood movement lost steam. In January 1894, Arkansas congressman Thomas C. McRae introduced a bill calling for single state for the twin territories. It failed. From 1894 to the end of the century, Congress entertained several more bills on the issue, but only two of them called for joint statehood. The others called for single statehood for either Oklahoma Territory or Indian Territory.[30] At least one federal official noticed the strong opposition to joint statehood in Indian territory. In late September 1897, Commissioner of Indian Affairs William A. Jones noted that "the Five Tribes do not want statehood with Oklahoma at this time," because "the tribes are struggling to settle their land tenure and to meet the new and vital issues that confront them."[31]

In the Fifty-Fifth Congress, Charles Curtis of Kansas, a mixed-blood Kaw, introduced his House Resolution 8581, "for the protection of the people of the Indian Territory, and for other purposes" on December 7, 1897. The Curtis bill provided this protection to the people of Indian Territory by placing them under federal law. The act also authorized incorporated towns and lots to be surveyed and sold. The proposed law would also establish public schools.[32] In addition, the bill allowed the federal government to collect taxes from "white citizens of the Indian nations in the territory."[33] It also sought to confer individual land ownership upon the Natives of Indian Territory.

HR 8581 was referred to the Committee on Indian Affairs, but it was tabled. Determined to help Native people, Curtis reintroduced his bill on January 17, 1898, and it went to the same committee and died there again.[34] The congressman revised his bill and introduced it for a third attempt on February 24. The bill made it to the Committee on Indian Affairs, which recommended that it to be a law. But impending war with Spain delayed the congressional vote on the bill, and it remained in the background until Republican senator James S. Sherman from New York championed it.[35] Many years later, Curtis recalled, "I little thought when I was traveling in the old Indian Territory, as a boy, in 1872 and 1873, that twenty-five years later,

I would be in Congress drawing a measure to settle the affairs of the Members of the Five Civilized Tribes of Indians, but that is what happened, for the bill I drew, introduced and passed in the summer of 1898 was intended to protect the interest of the people of the Indian Territory."[36]

While the bill was under consideration, delegates from the Five Nations arrived in Washington to protest the bill. The delegates and most of the Five Tribes' members believed that individual land ownership conflicted with their tradition of communal land ownership. They feared that their people would be cheated out of their lands. One of the most damaging parts of the Curtis bill was section 28, "That on the first day of July, eighteen hundred and ninety-eight, all tribal courts of Indian Territory shall be abolished, and no officer of said courts shall thereafter have any authority whatever to do or perform any act theretofore authorized by any law in connection with said courts, or to receive any pay for same; and all civil and criminal cases then pending to any such court shall be transferred to the United States court in said Territory."[37] Unfortunately, the delegates' complaints failed to stop the bill. After both houses of Congress approved it on June 27, President William McKinley signed the bill into law one day later.[38] Commissioner of Indian Affairs William Jones had helped draft the bill, and he made the case "that allotment of Indian lands in severalty has come, and has come to stay. By its strict enforcement tribal autonomy will disappear, and monopolies will be overthrown, and the homeless Indian—driven from pillar to post—will be guaranteed a homestead in his own right and will be protected in the enjoyment of his liberty and allowed to worship God according to the dictates of his conscience under his own vine and fig tree."[39]

While Curtis and Jones believed the Curtis Act would help Native people, it inspired a fierce backlash in Indian Territory. In mid-December 1899, Principal Chief Pleasant Porter of the Muscogees criticized the Curtis Act and "its terms, its radical changes, penal exactions, its conditions and inconsistencies," which would destroy the impressive progress that the Muscogees and other tribes had achieved.[40]

The Five Nations were not alone in having to deal with allotment. In 1906, Congress passed the Osage Allotment Act, despite considerable opposition from what was sometimes called "the sixth civilized tribe."[41] This law came after years of political turmoil and federal interference. The Interior Department had dissolved the Osage national government on May 21, 1900, except for the offices of principal chief and assistant principal chief.[42] This move raised questions about the legality of the federal government dissolving the government of a tribe that had made treaties with the United States.[43]

The region's non-Indigenous settlers fared somewhat better in Congress. Oklahoma Territory delegates Dennis Flynn and James Y. Callahan introduced the Free Homes Bill in early 1900. The measure provided relief to settlers on former tribal lands in both Oklahoma and Indian territories and freed them of all debts except for the land filing fee of $14.[44] Their total estimated debts amounted to $15 million. The Free Homes Act, also known as Public Law 105, was passed on May 17, 1900.

The movement for statehood gained steam after the turn of the century. On December 10, 1900, a meeting in support of joint statehood for the twin territories was held in McAlester. Delegates represented most of the counties of both territories.[45] Another statehood gathering occurred at Muskogee on November 14, 1901. The delegates agreed to joint statehood for Oklahoma Territory and Indian Territory.[46] In Washington, Congressman John Hall Stephens of Texas and Senator Thomas M. Patterson of Colorado introduced statehood bills to their colleagues. Immediate opposition rose from the Five Tribes, who protested the idea of joint statehood. The bills ultimately failed.[47] In January 1902, delegates gathered in the city of Oklahoma for the largest gathering in support of statehood to date. The delegates of the convention adopted a resolution, "We, the people of Oklahoma and Indian Territory, in convention assembled . . . favor the creation of a single state out of the area now embraced within both of these territories."[48]

The statehood initiatives for both Oklahoma and Indian territories were a regular concern for the Fifty-Seventh Congress in 1901 and 1902, as were similar measures for Arizona and New Mexico territories. Some bills proposed dividing Indian Territory into two parts, splitting it into counties, or making Indian Territory and Oklahoma Territory into one new state.[49] The House Committee on Territories received nine bills requesting statehoods. One bill supported New Mexico statehood, two called for statehood in Oklahoma, and a third promoted Arizona statehood. Yet another measure wanted to merge Oklahoma Territory and Indian Territory into one state. Not surprisingly, there were also measures that covered all four. Congressman William S. Knox of Massachusetts, chair of the House Committee on Territories, introduced HR 12543 on March 14, 1902, which would "enable the people of Oklahoma, Arizona and New Mexico to form constitutions and state governments and be admitted into the Union." Congressman

Thomas McRae of Arkansas amended the bill with a stipulation that Oklahoma and Indian territories be combined into one state.[50] The bill emerged from committee on April 1 with a recommendation for approval. Powerful Pennsylvania senator Matthew Quay flexed his power to push a similar bill through the Senate. Quay had a long-standing affinity with American Indians dating to his service on the Senate Indian Affairs Committee (additionally, two of his relatives, John Quay and John Quay Jr., were married to Native women).[51]

The Senate bill was held up by Albert J. Beverage, a Progressive from Indiana, who claimed Arizona and New Mexico did not have enough white citizens and possessed far too many Indians and Mexicans for statehood. Always determined to get his way, Senator Quay argued fervently for the bill. Despite Beverage's continuing opposition, by June 23, 1903, Quay believed that he had obtained enough votes to get the bill approved. But his motion to move the bill to the Senate floor ended in a tie, delaying it again.[52] The delay provided another opportunity for Beverage to try to defeat the bill. That autumn, a Senate Committee—Senators Albert J. Beverage, William P. Dillingham, Henry E. Burnham, and Henry A. Heitfeld—traveled to the four territories to hold hearings. After visiting Indian Territory in late November, the subcommittee concluded that it was not ready for single statehood and needed to improve its economy.[53]

Party politics must also be considered as a source of opposition. The addition of several new states in the later decades of the nineteenth century certainly helped Republicans maintain their dominance in national politics, but the political leanings of the new possibilities were not as favorable to the Grand Old Party. The Republican-dominated Congress and President Roosevelt did not want to risk adding four new Democratic states. The proposed state of Sequoyah, for example, leaned Democratic.[54]

Opposition to the bill was also evident in Indian Territory. A group calling itself the Indian Territory Executive Committee on Territorial Legislation met on November 25, 1902, at the three-story Scott Hotel at North Broadway and Seventh Street in Holdenville. The group passed resolutions opposing the statehood omnibus bill and arguing that Indian Territory needed more time to prepare itself for statehood on its own. To assist the Indians, Congressman John W. Moon of Tennessee introduced a bill to organize a territorial government for Indian Territory, but the measure went nowhere.[55]

Discussion of the omnibus statehood bill in the Senate began again on December 10. Quay stood stubbornly on one side of the debate and Beverage stood firmly on the other. For three weeks, Beverage and his committee members led a successful filibuster that once again stalled the measure. A long-winded Republican from Minnesota, Senator Knute Nelson, spoke five straight days against the bill in a boring monotone. Nelson aimed to wear down the other side when he read the voluminous testimonies of citizens in the territories. He succeeding in delaying the vote until early the next year.[56]

As the second session of the Fifty-Eighth Congress was ending, E. L. Hamilton, chair of the House Committee on Territories, introduced a statehood measure on behalf of Indian Territory. Republican congressman Reuben Moon of Pennsylvania also introduced a bill that called for the creation of Jefferson Territory from the Indian Territory.[57] Hamilton received some support from Indian Territory. Choctaw chief Green McCurtain explained that "the sentiment of the great majority of the Indians of the Five Tribes . . . are in favor of any statehood that Congress may provide, so long as it is statehood for Indian Territory alone, independent of Oklahoma."[58] While the measure was under consideration, Matthew Quay died on May 28, 1904.[59] Albert Beverage's great opponent was no more.

The Hamilton bill was still alive on February 7, 1905, when it passed in the Senate with no less than forty-seven amendments. The bill then went to committee, but before any final action could take place, Congress adjourned.[60] In the remaining days of the session in early March 1905, Senator Beverage gave a resounding speech and proclaimed only one was ready for statehood. Senator Beverage insisted that the people of proposed Oklahoma had made tremendous progress in the last two years. Senator Beverage declared,

> Not only that, but the idea of single statehood captured the country, and I hold here in my hand editorials from papers all over this nation advocating this course, regardless of party. In addition, the idea has grown until in this body itself it receives almost the overwhelming approval of senators. And now we are to have a single magnificent state made by the reunion of these two territories, a commonwealth unsurpassed in the Republic in generous resources, delightful climate, and a splendid citizenship—for such is the greater Oklahoma for which this bill provides and the only Oklahoma that is possible to be made a state.[61]

The measure also had the support of the White House. On his way to Texas, President Roosevelt stopped in Indian Territory to speak in support of combined statehood. At Muskogee on April 5, 1905, Roosevelt stood on a special grandstand and proclaimed, "Your territory, probably in conjunction with Oklahoma will soon be one of the great states of the Union. I look forward to meeting your congressmen and senators not long hence. I earnestly hope that as you enter statehood you will realize the immense responsibility that rests upon you."[62] On April 8, in the small town of Frederick in Oklahoma Territory, President Roosevelt said, "The next time I come to Oklahoma I trust I will come to a state and it won't be my fault if this is not so."[63]

On July 12, 1905, joint statehood promoters organized a large meeting at the popular Delmar Garden in the city of Oklahoma.[64] An impressive one-thousand delegates attended, five hundred representing Oklahoma Territory and five hundred representing Indian Territory.[65] The delegates argued that the two territories "had sufficient land area, population, resources and character," and passed a resolution advocating that "immediate joint statehood be granted to Oklahoma and Indian territories, on their own merits, and without reference to any right or claim of other territories seeking admission to the American Union."[66]

Advocates for both joint and separate statehood battled it out throughout the twin territories in the following months. On Saturday, October 14, 1905, the largest meeting on statehood so far took place in the city of Oklahoma, and it turned out to be the most heated gathering yet. The program called for a "session of the Constitution Convention Saturday morning followed by the statehood discussion in the afternoon and night." In this heated exchange of words, C. E. Castle and Judge William Hunter of Wagoner argued for joint statehood against Charles Haskell and Judge John Thomas, who argued for separate statehood.[67] Neither side could convince the other to change its mind.

Meanwhile, racial violence marred both of the twin territories. On August 29, 1901, the *Indian Chieftain* newspaper reported that Mayor H. C. Miller had issued a proclamation that if the local citizens were determined to drive African Americans from Sapulpa, that it be done in a peaceful manner.[68] In April of the following year, a race riot broke out in Lawton, Oklahoma Territory, when whites tried to force Black residents out of town. The escalation of violence there and elsewhere necessitated calling out the Oklahoma National Guard.[69] Racial outbursts increased in the following months and seemed to become a part of daily life. On November 29, the *Beaver Journal* reported that a vigilance committee posted notices proclaiming that Blacks had twenty-four hours to leave Waurika. The following three years recorded no improvement in race relations. The *Cherokee Messenger* reported in August 1905 that whites organized to force African Americans out of Claremore. In the ensuing violence, leaving one Black and one white wounded.[70] During these troubled years, thirty-three of the forty lynching victims were Black.[71]

In 1905, the future, political and otherwise, for everyone, regardless of race or ethnicity, was up in the air and pending congressional action. Delegates from Indian Territory and Oklahoma Territory lobbied in Washington to promote their interests. Fred Parkinson, a delegate for Indian Territory in favor of Oklahoma statehood, had a chance to meet with the president. Roosevelt assured Parkinson and the others of his group "that he was in hearty sympathy with the aspiration for joint statehood" and "believed it was the desire of a majority of the people of the two territories; that it was not a political question, but a broadly patriotic one; that one splendid state could be made of the two."[72]

On January 22, 1906, Congressman Edward L. Hamilton, a Republican from Michigan, introduced the Oklahoma Enabling Bill, HR 12707, to the House of Representatives. The bill offered "to enable the people of Oklahoma and of the Indian Territory to form a constitution and State government and be admitted into the Union on an equal footing with the original States; and to enable the people of New Mexico and of Arizona to form a constitution and State Government and be admitted into the Union on equal footing with the original States." The act provided, "that the inhabitants of all that part of the area of the United States now constituting the Territory of Oklahoma and the Indian Territory, as at present described, may adopt a constitution and become the State of Oklahoma, as hereafter provided: Provided, That nothing contained in the said constitution shall be construed to limit or impair the rights of persons or property pertaining to the Indians of said Territories."[73] After two days of heavy debate in the House, the bill returned to the House Committee on Territories. A serious point of contention was making New Mexico and Oklahoma, including Indian Territory, states at the same time. After considerable discussion, Speaker of the House "Uncle Joe" Cannon, a Republican from Illinois, succeeded in getting the bill passed on January 25.

The next step for the bill was to pass the Senate. Discussion started there on March 5. Minnesota senator Knute Nelson pointed out the vast differences between Oklahoma Territory and the combined territories of New Mexico and Arizona. Both New Mexico Territory and Arizona Territory had a lot of debt and Arizona had a lot of underdeveloped lands that needed irrigation.[74] On March 9 the Senate voted thirty-seven to thirty-five to separate Arizona and New Mexico from the bill.[75] The heatedly debated bill entered a joint congressional conference on June 13, and the House approved the bill the next day. Two days later, on June 15, 1906, the Senate passed the Oklahoma Enabling Act, and President Roosevelt signed the bill into law on June 16.[76] The new law laid out the process for electing delegates and included $100,000 to fund the convention.[77] The law purported "to enable the people of New Mexico and of Arizona to form a constitution and State government and be admitted into the Union on an equal footing with the original States."

The Oklahoma Enabling Act merged the twin territories into one called Oklahoma and authorized the citizens to form a government and draft a constitution. Indian delegates, mostly mixed bloods, attended the constitutional conventions held at Muskogee and Guthrie. People of various races had the right to vote. The enabling act included provisions that directly affected Native people. It made the Osage Reservation into a county, and although it protected the religious practices of various Indian nations, plural marriages were prohibited, which went against the cultural practices of some tribes, including the Muscogees, Cheyennes, and Comanches.

The prospect of statehood was met with protest in some corners of Indian Territory. In early June 1907 the *Vinita Chieftain* reported stiff opposition from the Keetoowah Cherokees. Among the Muscogees, Chitto Harjo and the traditionalist Snake full bloods also expressed their dissatisfaction. In fact, Harjo and the Snakes planned to move to Mexico with proceeds from selling their land allotments.[78] The Muscogee Snakes' resistance to federally imposed change dated back several years and included several hundred supporters that also included opponents of allotment from the Choctaws, Chickasaws, Seminoles, and Cherokees. And the Snakes were occasionally involved in violent confrontations.[79]

Despite such dissatisfaction, organizing efforts for the new state continued apace. A total of 112 delegates arrived at Guthrie on November 20, 1906, to form the constitutional convention. Two of the delegates represented the Osage Nation, while fifty-five came from each of the twin territories.[80] Most of the delegates were white and were not from the territories originally. At least sixty-four delegates were born east of the Mississippi River; the remaining forty-nine hailed from states in the West.[81]

Just after 2:00 p.m., temporary chairman Henry S. Johnston banged the gavel to officially open the convention at the three-story limestone Brooks Opera House. The convention overwhelmingly elected Democrat Alfalfa Bill Murray as the convention president over the Republican, Philip B. Hopkins of Muskogee.[82] Murray advocated his progressive reform ideas, which became an agenda for the convention. Some controversy arose over the wording of the preamble, "We, the people of the State of Oklahoma, wishing the guardianship of the Supreme Ruler of the Universe." Reverend J. H. N. Cobb from Sapulpa asked the assembly if their mothers taught them to say "Supreme Ruler of the Universe" in their prayers while growing up? "Damn it," yelled Murray, "you cannot leave God out of the constitution!"[83] On July 10, 1907, the constitutional convention drafted a constitution, and twelve days later it arrived at the office of the secretary of the territory.[84] The delegates of both territories voted for single statehood as outlined in the Oklahoma Enabling Act. When it was ready, the constitution was placed before Alfalfa Bill Murray to sign. While he signed, tears of joy filled the weary blue eyes of the tough native Texan who was now an Oklahoman. He was so overcome with emotion that Henry S. Johnston had to finish his official remarks for him.[85]

While taking in the moment, William Murray penned his name in black ink, and then completed his duties as president of the Oklahoma constitutional convention by adjourning the historic meeting.[86] The Oklahoma constitution sailed through Congress and was approved on September 17, 1907.[87] The Oklahoma constitution did include at least one important provision in favor of Indigenous residents. It stated that Oklahoma could not interfere with the federal government's sixty-eight treaties with the Indian nations in the new state. This was not an easy lesson for state bureaucrats to learn, considering that the treaties involved nearly forty tribes in Oklahoma.

The overwhelming majority of delegates were Democrats, and they controlled the statehood convention. They selected Charles N. Haskell of Muskogee to be the first governor.[88] Haskell served only one term as governor from 1907 to 1911, according to the term limit in the constitution. The first two senators were Robert L. Owen, a mixed-blood Cherokee from Lynchburg, Virginia, and Thomas Gore, a Populist from Mississippi.[89] The son of the president of a railroad company, Owen attended private schools and later Washington and Lee University. After arriving in the Cherokee Nation, Owen taught at the Cherokee Orphan Asylum from 1879 to 1880. He started practicing law in 1880 and owned the *Indian Chieftain* newspaper in Vinita. Owen was secretary of the Board of Education of the Cherokee Nation from 1881 to 1884, and from 1885 to 1890, he served as the Indian agent for the Five Tribes.[90]

Thomas Gore endured hardship at an early age when he suffered serious injuries to both eyes in different accidents, but he still made a success of himself.[91] In fall of 1891 he entered the law school at Cumberland University in Lebanon, Tennessee. After moving to Texas and entering law practice and politics, he realized the opportunity to politically help the farmers of Oklahoma Territory, something in line with the populist values he was raised with. His talent for oratory would help him to become elected as one of Oklahoma's first two senators, fulfilling his childhood dream.[92]

Prior to Haskell taking his oath of office on November 17, 1907, at the Carnegie Library in Guthrie, there was a symbolic wedding of a man dressed like a cowboy and a woman dressed like an Indian.[93] Miss Indian Territory was represented by Mrs. Leo Bennett, a young mixed-blood Cherokee who wore a "lavender satin dress made in the latest fashion of the time, floor length princess style with long sleeves and high collar; and a large picture hat and gloves, carrying one large, mauve colored chrysanthemum."[94] Mr. Oklahoma Territory was represented by Mr. C. G. Jones, a noted businessman from the city of Oklahoma, who was "tall, fair haired, and—noted for his punctilious appearance." He wore "striped trousers" and a black coat.[95] The event marked the union of the twin territories in a new state called Oklahoma. The *Oklahoma State Capital* reported that this famous day started with a "big parade" of "sixteen carriages with officials of Oklahoma Territory and others, one open carriage with the chiefs of the Five Tribes, these Indian Territory leaders fine looking in white collar, dark tie and citizen clothes; there was a marching band resplendent in their band regalia, and a large crowd of white people and Indians walking—some of the Indians in feathered headdress and blanket, with the women carrying baby cradle boards bright with decoration and bead work; there was a company of mounted police and another of Muscogee lighthorse troops. The parade ended at the steps of the [Carnegie] Library where an immense crowd had gathered."[96]

On November 16, the day before the grand parade, Charles Haskell and his family gathered with a few close friends in Room 47 of the Royal Hotel in Guthrie. About 11,000 people waited anxiously in the new state capital.[97]

Over 1,300 miles away in Washington, D.C., President Roosevelt scribbled his signature across the bottom of Presidential Proclamation 780, and Oklahoma Territory became the forty-sixth state of the Union. Then the president said, "Oklahoma is now a state."[98] Not long after, on the first of December, President Roosevelt declared in his annual message to Congress, "Oklahoma has become a state, standing on full equity with her elder sisters, and her future is assured by her great natural resources. The duty of the National Government to guard the personal and property rights of the Indians within her borders remains of course unchanged."[99]

In signing his name to the proclamation, Roosevelt shattered the dream for the Native state of Sequoyah. Roosevelt's friend, Pleasant Porter, passed away on September 3 from a heart attack. He had not lived to see the union of Indian and Oklahoma territories that ended the quest for an Indian state. He was the last elected Muscogee chief until 1971.[100]

Roosevelt's death blow to the idea of state of Sequoyah was of a piece with his long history of anti-Indian racism. Much earlier, in 1886, Roosevelt gave a speech, "Ranch Life in the West," during which he revealed his prejudice toward Native people when he said, "I don't go so far as to think that the only good Indians are dead Indians, but I believe nine out of every ten are. And I shouldn't like to inquire too closely into the case of the tenth."[101] Roosevelt believed that Indians were savages and inferior to whites, and that savageness was lowest level of existence.[102] Roosevelt argued that whites and Indians should interbreed until the latter no longer existed as a race.[103] His ethnocentrism blinded him to the great losses suffered by American Indians, who had lost over 90 percent of their original homelands, including Indian Territory, even though the Five Tribes and other tribes had been forcibly moved there. In Roosevelt's worldview, "the Indian would always remain a victim of white racial destiny." He died in 1919 from a coronary embolism with his famous glasses resting on a table next to his bedside.[104]

SIX

A Dream of a Black State and the Rise of Indian Nationalism

Edward P. McCabe stood out as one of the most extraordinary individuals of his time. He was a mixed-race African American and had many impressive accomplishments. Born in Troy, New York, in 1850, Edward was sometimes called "Edwin," sometimes just "E. P." He would become a land developer, lawyer, newspaper owner, state auditor, and a politician. Later in life, his close friends called him "Mac." But he came from humble origins. In his youngest days, Edward and his parents moved around a lot, but at some point, the young boy became an orphan and had to learn to make it on his own.[1]

As a young man, Edward found work on New York's Wall Street. Employed as a clerk and porter, he watched white people, saw how they dressed, and listened to their conversations. He learned their manners, refined his speech, and added new words to his vocabulary. He mastered the art of using words to persuade others. He became known as "a good talker."[2] Young Edward had dreams and ambition, including a desire for a better life. He read newspaper articles about the droves of people going west, especially to Kansas. He studied law, and realized that combining these two things—land and the law—would lead to success in life.[3] Although he learned well how to adapt himself to the image of the flourishing Wall Street denizen, he never forgot where he came from and hoped to improve life for other Black people.

Edward McCabe's vision for a Black state began during the Civil War. The Emancipation Proclamation on January 1, 1863, effectively freed roughly 3.5 million slaves in Confederate states, ushering in a period of drastic change.

The end of the war in 1865 brought even more upheaval. The four treaties of 1866 the US government signed with the Cherokees, Muscogees, Seminoles, and Choctaws and Chickasaws freed the slaves belonging to the Five Nations and called for the freed slaves, or freedmen to be treated as citizens of the tribes.

The freedmen generally opted to stay in Indian Territory rather than move elsewhere.[4] Some significant conflicts arose with the Five Nations. The Cherokee treaty of 1866 stipulated that every African American head of family was entitled to have 160 acres, although the tribe preferred communal ownership. While the Choctaws made their former slaves tribal citizens in 1883, the Chickasaws denied freedmen tribal citizenship and compelled them to leave the reservation.[5] The Muscogees were also resistant to making former slaves citizens. The Seminoles, on the other hand, were more willing to accept the presence of freedmen and allowed them to stay on their reservation.[6] Throughout the Five Nations, settlements of former slaves became Black communal towns, especially on the Muscogee and Seminole reservations. Although the Black residents of post–Civil War Indian Territory found variable receptions, others saw the place as a potential haven for African Americans. For example, Congressman William Lawrence of Ohio introduced a bill in 1866 for the creation of the territory of Lincoln for "Americans citizens of African descent."[7]

Lawrence was not alone in his dreams of a Black utopia on the Great Plains. Edward McCabe settled in the all-Black town of Nicodemus, Kansas, in 1878 and thereafter achieved notable success. He studied law and became a lawyer, a land agent, and a Republican. He received an appointment as county clerk for the newly established Graham County and then won an election for a full term in the position. McCabe married Sara Bryant in 1880, and they eventually had two daughters. When McCabe was in his early thirties, in 1882, both Black and non-Black voters elected him to the position of state auditor of Kansas in 1882.[8] Good with numbers, McCabe did his job effectively and served two terms. Although he was defeated in his quest for a third, he set his mind on a career in politics. In 1890, McCabe and his family moved to Oklahoma Territory.[9] Immediately, he began encouraging Black settlers to move to the territory to help realize his dream of a Black state.

The subject of a Black state was a considerable topic of discussion in the twin territories. McCabe was surely aware of the Oklahoma clubs in Kansas that hoped to establish Black homesteads in Indian Territory. They were well aware of the boomer movement and wanted to be a part of the opening of the Unappropriated Lands. Rumors spread like a prairie fire, and the hopes of Blacks in Kansas rose when the *Leavenworth Advocate,* a Black Republican newspaper, published a story about the government opening the former Muscogee and Seminole lands to settlers.[10] The era's racial tumult, Black efforts for self-sufficiency, and fast-moving rumors sometimes resulted in confusion. For example, Cyrus Leondus Blackburn, a Cherokee freedman, wrote to the *Indian Chieftain* in Vinita and asked if all of the "white men" in Indian Territory were trying to drive out the "colored people" who wanted "a chance to come in and settle" [in the] "country." He had also heard about "a bill" in Congress that promised to do the opposite: to drive out all whites and allow African Americans to stay in the territory.[11] Meanwhile, McCabe worked to achieve his dream for a Black state with the support of interested African Americans.[12]

Drawing on his experience as a state auditor, McCabe acquired 320 acres outside of Guthrie in 1891.[13] This land base provided a place for freedmen to live. In other efforts, African Americans organized the First Grand Independent Brotherhood, a loose political association with the general goal of colonizing the Guthrie area, and founded all-Black towns in Indian Territory and later Oklahoma Territory. A Black settlement took root near Purcell, two smaller ones developed east of the Canadian River, and others could be found west of Kingfisher. During the summer after the 1889 land rush, a colony of about three hundred African American settlers quietly left Topeka, Kansas, and organized a town called Lincoln City, which stood proudly about a dozen miles north of Kingfisher.[14] Red Wing and Wanamaker were also founded in the Cimarron River Valley in the wake of the 1889 land run. Unfortunately, not all of these communities were destined to survive. Poor soil doomed the efforts of potential wheat farmers at Lincoln City, and the town withered away by 1894, and Wanamaker also fell by the wayside. Along with adverse weather conditions and isolation, Black settlers encountered resistance and violence from white boomers and sometimes took an aggressive stance themselves toward Natives. In the Cherokee Nation, about two-hundred African Americans settled in an area called Gooseneck, and armed themselves with rifles, shotguns, pistols, and a cannon.[15] Fortunately no fighting broke out, and the Black settlers claimed the area.

During the first anniversary celebration of the 1889 land run, McCabe and two African Americans co-established a town called Langston City, named after an African American US congressman from Virginia. The former dean of the Howard University law school and president of Virginia Normal and Collegiate Institute, Congressman John Mercer Langston promised his support for an African American college in the town, which opened its doors to forty-one students on March 12, 1897. On May 2, 1891, McCabe started the *Langston Herald,* the first African American weekly newspaper in Oklahoma Territory. Interestingly, most of its subscribers lived outside of the territory.[16] Langston City and its college, the Colored Agricultural and Normal School (later renamed Langston University), became the beacon of Black progress in Oklahoma.

McCabe's efforts and speeches on behalf of a Black state provoked fiery criticism from regional newspapers.[17] Still, he persisted with his grand political ambitions and would not let racial prejudice stand in his way. Due to his persistence, he earned the nickname "pushahead."[18] Bold and determined, McCabe moved in with a Black politician friend, J. J. Jennings, in Washington, DC, and lobbied to be appointed the governor of Oklahoma Territory.[19] Other African Americans believed in McCabe and joined his efforts.

In late April 1890 twenty young Black men from the African American press and E. L. Thornton of New York arrived at the White House to see President Benjamin Harrison. The group reminded the president of McCabe's successful record as an auditor in Kansas and urged the president to consider "the appointment of Edward P. McCabe of Oklahoma as secretary of that territory." President Harrison "promised to consider their wishes." But the idea of a Black man in any political office in Oklahoma Territory provoked sharp criticism. One territorial politician outright rejected a "Negro government" and said of McCabe that he would not "give five cents for his life."[20] One individual argued in the *New York Times* that if President Harrison appointed McCabe as the governor of Oklahoma Territory, the latter would be assassinated within a week.[21]

The racial tensions called for a steady hand and a calm mind to govern the territory, preferably a leader from the outside, and President Harrison had someone in mind. He appointed George Washington Steele, a lawyer from Illinois, as the first governor of Oklahoma Territory, but McCabe was not left empty-handed. On May 22, 1890, Governor Steele appointed Edward McCabe as the first treasurer of Logan County. Not surprisingly, news of this appointment was not received well by everyone. The *Oklahoma State Capital* went as far as to claim, "McCabe's appointment is an insult to every honest white man in Oklahoma. He is not a citizen, cannot vote and represents no property."[22]

African Americans like Edward McCabe certainly were citizens and legally entitled to the vote by 1890, and to say that McCabe represented no property was also erroneous. By the turn of the twentieth century, African Americans possessed an estimated 1.5 million acres of farmland in Oklahoma Territory. Roughly 55,000 African Americans lived in Oklahoma Territory and Indian Territory at the time.[23] These included the residents of the town of Boley, officially established on the Muscogee reservation on September 22, 1904.[24] The town grew steadily to become one of the wealthiest African American towns in the country during the early twentieth century.[25]

The first decade of the twentieth century saw several efforts for statehood in the twin territories, and African Americans added their voices to the mix. At the same time of the Sequoyah Convention in August 1905, African Americans of both Oklahoma Territory and Indian Territory met and "held a single statehood convention at the same time in Muskogee." About three hundred delegates attended, and "they passed resolutions for a single state and for a liberal organic act by congress, fully protecting their rights," according to the *Oklahoma State Register* published in Guthrie.[26] Not long before, the single statehood convention in the city of Oklahoma had been held July 12. Hundreds of Indians, whites, Blacks, and mixed bloods were involved in these three conventions.[27] Discrimination offers an explanation for these separate efforts. A few days prior to the Sequoyah Convention, the *Muskogee Cimeter* reported the exclusion of African American interests, "The separate [*sic*] statehood convention should they succeed mean nothing of a progressive nature to us. Robt. L. Owen, the High Priest, and Thos. Owen and [S. M.] Rutherford, are one and the same in eliminating of the Negro."[28]

As African Americans continued to move into Indian Territory, white settlers responded with fear and panic. On November 2, 1906, the *Alva Weekly Pioneer* reported, "White men went into the Indian Territory, bought property, engaged in business, and were satisfied. Coal, gas and oil were discovered and [African Americans] flocked in by the hundreds and thousands until in many localities they hold the balance of power when combined with the carpet bagger republican politicians whose white skins are the only evidence of true Americans . . . white men CANNOT SELL OUT, and cannot leave without sacrificing almost everything."[29] The vitriol was not just verbal. White racists used Jim Crow tactics throughout Oklahoma Territory to intimidate Blacks, sending a clear message that they were not wanted.

The first decades of statehood were filled with racial violence. In 1908 the *Muskogee Cimeter* reported on the lynching death of James Garden of Henryetta.[30] The newspaper's editor, William H. Twine, advised Black people to "respect the law, but fight for your rights." He argued that "best way to stop lynching mobs was for every black man to get himself a gun and protect himself!"[31] He also organized an Anti-Jim Crow Club. His efforts led to the anti-Jim Crow League state convention.[32] The most infamous example of racial violence in the early statehood years came with the Tulsa Race Massacre of 1921, when some three hundred African Americans were killed and many more wounded.[33] Originally, Tulsa was a Muscogee town-community, but the heavy influx of new arrivals, especially during the early years of the twentieth century, created a mixed population of whites, Indians, and Blacks.

Edward McCabe's dream of a Black state in what is now Oklahoma seems to have dissipated by the time the Oklahoma Enabling Act was passed in 1906. But the dream of the state of Sequoyah did not fade away. With the political winds favoring Oklahoma statehood, could the state of Sequoyah still come into being? Efforts continued within the homelands of the Five Nations and outside.

As early as December 4, 1905, the House of Representatives considered a bill by Congressman Arthur Murphy of Missouri to create the state of Sequoyah. A clean-cut young Republican from Hancock, Missouri, Murphy worked for the Muscogees as a lawyer from 1902 to 1904. The bill failed. Evidence suggests that Pleasant Porter had hoped to meet with Murphy, but apparently he did not. Feeling frustrated, Pleasant Porter left Washington to return to Muskogee two days before Christmas. He told the *Muskogee Phoenix* that politicians in Washington favored merging Oklahoma and Indian territories into a single state.[34] On January 24, 1906, Senator Joseph B. Foraker of Ohio introduced Document No. 143, an eighty-seven page document called "Proposed State of Sequoyah," to his colleagues. Foraker had a passion for racial justice and he tried to make a convincing argument to his colleagues to admit Sequoyah as the next state of the United States, but the bill died in committee.[35]

Due to the lobbying of the settlers and politicians in Oklahoma Territory for joint statehood, the dream of the state of Sequoyah began to fade. As required by the Curtis Act of 1898, the tribal governments of the Five Nations were abolished in early March 1906. Adding injury to wound, Congress passed a law on the last day of April 1908 allowing Secretary of the Interior James R. Garfield to "take possession of all buildings on land belonging to the Five Civilized Tribes, now or hereafter used for Governmental, school or other tribal purposes." They were to be appraised and sold with the accumulated moneys to be put in accounts held by the government for the tribes.[36]

But some stalwarts did not give up on the Sequoyah dream so easily. Charles H. Sawyer was one of them. He had served as an assistant US attorney and clerked for the Dawes Commission. Although he hailed from Connecticut, he kept up with the affairs of the Indian Territory. Sawyer even designed a seal for the proposed state of Sequoyah, as well as one for Oklahoma. The "Great Seal of the State of Sequoyah" exhibited a circle with a five-pointed star in the middle, which had a small picture of Sequoyah at the top. The star featured images to represent each of the Five Tribes. From clockwise, a plow and haystack represented the Muscogees, an Indian paddling a canoe symbolized the Seminoles, a standing warrior represented the Chickasaws, three arrows with a bow represented the Choctaws, and a wreath almost encircling a star symbolized the Cherokees. The large five-pointed star rested on a background of smaller stars with an outer ring featured the words, "Great Seal of the State of Sequoyah." The year 1905 was inscribed at the bottom.[37]

Even if Sequoyah the state seemed destined to be forgotten, Sequoyah the man was not. Capping off ten years of effort by Oklahoma senator Robert Owen, the namesake of the proposed Indian state was honored in the Statuary Hall of the US Capitol on June 6, 1917, sculpted by Vinnie Ream Hoxie. Sequoyah was Oklahoma's first contribution to Statuary Hall.[38] In 1939, Oklahoma honored entertainer Will Rogers in its second and final contribution. Both individuals were Cherokee.[39] Even the traditionalist Keetoowah Cherokees celebrate Sequoyah as one of their two most important leaders alongside Red Bird Smith, who led them in opposing land allotments after the turn of the twentieth century.[40] In 1931 roughly 2,000 Keetoowah Cherokees and other Indians gathered to dance and celebrate these two leaders.[41] The Keetoowahs have continued these commemorations to this day.

When Oklahoma finally adopted a state flag in 1925, it also highlighted its Indigenous heritage. The background field was "sky blue (cobalt with [a] little white mixed); shield light tan (buckskin); stars (represented by crosses on face of shield) darker tan, and also thongs lacing with dark brown tips; pipe bowl and pendant decoration, red; pipe stem, pale yellow; olive branch, gray green)."[42] Although Oklahoma did not become an Indian state, the state flag consists of an Osage shield with seven eagle feathers symbolizing an Indian presence, and the state seal celebrates the Five Tribes.

As the dream of the state of Sequoyah faded, the great events of the age continued to affect American Indians. The Five Tribes and other tribes across Indian Country sent about 10,000 of their young men to fight in World War I, even though many were not citizens of the United States. Roughly five hundred American Indian men died in the Great War, but it is not known how many were members of the Five Tribes. About six-hundred Indian men, mostly Cherokees, Choctaws, Chickasaws, Muscogees, and Seminoles, served in the 142nd Infantry Regiment of the Thirty-Sixth "Panther" Division.[43] All honorably discharged Native men from the service were automatically granted US citizenship by a law passed in 1919.[44] Five years later, the US government passed the General Citizenship Act of 1924, which made all Indigenous Americans citizens of the country if they were not already.

As the Sequoyah movement faded from memory, one of its great champions died. After surviving a major stroke and a following bout of pneumonia, Charles Haskell lost consciousness, and the first governor of Oklahoma passed away on July 6, 1933, at the age of seventy-three. He was remembered by many people in Oklahoma and elsewhere, and one of his greatest friends was William "Alfalfa Bill" Murray, another former proponent of the Sequoyah statehood movement. Murray eulogized Haskell with these words: "From that standpoint, the nearest man to God I ever knew was C. N. Haskell. And I ought to know. In 1905 I came out of the Chickasaw nation to the Sequoyah convention at Muskogee. I was there all the time, attended every meeting and I ground my own puny mind against that of him who we honor here."[45]

The Great Depression witnessed considerable change in Indian Country, including the Five Nations in Oklahoma. Many of the arguments of the architects of the Sequoyah movement had been proven correct. One year prior to the Wall Street crash of 1929, the federal government published a report entitled *The Problem of Indian Administration* (also known as the Meriam Report). It argued that the land allotment policy introduced by the Dawes Act of 1887 and the Curtis Act of 1898 had failed.[46] The report ushered in fresh thinking and a new approach to federal-Indian relations. The Indian Reorganization Act in 1934 overturned the land allotment policy under the Dawes Act of 1887 and introduced a new federal Indian policy. Sometimes referred to as the Indian New Deal, this new Indian policy was led by a stark-looking man with spectacles who proved to be as formidable as his appearance suggested. Congressmen walked away in order to avoid being cornered by John Collier, the crusader for Indian reform.

The Indian Reorganization Act, also called the IRA, excluded the Five Tribes. This exemption was largely achieved by Senator Elmer Thomas of Oklahoma, who served on the Senate Committee on Indian Affairs and firmly believed that the members of the Five Nations were well on their way to assimilation into the American mainstream. But after a tour of Oklahoma in 1934 Commissioner John Collier convinced the senator that a new law was needed to provide the same IRA benefits to the Cherokees, Muscogees, Seminoles, Choctaws, and Chickasaws. With the help of Oklahoma congressman Will Rogers (not to be confused with the entertainer Will Rogers or the Cherokee chief William Rogers), Senator Thomas introduced a bill to include the Five Nations in the IRA.[47] The IRA was amended two years in later in 1936 to produce the Alaska Native Reorganization Act and the Oklahoma Indian Welfare Act. The latter provided IRA provisions to the Five Nations and tribes outside of Oklahoma.[48] Under the so-called OIWA, eighteen tribes produced constitutions to reorganize their governments, and another thirteen tribes reorganized under tribal charters.[49] Roughly six weeks after the passage of the Oklahoma Indian Welfare Act, Congress passed PL 715. This law federally recognized the group of dedicated traditionalists as the United Keetoowah Band of Cherokee Indians in Oklahoma.[50]

The post–World War II years saw wild swings in federal Indian policies. One was the termination of the US trust in 109 cases involving tribes, bands, and tribal communities. More upheaval came with the relocation program, which moved two-thirds of the Indian population to urban areas. Even during these hard years in Indian Country, echoes could be heard of the Sequoyah idea. Congressman Victor Wickersham of Oklahoma introduced House Joint Resolution (HJR) 181 on January 27, 1955. HJR 181 reminded Congress that the

Five Tribes had ceded their eastern lands via treaties for new lands in "the Indian Territory, part of this consideration for the exchanges of properties was that the lands of the Indians should never be embraced within a State, that the Indians should never be made subject to control by any State, and that the United States would guarantee and protect these Indians in these rights forever."[51] The election of John F. Kennedy in 1960 and his New Frontier platform halted the termination policy, and called for more Indian input in federal-Indian affairs. In February of his first year in office, President John Kennedy appointed John Orien Crow, who was one-fourth Cherokee, as acting commissioner of Indian Affairs.[52]

Roughly a decade later, a new law was passed that supported Indigenous sovereignty in Oklahoma. On October 22, 1970, Congress passed Public Law 91–495, which stated that, subject to the approval of the secretary of the Interior, the Five Tribes of Oklahoma would have authority in electing their tribal leaders.[53] The later enactment of the Self-Determination and Education Assistance Act of 1975 (PL 93–638) provided abundant funding for tribal programs. The legislation stressed tribal control in supervising services.[54] The Republican administrations of Richard Nixon and Gerald Ford and the Democratic administration of Jimmy Carter confirmed Indian self-determination as the primary directive of federal Indian policy.

The effects of the new laws could be seen immediately. The Muscogees held their first "official" election in 1971 for the principal chief since Pleasant Porter's election in 1903. Claud Cox started his first four-year term in humble surroundings. His administrative staff consisted of himself and a part-time secretary, with both of them working out of their own homes. Construction for a new capitol complex began on the north side of Okmulgee and within the next few years, the Cox administration flourished into a growing bureaucracy. The newly completed complex included administrative offices, housing authority, Indian Health Service offices with a dental health clinic and an environmental health office. In October 1975, the Muscogees held a dedication ceremony for the tribal complex. This act officially marked the most progressive period that the Muscogee tribe had ever known. The tribe ambitiously introduced a series of various programs to address the needs the people. A new dental clinic began operating and additional plans called for extended health care. By 1975 four clinics were operating at Wetumka, Holdenville, Okemah, and Sapulpa.[55]

In 1971 the Cherokee people elected W. W. Keeler as their first principal chief since Oklahoma statehood. He would go on to serve in the role for sixteen years, and his election enabled the Cherokees to pursue their ambitions and plans for a tribal complex similar to what the Muscogees had developed. The tribe opened the Cherokee National Museum, and they completed a replica of a historic village called Tsa-La-Gi in 1971, which featured an outdoor drama called "Trail of Tears" during the summer months. The cultural complex attracted 30,000 visitors during its first year.[56] During the 1970s and 1980s, the Cherokees worked diligently to advance their tourism industry and to preserve their culture. The Cherokee Heritage was created to be the base of operations for the tribe's cultural preservation efforts. The other Five Tribes also began to develop plans for heritage centers or museums to preserve their histories based on their perspectives.

A branch of the Five Nations still in the eastern United States would be the first to institute a change that has had widespread effects on Indian Country since the late twentieth century. In 1979, inspired by what they had seen at a Catholic church, the small population of Seminoles who had remained in Florida started holding tribal bingo games on their Hollywood Reservation. While the gaming industry has been a boon for some tribes, the presumption that it has led to widespread Native prosperity is not accurate. Only about 25 percent of Native communities in gaming succeed or break even to pay their operating expenses.

On November 16, 1990, the Cherokees of Oklahoma entered a new era when they held a ribbon-cutting ceremony for opening the tribe's first bingo hall, the Bingo Outpost. "This will be, in my opinion, the major tourist attraction in this area [of Oklahoma]," said Chief Wilma Mankiller to more than three hundred guests. Mankiller followed in the footsteps of Alice Davis of the Seminoles, who served as principal chief of her tribe from 1922 to 1935, and would set an example for more Indian women to become tribal leaders. With a final cost of $700,000, the new Cherokee bingo hall occupied 23,000 square feet at the intersection of Interstate 40 and Oklahoma Highway 64, just west of Fort Smith, Arkansas, and about fifteen miles from the Blue Ribbon Downs horse-racing facility. The Bingo Outpost could seat 884 players and offered about $2.25 million in prizes during its first year of operation.[57]

Profits from the Indian gaming industry has enabled each of the Five Nations to produce revenue and become less dependent upon the federal government for grants and funding. It has enabled the Five Tribes to stabilize their five governments and helped their town communities. Throughout the modern Indian Territory of the Muscogees, Seminoles, Cherokees, Chickasaws, and Choctaws are hospitals, clinics, tribal museums, businesses of various sorts, and a tribal college. In addition, roads and highways are maintained, and health services are available to non-Indians as well as Indians.

Along with their separate efforts, the Five Tribes have a long track record of working together to address common concerns. Important milestones include the 1842 Inter-Tribal Council of the Deep Fork River, which included the Osages, the 1861 meeting of the United Nations of Indian Territory, and the Okmulgee Council held in 1866. In 1870, the Five Tribes met with eight other tribes to write the Okmulgee Constitution. In 1949, the Cherokees, Muscogees, Seminoles, Chickasaws, and Choctaws officially formed the Inter-Tribal Council of the Five Civilized Tribes and drafted a constitution for the organization. One year later, on February 3, 1950, the council approved its own constitution. To this day, the intertribal council holds quarterly meeting to discuss common issues and concerns.[58] Perhaps the idea of an Indian state, as imagined by the delegates at the Sequoyah convention more than a century ago, is not so far-fetched.

Like the leaders of the state of Sequoyah movement, Edward McCabe had a dream, but Oklahoma statehood ended his vision of a Black state. The town of Langston would become his legacy when he and his wife decided to leave the former Indian Territory, now called Oklahoma. Disenchanted by persistent racism, many other Blacks felt like McCabe and hoped to leave. The McCabes had their sights set on an island off the coast of western Canada. One can imagine how Edward McCabe felt determined as he clutched his train ticket at the start of a journey bound for Victoria, British Columbia.[59] But McCabe's plans did not work in Canada or in Chicago, where he moved later. In the end, McCabe died in poverty in February 1920 at the age of seventy-one. His wife had a private funeral for him in Topeka, Kansas, where he had done so well decades earlier.[60]

In the former Indian Territory, the cycles of life in the Medicine Way continue, and the seasons come and go as they have done for centuries. Spring brings new life as animals are born and plants emerge from the earth. For the

Muscogees, Seminoles, Cherokees, Choctaws, and Chickasaws, tribal nationalism and inherent sovereignty are a part of the renewal ceremony. They invite everyone in the spirit of togetherness, the feeling of being one with the universe. The Five Nations hold their stomp dances, inviting everyone, leading up to the Green Corn Ceremony of songs and dancing, with men wearing their eagle feathers and women shaking shells in rhythm with the earth through the night until dawn. The ceremony is traditional sovereignty in action and it is a central part of the cultural continuum that the Five Tribes have carried for centuries.

Epilogue

McGirt v. Oklahoma *and the Future of Indian Country*

The most important question we can ask about the state of Sequoyah is, "Why didn't it happen?" The most obvious answer is "politics." But politics is not an abstract concept. There can be no politics without individuals, whether they be well-known leaders or lesser-known players. Politics also has two sides to it: the internal and the external. For the Five Tribes, the internal relates to factionalism, whereas the external relates to those wielding power from outside of Indian Territory.

This understanding of tribal politics leads to three more questions. Who wielded power, what was the factionalism dividing the Indian nations from within, and how did rhetoric influence people to believe in a cause? The cause began with an idea that transformed into a political movement called the state of Sequoyah. This leads us to even more questions. Where did the idea for an Indian state come from? Who was behind it? And how did the state of Sequoyah movement keep going? Was it a vision or a dream, and did it have any impact? Is it still alive today? Further answers to these inquiries are found through an understanding of two important concepts: American Indian, or "tribal," nationalism and Indigenous sovereignty. This tribal nationalism was embedded in the subconscious and conscious identities of the nearly six hundred tribal nations across Indian Country. This consciousness was historical, dating back centuries, and it shaped the identities of the Cherokees, Muscogees, Seminoles, Chickasaws, and Choctaws.[1]

A common denominator in the answers to the above questions is leadership. Leadership was a major driving force of the state of Sequoyah movement. In particular, Charles Haskell, Pleasant Porter, William "Alfalfa Bill" Murray, Dennis Bushyhead, James Norman, and others led the way at various times, both separately and together. Some leaders were one-of-a-kind characters. Native and non-Native leaders worked together for one cause on behalf of the Five Tribes. Bushyhead was a proactive Cherokee leader who kept his tribe in the forefront to sustain momentum. Norman, a Cherokee mixed blood, worked more behind the scenes, but was devoted to the proposed state of Sequoyah. As principal chief of the Muscogees, Porter was a key insider.

William Murray's path to the Sequoyah movement is instructive in showing how it encompassed outsiders and insiders. He was an outsider who played a vital role in Chickasaw politics and the state of Sequoyah movement. With his homespun oratory, he spoke up for the interests of Indians and farmers, earning him the nickname "Alfalfa Bill." Alfalfa Bill befriended another outsider, Charles Haskell, an Ohioan who moved to Muskogee in 1901. Like Murray, Haskell was a non-Indian and an outsider who became an insider in the state of Sequoyah movement.

Outsiders befriended other outsiders and allied with insiders. Haskell, for example, also befriended Muscogee principal chief Pleasant Porter. Although not admired by everyone, Porter proved to be the most influential leader at the height of the Sequoyah movement in 1905. Porter had learned from the Muscogee past that his people had worked with allies, bonded by friendships. Porter and other leaders of the Five Nations became friends with Murray and especially Haskell. A mixed-blood progressive, Porter was seen by federal officials as a model for other Native people.

Before the movement had leaders, there first had to be an idea, and it came into being with a conversation between Charles Haskell and Pleasant Porter in early August 1904. But there were antecedents. As one historian put it, the idea "had been advocated for a hundred years of forming an Indian state," from "1778 to 1887."[2] The earliest precedent was the Treaty of Fort Pitt, signed by Delaware Indian leaders in 1778. In this treaty, the newly formed United States promised the creation of an Indian state, which would be called Delaware.[3] From this broken promise came the idea for an Indian territory that spanned the next several decades. In this political context, Indian Territory was envisioned as a part of the United States where Native sovereignty prevailed, not as an independent nation-state. The landmark 1832 Supreme Court case *Worcester v. Georgia* established the independent sovereignty of the Cherokees, therefore setting a precedent of recognized autonomy for all Indian nations, albeit within an American context.[4] Of course, the Cherokees had known all along that they possessed an inherent sovereignty, which US leaders had to recognize. Furthermore, the sixty-eight treaties that the United States signed with the Cherokees, Choctaws, Chickasaws, Muscogees, and Seminoles on a sovereign-to-sovereign basis demonstrated the federal government's recognition of the independent autonomy of the Five Tribes. This number of agreements represents roughly 20 percent of the total 374 ratified US-Indian treaties. The takeaway here is that Indigenous sovereignty is a basic right of identity manifested by the peoples' historical presence and worldview. While most tribal leaders supported the idea of an Indian state becoming a part of the United States, a minority of individuals, such as Chitto Harjo, a full-blood Muscogee traditionalist, advocated for a fully independent nation-state.

While US courts and the Five Nations continued to understand the idea of tribal sovereignty according to *Worcester v. Georgia,* some federal politicians intended for the Five Tribes to become a US territory under federal law. After the Civil War, "several sessions of both houses" of Congress, from 1870 to 1905, listened to a dozen bills proposing to change the status of Indian Territory. (At this time, Indian Territory was not an organized territory of the United States.) These initiatives never materialized.[5] But these periodic bills established the hope among the Five Nations that there might be an Indian state comparable to neighboring ones like Kansas and Arkansas.

As for the physical requirements for statehood, Indian Territory easily surpassed them. By the end of the nineteenth century, almost 400,000 people lived in Indian Territory, and there were "ambitious and rival cities in every portion of this region; there were a dozen or more railroads, rich oil and coal fields, all to be affected in no small degree by the arbitrary running of county lines and the designating of county seats," as noted by author C. M. Allen [6] Considering its substantial population and natural resources, Indian Territory as a potential state offered many opportunities to outsiders. In addition to 74,000 square miles of fertile lands for crops and grasslands for cattle, the territory possessed rich veins of coal and underground pools of oil. With its abundant resources, the region developed a "sense of place."[7]

By the late 1800s, the leaders of the Five Nations understood well how the US government and its bureaucracy functioned. They comprehended the power of the committees on territories in Congress, and they knew which politicians held important influence. The insiders of tribal politics had learned about the politics of Washington, and they took on the tall task of persuading Washington bureaucrats to support their cause even as many other territories made their own cases for statehood.

The progress of tribal governments came to a halt in the wake of the Dawes Commission and the Atoka Agreement of 1898, which called for the allotment of Choctaw and Chickasaw lands. But these actions by the US government did not diminish the legal rights of the Five Tribes, which were vested in the treaties they had made with the United States. The 1898 Curtis Act, which furthered allotment and worked to abolish tribal governments, also stipulated that if the "tribal governments will prove so satisfactory," then "the Five Civilized Tribes shall, in the opinion of Congress, be prepared for admission as a State to the Union."[8] On January 14, 1899, the Dawes Commission struck an agreement with the Cherokees that was similar to the Atoka Agreement. During their negotiations, the commission affirmed that the Cherokees "would never be made a part of any state or territory without their consent; or that if made a part of a state without such consent the state or territory would include only the lands of the Five Civilized Tribes."[9] In keeping with this stance, some members of Congress wanted the Five Nations to have their own Indian state. But the majority of Congress opposed the idea.

Another possible option for Indian Territory was to join with neighboring Oklahoma Territory, carved from the western part of Indian Territory in 1890, and become a single state. But tribal leaders from the Five Nations resisted this idea. On November 28, 1902, tribal leaders met in Eufaula. Pleasant Porter of the Muscogees chaired the meeting.[10] After much discussion about joint statehood with the newly formed Oklahoma Territory, the delegates decided against it. They wanted statehood only for Indian Territory. Principal chiefs Pleasant Porter of the Muscogees and William Rogers of the Cherokees issued a proclamation stating that "a majority of the Five Civilized Tribes" wanted "separate and independent statehood."[11]

While insiders and supportive outsiders such as Alfalfa Bill Murray and Charles Haskell made the case for statehood, other outsiders impeded the Sequoyah movement's progress. These outsiders, including President Theodore Roosevelt and Washington bureaucrats, did not outright reject the plan for Indian Territory becoming a state, but the favor they gave to Oklahoma Territory's push for statehood left little room for movement on the development of an Indian state. At the same time, the bureaucrats were more willing to entertain the prospect of making Indian Territory and Oklahoma Territory into one state. Insiders began to doubt that there was much of a chance of an Indian state becoming reality.

Still, many continued to lay the groundwork. The state of Sequoyah Convention in 1905 represented the climax of the movement for an Indian state and the culmination of the hard work put in by the likes of Pleasant Porter, Robert Owen, Charles Haskell, and Alfalfa Bill Murray. Within two years, Indian Territory would be combined with its western neighbor and enter the Union as the state of Oklahoma. Not only did the dream of Native state die, but so did the idea of a Black state, another possible destiny for the region dreamed of by Edward McCabe and others.

The twentieth century saw several shifts in federal Indian policy, all of which had important implications for tribal sovereignty. When the Curtis Act of 1898 called for the dissolution of the tribal governments in 1906, the Five Tribes had to endure the consequences of the allotment policy through the beginning of the Great Depression. The Oklahoma Indian Welfare Act of 1936 ended the assimilationist allotment policy and offered the opportunity for the Five Tribes to rebuild their governments. During the Cold War years, federal Indian policy changed direction again with an emphasis of Indian self-determination based on Indigenous sovereignty.[12] This new policy and at least two major court cases reaffirmed Indigenous sovereignty. The first case, *Harjo v. Kleppe,* reestablished the Muscogee Nation's tribal government.[13] Two years later, in 1978, the US Supreme Court again demonstrated support for Indigenous sovereignty when it ruled that the Santa Clara Pueblo in New Mexico could assert its full authority in determining its tribal membership.[14]

During the last part of the twentieth century and the first two decades of the twenty-first, the Five Nations and other Native groups exercised their sovereign rights, but in 2020, these rights were seriously challenged. *McGirt v. Oklahoma* (2020) is arguably one of the most important US Supreme Court cases ever when it comes to issues of American Indian sovereignty. The case involved a man named Jimcy McGirt, a Seminole and Muscogee, who in 1997 was convicted in the District Court of Wagoner County of sexually abusing a child. Oklahoma authorities arrested McGirt, and the state justice system sentenced him to prison. In appealing the conviction, his legal counsel argued that because the crime was committed on the Muscogee Reservation, their client could not legally be tried in the state of Oklahoma. They claimed that this case should instead be tried by a federal court, an argument based on the treaties the Muscogees made with the United States as well as the Major Crimes Act (1885), which covered fourteen crimes committed on Indian reservations.[15]

The US Supreme Court ruled against the state of Oklahoma, arguing that the Muscogee Nation's reservation had never been disestablished. The court based its ruling on the 1830s removal treaties and the Muscogee Treaty of 1866. In particular, the Muscogee treaties of 1832 and 1833 designated Indian homelands as reservations, although the word "reservation" did not appear in the two agreements, as it was not yet a term used in federal Indian law.[16] In writing the majority opinion for *McGirt,* Justice Neil Gorsuch explained that, according to federal law, Oklahoma cannot prosecute crimes committed on the reservation, but the state can maintain criminal jurisdiction over crimes committed by non-Indians anywhere in the state. As a basis for Gorsuch's ruling, the treaty of 1856 states that "'no portion' of the Creek Reservation 'shall ever be embraced or included within, or annexed to, any Territory or State.'"[17] It had already been established by the Supreme Court in *Worcester v. Georgia* in 1832 that Indian nations possessed sovereignty and therefore self-government.[18]

In the words of one legal scholar, "McGirt relies on the doctrine of 'Indian title,'" meaning "the right and occupancy and use" of the land. According to the 1823 Supreme Court ruling in *Johnson v. McIntosh,* European sovereigns could obtain "absolute ultimate title" to Indian lands.[19] This legal process of obtaining Indian lands via treaties provided the rationale for the Supreme Court's ruling in *McGirt.*[20] In sum, the *McGirt* decision supported Indian sovereignty and upheld the federal-Indian treaty relationship while denying state interference.

Three earlier court decisions established the case-law precedence for *McGirt.* In *Seymour v. Superintendent* in 1962, the Supreme Court ruled that a congressional law in 1906 did not disestablish the Colville Reservation in Washington. The *Maltz v. Arnett* case in 1973 cited the *Seymour* decision in reaffirming that the Klamath River Reservation still existed. *Solem v. Bartlett* in 1984 held that the Cheyenne River Sioux Reservation was not disestablished.[21] These cases supported the *McGirt* decision, and together they prove that not only was the Muscogee Reservation never disestablished, neither were those of the Cherokees, Chickasaws, Choctaws, and Seminoles.

The *McGirt* decision was so important to the Muscogee Nation that the tribe declared July 9 to be Muscogee Nation Sovereignty Day, in honor of the date of the *McGirt* ruling in 2020. By proclamation, Principal Chief David W. Hill stated, "Generations of Mvskokvlke (Muscogee) will always look to this historic day as a reminder of our remarkable past, our perseverance and survival and our inherent right to exist as a sovereign nation that predated both the United States and Oklahoma." The tribal fight for sovereignty continues. Treaty-based rights for all Native nations remain under threat from the plenary powers of Congress. In *Lone Wolf v. Hitchcock* (1903), the Supreme Court upheld the principle that tribal lands were under the jurisdiction of the US Congress and Congress had the authority to "abrogate the provisions of an Indian treaty."[22]

Under Oklahoma governor Kevin Stitt, state Republican leaders attempted to undo the *McGirt* decision and deny the existence of the Muscogee Nation reservation in an effort to preserve the legal authority of state intervention. But Indian nations continue to remind the state of Oklahoma that their legal relationship is with the federal government, based on sovereign-to-sovereign treaties, and not with a state government.

The *McGirt* decision also shows how the idea of an Indian state, such as the one proposed at the Sequoyah Convention, has not disappeared. The Supreme Court ruled in *McGirt v. Oklahoma* that the reservation boundaries were never disestablished and still remain.[23] Is it possible, then, that the Muscogee Nation of Oklahoma could unite with the Cherokee Nation, Choctaw Nation, Chickasaw Nation, and Seminole Nation, all of whose present reservation boundaries form the same collective area that the state of Sequoyah was to encompass in 1905?

Legally, the Five Tribes could unify their reservations of more than 31,000 square miles to form a new state. Many non-Native people would be residents of this Indian state. But such a new state, if approved by Congress, would operate according to a constitution just like Oklahoma or any other state. If the District of Columbia or Puerto Rico are possible candidates for statehood, then so should be the state of Sequoyah.

Why not fulfill past promises with a federal law creating the state of Sequoyah?

Notes

Preface

1. I have chosen to use the term "Five Tribes" throughout this book to refer to the alliance originally known as the "Five Civilized Tribes," namely the Cherokees, Muscogees, Chickasaws, Choctaws, and Seminoles. I also use the term "Five Nations" interchangeably with "Five Tribes." In many cases, I use the term "Indian" or "American Indian" to describe Native American or Indigenous peoples. Although many avoid using the term "Indian" nowadays due to its colonialist origins, I am comfortable using it because Native peoples have given it a new meaning. I use the adjective "Native" in reference to "Native people" and interchangeably with "Indian," but I avoid using "Native American" because it refers to anyone born in the Western Hemisphere. I use Five Civilized Tribes when the term appears in primary source documents.
2. Frank Bealey, *The Blackwell Dictionary of Political Science* (Malden, MA: Blackwell, 1999), 72–73.
3. Bealey, *Blackwell Dictionary of Political Science*, 286.
4. Bealey, *Blackwell Dictionary of Political Science*, 219. See also J. A. Armstrong, *Nations before Nationalism* (Chapel Hill: University of North Carolina Press, 1982).
5. Bealey, *Blackwell Dictionary of Political Science*, 308. See also A. P. D'Entreves, *The Notion of the State* (Oxford: Clarendon, 1967); and P. Dunleavy and B. O'Leary, *Theories of the State* (London: Macmillan, 1987).
6. Bealey, *Blackwell Dictionary of Political Science*, 309.

Chapter 1. The Birth of Indian Territory

1. John B. Davis, "The Life and Work of Sequoyah," *Chronicles of Oklahoma*, Vol. 8, No. 2 (June 1930), 149–180; "Sequoyah, the Cherokee: For Whom the Indians Propose to Name Their State," *Washington Post*, September 24, 1905.

2. James Mooney, *Historical Sketch of the Cherokee* (Chicago: Aldine, 1975), 101.

3. Althea Bass, *Cherokee Messenger* (Norman: University of Oklahoma Press, 1936), 35.

4. Grant Foreman, *Sequoyah* (Norman: University of Oklahoma Press, 1938), 37.

5. Marilou Awiakta, *Selu: Seeking the Corn-Mother's Wisdom* (Golden, CO: Fulcrum, 1993), 207.

6. James Adair was an Irish-English trader whose notes about Indian customs became *The History of American Indians* (London: n.p., 1775). See Samuel Cole Williams, ed., *Adair's History of the American Indians* (New York: Promontory Press, 1930), 238.

7. Tiya Miles, *Ties That Bind: The Story of an Afro-Cherokee Family in Slavery and Freedom* (Berkeley: University of California Press, 2006), 50.

8. Jean Chaudhuri and Joyotpaul Chaudhuri, *A Sacred Path: The Way of the Muscogee Creeks* (Los Angeles: UCLA American Indian Studies Center, 2001), 86–88.

9. Douglas A. Hurt, "The Shaping of a Creek (Muscogee) Homeland in Indian Territory, 1828–1907" (Ph.D. diss., University of Oklahoma, 2000), 38.

10. William C. Sturtevant and Jessica R. Cattlelino, "Florida Seminole and Miccosukee," in *Handbook of the North American Indians*, ed. Raymond Fogelson (Washington, DC: Smithsonian Institution, 2004), 14:431–432.

11. Patricia Galloway and Clara Sue Kidwell, "Choctaw in the East," in Fogelson, *Handbook of North American Indians*, 14:501.

12. James Taylor Carson, *Searching for the Bright Path: The Mississippi Choctaws from Prehistory to Removal* (Lincoln: University of Nebraska Press, 1999), 13.

13. Angie Debo, *The Rise and Fall of the Choctaw Republic* (Norman: University of Oklahoma Press, 1934), 15.

14. Carson, *Searching for the Bright Path*, 15.

15. Robert A. Brightman and Pamela S. Wallace, "Chickasaw," in Fogelson *Handbook of North American Indians*, 14:480.

16. Stephen Steacy, "The Chickasaw Nation on the Eve of the Civil War," *Chronicles of Oklahoma*, Vol. 49, No. 1 (Spring 1971), 52.

17. "Colin G. Calloway, *The Indian World of George Washington: The First President, the First Americans, and the Birth of the Nation* (New York: Oxford University Press, 2018), 451–476.

18. W. David Baird and Danney Goble, *The Story of Oklahoma* (Norman: University of Oklahoma Press, 1994), 128. See also Fred J. Patton, *History of Fort Smith, Arkansas, 1817–2003* (Hampton, VA: Prestige Press, 2003).

19. Brad Agnew, *Fort Gibson: Terminal on the Trail of Tears* (Norman: University of Oklahoma Press, 1980), 29–30.

20. "Arkansas Territorial Representative to the House of Representative, Henry W. Conway," in *Niles' Weekly Register*, December 25, 1824, quoted in George A. Schultz, *An Indian Canaan: Isaac McCoy and the Vision of an Indian State* (Norman: University of Oklahoma Press, 1972), 79–80.

21. Morris L. Wardell, *A Political History of the Cherokee Nation, 1838–1907* (1938; repr., Norman: University of Oklahoma Press, 1977), 6.

22. Baird and Goble, *Story of Oklahoma*, 130, and Treaty with the Western Cherokees, May 6, 1828, in *Indian Affairs 1778–1883*, ed. Charles J. Kappler (New York: Interland, 1972), 288–292.

23. Treaty with the Cherokees, July 8, 1817, in Kappler, *Indian Affairs*, 140–144, and Treaty with the Cherokees, February 27, 1819, in Kappler, *Indian Affairs*, 177–181.

24. Alfred A. Cave, *Sharp Knife: Andrew Jackson and the American Indians* (Santa Barbara: ABC-CLIO, 2017), 138.

25. Grace Steele Woodward, *The Cherokees* (Norman: University of Oklahoma Press, 1963), 133.

26. Gary E. Moulton, *John Ross: Cherokee Chief* (Athens: University of Georgia Press, 1978), 11.

27. This is one of three or four different accounts of how and who discovered gold in Georgia. See David Williams, *Georgia Gold Rush: Twenty-Niners, Cherokees, and Gold Fever* (Columbia, SC: University of South Carolina Press, 1993), 21–36.

28. James W. Parins, *Elias Cornelius Boudinot: A Life on the Cherokee Border* (Lincoln: University of Nebraska Press, 2006), 14; Woodward, *The Cherokees*, 224–225; Rennard Strickland, *Fire and the Spirits: Cherokee Law from Clan to Court* (Norman: University of Oklahoma Press, 1975), 52; and Robert J. Conley, *The Cherokee Nation: A History* (Albuquerque: University of New Mexico Press, 2005), 160.

29. Nancy N. Scott, ed., *A Memoir of Hugh Lawson White: Judge of the Supreme Court of Tennessee, Member of the Senate of the United States, Etc., Etc.* (Philadelphia: J. B. Lippincott & Company, 1856), 153–196.

30. Indian Removal Act, May 28, 1830, in *U.S. Statutes at Large*, Vol. 4, 411.

31. Tim Alan Garrison, *The Legal Ideology of Removal: The Southern Judiciary and the Sovereignty of Native American Nations* (Athens: University of Georgia Press, 2002), 107.

32. U.S. Const, amend XI, art. 3, § 2.

33. *Cherokee Nation v. Georgia*, 30 U.S. 5 Pet. 1 (1831).

34. *Cherokee Nation v. Georgia*, 30 U.S. 5 Pet. 1 (1831).

35. Jerran Burris White, "The Missionary Work of Samuel A. Worcester among the Cherokee: 1825–1840" (master's thesis, North Texas State University, 1970), 44.

36. Garrison, *Legal Ideology of Removal*, 195.

37. Bass, *Cherokee Messenger*, 137.

38. *Worcester v. Georgia*, 31 U.S. 6 Pet. 515 (1832).

39. W. Dale Weeks, *Cherokee Civil Warrior: Chief John Ross and the Struggle for Tribal Sovereignty* (Norman: University of Oklahoma Press, 2023), 38.

40. Bass, *Cherokee Messenger*, 176.

41. Memorial of the Headmen and Warriors, of the Creek Nation of Indians to the Honorable the Senate and House of Representatives of the United States of America in

Congress, February 6, 1832, Box 1, Folder 17, G. W. Grayson Papers, Western History Collections, University of Oklahoma.

42. Treaty with the Creeks, January 8, 1821, in Kappler, *Indian Affairs*, 195–198.

43. Andrew K. Frank, "The Rise and Fall of William McIntosh: Authority and Identity on the Early American Frontier," *Georgia Historical Quarterly*, Vol. 86, No. 1 (Spring 2002), 18–48.

44. Okmulgee Historical Society and the Heritage Society of America, ed., *History of Okmulgee County, Oklahoma* (Tulsa: Historical Enterprises, Inc., 1985), 1:24.

45. John T. Ellisor, *The Second Creek War: Interethnic Conflict and Collusion on a Collapsing Frontier* (Lincoln: University of Nebraska Press, 2010), 143–181.

46. Baird and Goble, *Story of Oklahoma*, 136.

47. Okmulgee Historical Society and the Heritage Society of America, *History of Okmulgee County, Oklahoma*, 1: 30, 33.

48. Daniel F. Littlefield Jr., *Africans and Creeks: From the Colonial Period to the Civil War* (Westport, CT: Greenwood Press, 1979), 135; Hurt, "The Shaping of a Creek (Muscogee) Homeland in Indian Territory," 93.

49. According to tradition, a circular area twenty to thirty feet across had to be leveled and cleaned. Then, "some clean dirt, about a wash-pan full, is piled where the fire is to be made and smoothed down on top. Two lines are made, one going exactly north and south, the other going east and west on the top of the dirt. Some herbs are put in the spaces between the lines. Four two and a half foot logs are placed with the end touching in the center. Then four roasting [corn] ears are places between them." See Nancy Grayson Barnett, interview by Grace Kelley, November 11, 1937, Interview 12128, 395, Indian-Pioneer History Project for Oklahoma, Western History Collections, University of Oklahoma.

50. Baird and Goble, *Story of Oklahoma*, 154.

51. Baird and Goble, *Story of Oklahoma*, 166.

52. See John K. Mahon, *History of the Second Seminole War* (Gainesville: University of Florida Press, 1967).

53. The generals were Brigadier General Walker K. Armstead, General Richard Keith Call, Brevet Brigadier Duncan L. Clinch, Brigadier General Abraham Eustis, Major General Edmund Gaines, Brigadier General Joseph Hernandez, Major General Thomas Jessup, Major General C. G. Macomb, Major General Charles Nelson, Major General Winfield Scott, Brigadier General Zachary Taylor, and Brigadier General William Worth. See Mahon, *History of the Second Seminole War*, 108–112, 138, 144, 150, 164, 179, 200, 214–215, 231, 240, 274, and 294.

54. Kevin Mulroy, *The Seminole Freedmen: A History* (Norman: University of Oklahoma Press, 2007), 84.

55. Baird and Goble, *Story of Oklahoma*, 154–155.

56. Baird and Goble, *Story of Oklahoma*, 141.

57. "Petition to Congress," September 28, 1836, in *The Papers of John Ross*, ed. Gary E. Moulton, vol. 1, *1807–1839* (Norman: University of Oklahoma Press, 1985), 458–461.

58. Allen Ross, "The Murder of Elias Boudinot," ed. Grant Foreman, *Chronicles of Oklahoma*, Vol. 12, No. 1 (March 1934), 19–25.

59. Baird Goble, *Story of Oklahoma*, 153.

60. Treaty with the Choctaws, September 27, 1830, in Kappler, *Indian Affairs 1778–1883*, 310–318.

61. Baird and Goble, *Story of Oklahoma*, 135.

62. Baird and Goble, *Story of Oklahoma*, 152.

63. Baird and Goble, *Story of Oklahoma*, 165.

64. George W. Harkins to Greenwood LeFlore, June 17, 1845, Box B-59, Folder 1, H. O. Boggs Collection, Western History Collections, University of Oklahoma.

65. Grant Foreman, "How the Chickasaws Got Here," *Daily Oklahoman* (Oklahoma City), April 11, 1937.

66. Grant Foreman, "How the Chickasaws Got Here," *Daily Oklahoman* (Oklahoma City), April 11, 1937.

67. Baird and Goble, *Story of Oklahoma*, 152–153.

68. Baird and Goble, *Story of Oklahoma*, 165–166.

69. Michael F. Doran, "Population Statistics of Nineteenth Century Indian Territory," *Chronicles of Oklahoma*, Vol. 53, No. 4 (Winter 1975–1976), 496.

70. Donald L. Fixico, ed., *Indian Treaties in the United States: An Encyclopedia and Documents Collection* (Santa Barbara and Denver: ABC-CLIO, 2018), xvi.

71. "Editorial on Indian Slave Holders," *Holdenville (I.T.) Times*, August 17, 1906.

72. "The Negro Insurrection," *Fort Smith (AR) Elevator*, February 12, 1897.

73. In Thomas Jefferson's view, those Indians who did not adopt farming and remained "savage" were to be removed to the lands acquired in the Louisiana Purchase. See Anthony F. C. Wallace, *Jefferson and the Indians: The Tragic Fate of the First Americans* (Cambridge, MA: Belknap Press of Harvard University Press, 1999), 225

74. Roy Gittinger, *The Formation of the State of Oklahoma, 1803–1906* (Norman: University of Oklahoma Press, 1939), 25.

75. Gittinger, *Formation of the State of Oklahoma*, 27.

76. Gittinger, *Formation of the State of Oklahoma*, 25.

77. An Act Making Appropriations for the Current and Contingencies of the Indian Department, *U.S. Statutes at Large*, Vol. 9, 574.

78. Gittinger, *Formation of the State of Oklahoma*, 58–59, 61.

79. William E. Unrau, *The Rise and Fall of Indian Country, 1825–1855* (Lawrence: University Press of Kansas, 2007), 9–10.

80. "The International Council, November 8–15, 1859," *The Vindicator* (Atoka, I.T.), ca. November 1859.

81. Interview with George Guess by Jeremiah Evarts, *Missionary Herald*, Vol. 24 (April 1828), 133–134; White, "Missionary Work of Samuel A. Worcester Among the Cherokee."

82. Foreman, *Sequoyah*, 37.

Chapter 2. The Idea of an Indian State

1. Walter Lee Brown, *A Life of Albert Pike* (Fayetteville: University of Arkansas Press, 1997), 4 and 7.
2. Brown, *Life of Albert Pike*, 355.
3. Fixico, *Indian Treaties in the United States*, xv.
4. Treaty with the Delawares, September 17, 1778, in Kappler, *Indian Affairs*, 2–5.
5. Ingrid P. Westmoreland, "Inter-Tribal Council of the Five Civilized Tribes," in *The Encyclopedia of Oklahoma History and Culture*, ed. Dianna Everett (Oklahoma City: Oklahoma Historical Society, 2009), 1:741–742.
6. Angie Debo, *The Road to Disappearance: A History of the Creek Indians* (1941; repr.; Norman: University of Oklahoma Press, 1979), 132.
7. Debo, *Road to Disappearance*, 133.
8. Sam J. Haynes, interview by Effie S. Jackson, February 18, 1938, Interview 12992, 329, Okmulgee, Oklahoma, Indian-Pioneer Papers, Western History Collections, University of Oklahoma. Muskogee is the spelling of the city, and Muscogee is the spelling of the tribe.
9. Andre Paul DuChateau, "Creek Nation on the Eve of the Civil War," *Chronicles of Oklahoma*, Vol. 52, No. 3 (Fall 1974), 296.
10. Okmulgee Historical Society and the Heritage Society of America, *History of Okmulgee County, Oklahoma*, 1:49.
11. Muriel H. Wright, "General Douglas H. Cooper, C.S.A.," *Chronicles of Oklahoma*, Vol. 32, No. 2 (Summer 1954), 157.
12. Wright, "General Douglas H. Cooper, C.S.A.," 162.
13. Baird and Goble, *Story of Oklahoma*, 171.
14. "Treaty with the Creek," July 10, 1861, in *Documents of American Indian Diplomacy: Treaties, Agreements, and Conventions, 1775–1979*, ed. Vine Deloria Jr. and Raymond J. DeMallie (Norman: University of Oklahoma Press, 1999), 589 and 594.
15. "Treaty with the Choctaws and Chickasaws," July 12, 1861, in Deloria and DeMallie, *Documents of American Indian Diplomacy: Treaties, Agreements, and Conventions*, 609.
16. Confederate Treaty, 1861, An act for the protection of certain Indian Tribes, identifier 38, Folder Confederate and Indian Territory Indian Treaty, 4826.17, Civil War Papers, Helmerich Center for American Research, Gilcrease Museum, Tulsa, Oklahoma.
17. Brown, *Life of Albert Pike*, 363.
18. Charles R. Freeman, "The Battle of Honey Springs," *Chronicles of Oklahoma*, Vol. 13, No. 2 (June 1935), 154.
19. Albert Pike quoted in Dean Trickett, "The Civil War in Indian Territory 1862 (Continued)," *Chronicles of Oklahoma*, Vol. 19, No. 4 (December 1941), 390.
20. Kenny A. Franks, "An Analysis of the Confederate Treaties with the Five Civilized Tribes," *Chronicles of Oklahoma*, Vol. 51 No. 4 (Winter 1972), 458–473, and "The

Implementation of the Confederate Treaties with the Five Civilized Tribes," *Chronicles of Oklahoma*, Vol. 51, No. 1 (Spring 1973), 21–33; Kinneth McNeil, "Confederate Treaties with the Tribes of Indian Territory," *Chronicles of Oklahoma*, Vol. 42, No. 4 (Winter 1964–1965), 408–420.

21. T. Paul Wilson, "Confederate Delegates of the Five Civilized Tribes," *Chronicles of Oklahoma*, Vol. 53, No. 3 (Fall 1975), 354–356.

22. Wilson, "Confederate Delegates of the Five Civilized Tribes," 354–356; Parins, *Elias Cornelius Boudinot*, 52.

23. Don Diehl, "The Civil War Ripped Creek Nation: Part 2," *Muscogee Nation News* (Okmulgee, OK), April 1, 2016.

24. Trickett, "Civil War in Indian Territory 1862 (Continued)," 385, and Wright, "General Douglas H. Cooper, C.S.A.," 165.

25. Arthur Shoemaker, "The Battle of Chustenahlah," *Chronicles of Oklahoma*, Vol. 38, No. 2 (Summer 1960), 181.

26. Carter Blue Clark, "Opothleyahola and the Creeks During the Civil War," in *Indian Leaders: Oklahoma's First Statesmen*, ed. H. Glenn Jordan and Thomas M. Holm (Oklahoma City: Oklahoma Historical Society), 1979), 61. See also, Lela J. McBride, *Opothleyahola and the Loyal Muskogee: Their Flight to Kansas in the Civil War* (Jefferson, NC: McFarland, 2000).

27. Baird and Goble, *Story of Oklahoma*, 175.

28. Okmulgee Historical Society and the Heritage Society of America, *History of Okmulgee County, Oklahoma*, 1:40.

29. Okmulgee Historical Society and the Heritage Society of America, *History of Okmulgee County, Oklahoma*, 1:41.

30. Gittinger, *Formation of the State of Oklahoma*, 85–87.

31. The original surrender treaty of Stand Watie, 1865, is in the Thomas L. Ballenger Collection, Special Collections, John Vaughan Library, Northeastern State University, Tahlequah, Oklahoma. See also Baird and Goble, *Story of Oklahoma*, 179.

32. Okmulgee Historical Society and the Heritage Society of America, *History of Okmulgee County, Oklahoma*, 1:38.

33. Baird and Goble, *Story of Oklahoma*, 183. See also, Treaty with the Seminoles, March 21, 1866, in Kappler, *Indian Affairs Laws and Treaties*, 910–915; Treaty with the Choctaws and Chickasaws, April 28, 1866, in Kappler, *Indian Affairs Laws and Treaties*, 918–931; Treaty with the Creeks, June 14, 1866, in Kappler, *Indian Affairs Laws and Treaties*, 931–937; and Treaty with the Cherokees, July 19, 1866, in Kappler, *Indian Affairs Laws and Treaties*, 944.

34. Message of Allen Wright to General Council, 1867, Allen Wright Collection, Box W-25, Folder 4, Western History Collections, University of Oklahoma.

35. Allen Wright to Cyrus Harris, January 21, 1868, Allen Wright Collection, Box W-25, Folder 7, Western History Collections, University of Oklahoma.

36. Baird and Goble, *Story of Oklahoma*, 205.

37. Baird and Goble, *Story of Oklahoma*, 232.

38. Baird and Goble, *Story of Oklahoma*, 198, 202.
39. The article from the *New York Sun* was reported in the *Cherokee Advocate* (Tahlequah, I.T.), "The Okmulgee Constitution," March 2, 1872.
40. Bass, *Cherokee Messenger*, 33.
41. Michael Cassity and Danney Goble, *Divided Hearts: The Presbyterian Journey through Oklahoma History* (Norman: University of Oklahoma Press, 2009), 46.
42. Guy Logsdon, "Oklahoma's First Book: Istutsi in Naktsoku," *Chronicles of Oklahoma*, Vol. 54, No. 2 (Summer 1976), 179.
43. Jack M. Schultz, *The Seminole Baptist Churches of Oklahoma: Maintaining a Traditional Community* (Norman: University of Oklahoma Press, 1999), 52.
44. Schultz, *Seminole Baptist Churches of Oklahoma*, 53. This source spelled Mekusukey this way, but it has been spelled other ways,
45. Frank A. Balyeat, "Joseph Samuel Murrow, Apostle to the Indians," *Chronicles of Oklahoma*, Vol. 35, No. 3 (Autumn 1957), 298–299.
46. W. A. Carleton, *Not Yours, But You* (Berkeley, CA: privately printed, c. 1954), 73.
47. Tash Smith, *Capture These Indians for the Lord: Indians, Methodists, and Oklahomans, 1844–1939*, 2nd ed. (Tucson: University of Arizona Press, 2014), 48.
48. Baird and Goble, *Story of Oklahoma*, 183.
49. Baird and Goble, *Story of Oklahoma*, 217.
50. "Letter of Tuskahoma to Editor Vindicator," *The Vindicator* (Atoka, I.T.), June 12, 1875.
51. David G. LoConto, "Discrimination Against and Adaptation of Italians in the Coal Counties of Oklahoma," *Great Plains Quarterly*, Vol. 24 (Fall 2004), 249–261.
52. "Coleman Cole to Editor of Vindicator, Sep 1, 1875," *The Vindicator* (Atoka, I.T.), September 4, 1875.
53. "Proclamation of Coleman Cole," September 25, 1875, *The Vindicator* (Atoka, I.T.), September 25, 1875.
54. H. F. O'Beirne, *Leaders and Leading Men of the Indian Territory with Interesting Biographical Sketches* (Chicago: American Publishers' Association, 1891), 22.
55. "Editorial On Message of Coleman Cole," *Cherokee Advocate* (Tahlequah, I.T.), October 17, 1877.
56. "Impeachment of Gov. Cole—Nolle Prosequi by the Senate," *Atoka Independent*, October 26, 1877.
57. Lochar Harjo to the Houses Kings and Warriors, December 6, 1875, Lochar Harjo Collection, Folder 1, Western History Collections, University of Oklahoma.
58. James McHenry, Presiding Court of Impeachment filed with Samuel Grayson, Clerk, December 5, 1876, Okmulgee, Creek Nation, Lochar Harjo Collection, Folder 3, Western History Collections, University of Oklahoma.
59. "Message of B. C. Burney to Hon. Members to the Senate and House of Representatives, ca September 16, 1880," *Indian Journal* (Eufaula, I.T.), September 16, 1880.
60. "Message of B. C. Burney to Hon. Members to the Senate and House of Representatives, ca September 16, 1880," in *Indian Journal* (Eufaula, I.T.), September 16, 1880.

61. D. W. Bushyhead and Cherokee Delegation to Henry M. Teller, August 9, 1882, *Cherokee Advocate* (Tahlequah, I.T.), August 25, 1882.

62. Dennis Bushyhead to Senate Branch of the National Council, November 3, 1885, Dennis Wolf Bushyhead Collection, Box 54, Western History Collections, University of Oklahoma.

63. L. B. Bell to D. W. Bushyhead, December 5, 1885, Dennis Wolf Bushyhead Collection, Box 2 (B54), Western History Collections, University of Oklahoma, Norman, Oklahoma.

64. See Harry Drago, *Great American Cattle Trails: The Story of the Old Cow Paths of the East and the Longhorn Highways of the Plains* (New York: Dodd, Mead, 1965).

65. Wendy St. Jean, "'You Have the Land, I Have the Cattle': Intermarried Whites and the Chickasaw Range Lands," *Chronicles of Oklahoma*, Vol. 78, No. 2 (Summer 2000), 187; Mary Jane Warde, "Fight for Survival: The Indian Response to the Boomer Movement," *Chronicles of Oklahoma*, Vol. 67, No. 1 (Spring 1989), 30–51.

66. St. Jean, "'You Have the Land, I Have the Cattle,'" 186.

67. St. Jean, *Remaining Chickasaw in Indian Territory*, 4.

68. Solon J. Buck, "The Settlement of Oklahoma," in *Transactions of the Wisconsin Academy of Sciences, Arts and Letters*, ed. Secretary, vol. 15, part 2 (Madison: Democrat Printing Company, 1907), 334.

69. "An Act to Prevent Monopoly," *Indian Chieftain* (Vinita, I.T.), January 19, 1883.

70. "A Protest by John Chupco, P. P. Ptichlynn, et al.," February 9, 1874, *Cherokee Advocate* (Tahlequah, I.T.), March 14, 1874.

71. Dennis Bushyhead to Lucien B. Bell, October 7, 1885, Dennis Wolf Bushyhead Papers, Box B-54, Western History Collections, University of Oklahoma.

72. Letter of D. W. Bushyhead, *Cherokee Advocate* (Tahlequah, I.T.), April 2, 1886.

73. Baird and Goble, *Story of Oklahoma*, 310.

74. Isaac Parker to W. A. Duncan, March 16, 1894, in Walter A. Duncan, *Letter to the President, Touching Statehood for Indian Territory* (Washington, DC: Gibson Bros, Printers and Bookbinders, 1894), 18.

75. "Letter of Pleasant Porter to Isparhecher, June 13, 1893, Muskogee, Indian Territory," *The Purcell (O.T.) Register*, June 26, 1891.

76. Article 12, Treaty with the Cherokees, July 19, 1866, in Kappler, *Indian Affairs Laws and Treaties*, 945; Article 7, Treaty with the Seminoles, March 21, 1866, in Kappler, *Indian Affairs Laws and Treaties*, 913; Article 8, Treaty with the Choctaws and Chickasawa, April 28, 1866, in Kappler, 921; and Article 10, Treaty with the Creeks, June 14, 1866, in Kappler, 935.

77. Baird and Goble, *Story of Oklahoma*, 309.

78. "First Annual Message of D. W. Bushyhead," *Cherokee Advocate* (Tahlequah, I.T.), November 26, 1879.

79. James D. Morrison, "The Union Pacific, Southern Branch," *Chronicles of Oklahoma*, Vol. 14, No. 2 (June 1936), 175.

80. Baird and Goble, *Story of Oklahoma*, 191.

81. Alaina E. Roberts, *I've Been Here All the While: Black Freedom on Native Land* (Philadelphia: University of Pennsylvania Press, 2021), 27.

82. Baird and Goble, *The Story of Oklahoma* (Norman: University of Oklahoma Press, 1994), 235.

83. Berlin B. Chapman, "Freedmen and the Oklahoma Lands," *Southwestern Social Science Quarterly*, Vol. 29, No. 2 (September 1948), 151–152; Norman Crockett, *The Black Towns* (Lawrence, KS: Regents Press, 1979), 100.

84. Fay A. Yarbrough, *Race and the Cherokee Nation: Sovereignty in the Nineteenth Century* (Philadelphia: University of Pennsylvania Press, 2008), 4, 7.

85. Baird and Goble, *Story of Oklahoma*, 189.

86. L. Edward Carter, *The Story of Oklahoma Newspapers, 1844–1984* (Oklahoma City: Oklahoma Heritage Association, 1984), 14.

87. Carter, *The Story of Oklahoma Newspapers*, 26.

88. Nudie Eugene Williams, "Oklahoma: Genesis and Tradition of the Black Press, 1889–1980," in *The Black Press in the Middle West, 1865–1985*, ed. Henry Lewis Suggs (Westport, CT: Greenwood Press, 1996), 276–277.

89. Baird and Goble, *Story of Oklahoma*, 193.

90. "Message of L. C. Perryman," *Muskogee (I.T.) Phoenix*, October 12, 1893.

91. "Letter of Pleasant Porter and A. P. McKellop," *Muskogee (I.T.) Phoenix*, January 16, 1894.

92. "Platform of the Choctaw and Chickasaw Union Party," in *Delegates of the Antlers' Convention, Before the Dawes Commission, Fort Smith, Arkansas, December 9th, 1896* (n.p.: Choctaw Herald Print, 1896), 3.

93. "Letter of D. W. Bushyhead to Dr. M. Frazer," *Cherokee Telephone* (Tahlequah, I.T.), June 6, 1891.

94. "Editorial on D. W. Bushyhead," *Cherokee Telephone* (Tahlequah, I.T.), July 9, 1891.

95. "Speeches by Bushyhead, Mayes and Benge, July 23, 1891," *Cherokee Telephone* (Tahlequah, I.T.), July 23, 1891.

96. "Cherokee Ultimatum (to the Dawes Commission), October 28, 1897," *Indian Chieftain* (Vinita, I.T.), November 11, 1897.

97. "Meeting of the Kee-Too-Wahs," *Wagoner (I.T.) Record*, August 2, 1900.

98. "The Fullblood Cherokees," *Chelsea (I.T.) Reporter*, August 31, 1901.

99. "Editorial on Enrollment of Family by F. J. Boudinot," *Francis Banner* (Newton, I.T.), November 16, 190.

100. Pleasant Porter to J. George Wright, November 9, 1905, Muskogee, Indian Territory, Grayson Family Collection, Box 2, Folder 9, Western History Collections, University of Oklahoma.

101. Pleasant Porter to Muskogee People, February 20, 1906, Grayson Family Collection, Box 6, Folder 16, Western History Collections, University of Oklahoma.

102. Principal Chief Pleasant Porter to George W. Grayson, September 14, 1906, Grayson Family Collection, Box 5, Folder 14, Western History Collections, University of Oklahoma.

103. "Editorial on Pleasant Porter," *Purcell (O.T.) Register*, February 16, 1893.

104. Treaty with the Choctaws, September 27, 1830, in Kappler, *Indian Affairs*, 310–319.

105. *Addresses and Arguments by Prominent Men in Favor of Separate Statehood for Indian Territory* (Kinta, I.T.: Kinta Separate Statehood Club, 1905), 13.

106. *Addresses and Arguments by Prominent Men in Favor of Separate Statehood for Indian Territory*, 13.

107. *Addresses and Arguments by Prominent Men in Favor of Separate Statehood for Indian Territory*, 17.

108. "Editorial on Creek Council," *Holdenville (I.T.) Tribune*, October 13, 1904.

109. Brown, *Life of Albert Pike*, 377.

Chapter 3. Boomers and Land Runs

1. Carl Coke Rister, "Free Land Hunters of the Southern Plains," *Chronicles of Oklahoma*, Vol. 22, No. 4 (Winter 1944–1945), 400.

2. Rister, "Free Land Hunters of the Southern Plains," 400.

3. Horace Greeley, "Editorial," *New York Tribune*, July 13, 1865.

4. An act to secure homesteads to actual settlers on the public domain, PL 37–64, May 20, 1862, ch. 75, *United States Statutes at Large*, Vol. 12, 392.

5. Abraham Lincoln, "Speech to Germans at Cincinnati, Ohio," February 12, 1861, in vol. 4, *Collected Works of Abraham Lincoln, 1809–1865*, ed. Roy P. Basler (New Brunswick, NJ: Rutgers University Press, 1953), 202.

6. Baird and Goble, *Story of Oklahoma*, 292.

7. David A. Chang, *The Color of the Land: Race, Nation, and the Politics of Landownership in Oklahoma, 1832–1929* (Chapel Hill: University of North Carolina Press, 2010), 77.

8. Carl Coke Rister, *Land Hunger: David L. Payne and the Oklahoma Boomers* (Norman: University of Oklahoma Press, 1942), 10.

9. Rister, *Land Hunger*, 41; Parins, *Elias Cornelius Boudinot*, 192; William T. Hagan, *Taking Indian Lands: The Cherokee (Jerome) Commission, 1889–1893* (Norman: University of Oklahoma Press, 2003), 9. The phrase, "Unassigned Lands," attributed to Elias Boudinot in his "The Indian Question" letter published by the *Chicago Times*, February 17, 1879, does not appear there, but five years earlier Boudinot stated, "the lands remaining unappropriated to be sold by the United States government to actual settlers at not less than $1.25 per acre, and the funds accruing to be invested for the benefit of the Indians,—the interest of which should be used in great part, if not entirely, as an educational fund," E. C. Boudinot, "The Indian Territory and Its Inhabitants," *Journal of the American Geographical Society of New York*, Vol. 5 (1874), 222–223.

10. "File: Unassigned Lands 1885.jpg," https://www.archives.gov/digital_classroom /lessons/federal_indian_policy/federal_indian_policy.html, accessed February 6, 2021.

11. Treaty with the Creeks, June 14, 1866, in Kappler, ed., *Indian Affairs*, 931–937.
12. Treaty with the Seminoles, March 21, 1866, in Kappler, ed., *Indian Affairs*, 910–915.
13. Treaty with the Choctaws and Chickasaws, April 28, 1866, in Kappler ed., *Indian Affairs Laws*, 918–931.
14. Coke Rister, *Land Hunger*, 37–38.
15. "The Indian Territory," *Kansas City Times*, May 13, 1879.
16. Francis A. Walker, *Report of the Commissioner of Indian Affairs, 1872* (Washington, DC: Government Printing Office, 1873), 93.
17. Bruce A. Glasrud and Michael N. Searles, eds., *Buffalo Soldiers in the West: A Black Soldiers Anthology* (College Station: Texas A&M University Press, 2007), 43.
18. Stan Hoig, *David L. Payne: The Oklahoma Boomer* (Oklahoma City: Western Heritage Books, 1980), 53.
19. Baird and Goble, *Story of Oklahoma*, 292.
20. Nell Irvin Painter, *Exodusters: Black Migration to Kansas After Reconstruction* (1977; repr., New York: W.W. Norton & Company, 1992), 184–201.
21. E. A. Hayt to Carl Schurz, November 1, 1879, in *Annual Report of the Commissioner of Indian Affairs, 1879* (Washington, DC: Government Printing Office, 1879), 44.
22. J. D. C. Atkins to Lucius Q. C. Lamar II, September 28, 1886, in *Annual Report of the Commissioner of Indian Affairs, 1886* (Washington, DC: Government Printing Office, 1886), 44.
23. St. Jean, *Remaining Chickasaw in Indian Territory*, 5.
24. Affairs Hiram Price to Carl Schurz, October 24, 1881, in *Annual Report of the Commissioner of Indian Affairs 1881* (Washington, DC: Government Printing Office, 1881), 68
25. "On to Oklahoma," *Kansas City Times*, May 4, 1879.
26. Rister, *Land Hunger*, 41.
27. Roy W. Meyer, "Ezra A. Hayt 1877–80," in *The Commissioners of Indian Affairs, 1824–1977*, ed. Robert M. Kvasnicka and Herman J. Viola (Lincoln: University of Nebraska Press, 1979), 162–163.
28. The theme of Manifest Destiny in American history is explored by Reginald Horsman, *Race and Manifest Destiny: The Origins of American Racial Anglo-Saxonism* (Cambridge, MA: Harvard University Press, 1981); Patrick Wolfe, "Settler Colonialism and the Elimination of the Native," *Journal of Genocidal Research*, Vol. 8, No. 4 (2006), 387–409; Wolfe, *Settler Colonialism and the Transformation of Anthropology: The Politics and Poetics of an Ethnographic Event* (London: Cassell, 1999), 1–42; and Lorenzo Veracini, *Settler Colonialism: A Theoretical Overview* (London: Palgrave, 2010), 1–15.
29. E. M. Marbel to Carl Schurz, November 1, 1880, in *Annual Report of the Commissioner of Indian Affairs, 1880* (Washington, DC: Government Printing Office, 1880), 20.
30. Glasrud and Searles, *Buffalo Soldiers in the West*, 43.

31. Rutherford B. Hayes, Proclamation Against Intruders in Indian Territory, February 12, 1880, in Annual *Report of the Commissioner of Indian Affairs, 1880,* 201.

32. Buck, "Settlement of Oklahoma," 338; Rister, *Land Hunger,* 54.

33. E. M. Marbel to Carl Schurz, November 1, 1880, in *Annual Report of the Commissioner of Indian Affairs, 1880,* 21.

34. Buck, "Settlement of Oklahoma," 338; E. M. Marbel to Carl Schurz, November 1, 1880, in *Annual Report of the Commissioner of Indian Affairs, 1880,* 21.

35. Roger H. Tuller, *"Let No Guilty Man Escape": A Judicial Biography of 'Hanging Judge' Isaac C. Parker* (Norman: University of Oklahoma Press, 2001), 112.

36. Hiram Price to Carl Schurz, October 10, 1882, in *Annual Report of the Commissioner of Indian Affairs, 1882* (Washington, DC: Government Printing Office, 1882), 18.

37. "David Lewis Payne to Editor Indian Journal," August 3, 1880, David Payne Collection, Box P-24, Folder 24, Western History Collections, University of Oklahoma.

38. "Proclamation by Capt. Payne," *Wichita Beacon,* November 3, 1880.

39. Stan Hoig, *The Oklahoma Land Rush of 1889* (Oklahoma City: Oklahoma Historical Society, 1984), 16.

40. Chester A. Arthur, "July 1, 1884: Message Regarding Settlement on Indian Territory," Transcript [Proclamation], University of Virginia Miller Center, https://millercenter.org/the-presidency/presidential-speeches/july-1-1884-message-regarding-settlement-indian-territory, accessed June 12, 2020.

41. Hoig, *David L. Payne,* 199.

42. Michael J. Hightower, *1889: The Boomer Movement, the Land Run, and Early Oklahoma City* (Norman: University of Oklahoma Press, 2018), 102–103. Hiram Price to Carl Schurz, September 12, 1884, in *Annual Report of the Commissioner of Indian Affairs, 1884* (Washington, DC: Government Printing Office, 1884).

43. A. Suman Morris, "Captain David L. Payne: The Cimarron Scout," *Chronicles of Oklahoma,* Vol. 42, No. 1 (Spring 1964), 23.

44. Hightower, *1889,* 107, and *United States v. Payne,* November 11, 1884, 22 Fed. Rep. 426, in Frank Dale, *Reports of Cases Argued and Determined in the Supreme Court of the Territory of Oklahoma* (Guthrie, O.T.: Union Label, 1897), 4:424.

45. "Oklahoma's Chief Fallen," *Sumner County Standard* (Wellington, KS), November 29, 1884.

46. Hightower, *1889,* 108.

47. Memorial of Payne's Oklahoma Colony of Boomers, presented to the Senate by Preston B. Plumb of Kansas, January 7, 1885, Box 1, Folder 9: Boomer movement, undated, Berlin B. Chapman Collection, Oklahoma History Center, Oklahoma City.

48. Chapman, "Freedmen and the Oklahoma Lands," 150–159.

49. Baird and Goble, *Story of Oklahoma,* 284.

50. Buck, "Settlement of Oklahoma," 342.

51. Worth Robert Miller, *Oklahoma Populism: A History of the People's Party in the Oklahoma Territory* (Norman: University of Oklahoma Press, 1987), 12.

52. Dan W. Peery, "Colonel Crocker and the Boomer Movement," *Chronicles of Oklahoma*, Vol. 13, No. 3 (September 1935), 282.

53. Baird and Goble, *Story of Oklahoma*, 297; Peery, "Colonel Crocker and the Boomer Movement," 285–286.

54. Buck, "Settlement of Oklahoma," 344.

55. Berlin B. Chapman, "The Legal Sooners of 1889," *Chronicles of Oklahoma*, Vol. 35, No. 4 (Winter 1957–1958), 387.

56. James K. Hastings, "The Opening of Oklahoma," *Chronicles of Oklahoma*, Vol. 27, No. 1 (Spring 1949), 71.

57. Gittinger, *Formation of the State of Oklahoma*), 187.

58. Baird and Goble, *Story of Oklahoma*, 298.

59. Chapman, "The Legal Sooners of 1889," 390.

60. Gordon Hines, *Alfalfa Bill: An Intimate Biography* (Oklahoma City: Oklahoma Press, 1931), 161.

61. Gittinger, *Formation of the State of Oklahoma*, 190.

62. Buck, "Settlement of Oklahoma," 345, 349.

63. Miller, *Oklahoma Populism*, 29.

64. Williams, "Oklahoma: Genesis and Tradition of the Black Press," 267.

65. Bonnie Lynn-Sherow, *Red Earth: Race and Agriculture in Oklahoma Territory* (Lawrence: University Press of Kansas, 2004), 32.

66. Lynn-Sherow, *Red Earth*, 44.

67. Yarbrough, *Race and the Cherokee Nation*, 105–106.

68. Chang, *Color of the Land*, 149–150.

69. Chang, *Color of the Land*, 151.

70. James M. Smallwood, "Segregation," in Everett, *Encyclopedia of Oklahoma History and Culture*, 2:1344–1346.

71. Veda Giezentanner, "In Dugouts and Sod Houses," *Chronicles of Oklahoma*, Vol. 39, No. 2 (Summer 1961), 142–143, and Orvoe Swartz, "A Pioneer's Sod House Memories," *Chronicles of Oklahoma*, Vol. 41, No. 4 (Winter 1963–1964), 412–413.

72. "Editorial on W. L. Byrd," *Purcell Register*, August 7, 1891.

73. "An Interview with W. L. Byrd," *Purcell Register*, August 28, 1891.

74. "Editorial on the Message of W. L. Byrd, *Indian Citizen* (Atoka, I.T.), September 19, 1891.

75. George W. Stiles, "Early Days in the Sac and Fox Country," *Chronicles of Oklahoma*, Vol. 33, No. 3 (Autumn 1955), 323.

76. Mary Ann Blochowiak, "'Justice is our Battle Cry': The Territorial Free Home League," *Chronicles of Oklahoma*, Vol. 62, No. 1 (Spring 1984), 38.

77. Miller, *Oklahoma Populism*, 84–85, 94.

78. Berlin B. Chapman, "The Land Run of 1893 as Seen at Kiowa," *Kansas Historical Quarterly*, Vol. 31, No. 1 (Summer 1965), 71.

79. Chapman, "Land Run of 1893 as Seen at Kiowa," 73.

80. Chapman, "The Land Run of 1893 as Seen at Kiowa," 71; Clara Williamson Warren Bullard, "Pioneer Days in the Cherokee Strip," *Chronicles of Oklahoma*, Vol. 36, No. 3 (Autumn 1958), 259–260.

81. Bullard, "Pioneer Days in the Cherokee Strip," 259–260.

82. Lynn-Sherow, *Red Earth*, 84.

83. Edwin McReynolds, *Oklahoma: A History of the Sooner State* (Norman: University of Oklahoma Press, 1954), 298–301; LeRoy H. Fisher, "Oklahoma Territory, 1899–1907," *Chronicles of Oklahoma*, Vol. 53, No. 1 (Spring 1975), 5.

84. Lewis N. Hornbeck, "Editorial on Election of W.L. Byrd," *Minco (O.T.) Minstrel*, July 13, 1894.

85. "About the Territories: Items of Interest to the Dwellers in the New Country," *Edmond (O.T.) Sun-Democrat*, June 28, 1895.

86. Kevin L. Cook, "Oklahoma's Land Lottery: The last Great Opening," *HistoryNet*, https://www.historynet.com/oklahomas-land-lottery-last-great-opening.htm, accessed December 24, 2019.

87. Cook, "Oklahoma's Land Lottery: The last Great Opening."

88. Buck, "Settlement of Oklahoma,"369–370.

89. Buck, "Settlement of Oklahoma," 366.

90. Larry G. Johnson, *Tar Creek: A History of the Quapaw Indians, the World's Largest Lead and Zinc Discovery, and the Tar Creek Superfund Site* (Mustang, OK: Tate, 2008), 112.

91. Gittinger, *Formation of the State of Oklahoma*, 184.

92. "Distributing Homesteads by Lot," *Outlook*, August 10, 1901.

93. "Excitement," *Oklahoma Democrat* (El Reno, OK), February 13, 1892.

94. Hoig, *David L. Payne*, 55; Stan Hoig, "Carpenter, Charles C.," in Everett, *Encyclopedia of Oklahoma History and Culture*, 1:223–224.

Chapter 4. The State of Sequoyah Convention

1. John B. Meserve, "Chief Pleasant Porter," *Chronicles of Oklahoma*, Vol. 9, No. 3 (September 1931), 322.

2. Amos D. Maxwell, "The Sequoyah Convention," *Chronicles of Oklahoma*, Vol. 28, No. 2 (Summer, 1950), 163–164.

3. Gittinger, *Formation of the State of Oklahoma*, 103–104.

4. Maxwell, "Sequoyah Convention," 163–164.

5. Maxwell, "Sequoyah Convention," 164.

6. Maxwell, "Sequoyah Convention," 164.

7. Miles, *Ties That Bind*, 195.

8. Gittinger, *Formation of the State of Oklahoma*, 212.

9. Gittinger, *Formation of the State of Oklahoma*, 214.

10. Maxwell, "Sequoyah Convention," 165–166.

11. Maxwell, "Sequoyah Convention," 166.

12. Amos D. Maxwell, *The Sequoyah Constitutional Convention* (Boston: Meador, 1953), 23–24.

13. Indian Populations of Reservations, "Oklahoma," Indian Population as of June 1, 1890, 528, https://www2.census.gov/prod2/decennial/documents/1890a_v10-23 .pdf, accessed February 25, 2023.

14. Maxwell, *Sequoyah Constitutional Convention*, 24.

15. "Editorial on D. W. Bushyhead," *Muskogee Phoenix*, December 29, 1894.

16. Abraham Lincoln, "Proclamation 100—Admitting West Virginia Into the Union," April 20, 1863, *The American Presidency Project*, https://www.presidency.ucsb.edu /node/203153, accessed July 17, 2023.

17. Albert H. Ellis, *A History of the Constitutional Convention of the State of Oklahoma* (Muskogee, OK: Economy, 1923), 8.

18. Maxwell, *Sequoyah Constitutional Convention*, 26.

19. Maxwell, *Sequoyah Constitutional Convention*, 27.

20. "Editorial on Message of Pleasant Porter," *South McAlester (I.T.) Capital*, October 11, 1900.

21. The name of Hulbutta Micco is also spelled Hulputta Mekko.

22. "An Indian Conference," *Collinsville (I.T.) News*, September 25, 1902. See also Pleasant Porter to Green McCurtain, October 13, 1902, Green McCurtain Collection, Box 12, Folder 2, Western History Collections, University of Oklahoma.

23. "News Item of Hulbutto Micco," *South McAlester News*, November 13, 1902.

24. Maxwell, *Sequoyah Constitutional Convention*, 33.

25. *Five Civilized Tribes Protest Against Congressional Legislation Contemplating Annexation of Indian Territory to Oklahoma or Territorial Form of Government Prior to March 4th, 1906* (n.p., 1906), 3, Green McCurtain Collection, Box 17, Folder 19, Western History Collections, University of Oklahoma.

26. "Resolutions Approved by Pleasant Porter, Swimmer, Et Al," *Sallisaw (I.T.) Star*, December 5, 1902.

27. Maxwell, *Sequoyah Constitutional Convention*, 34, and Daniel F. Littlefield Jr., *Seminole: A Story of Racial Vengeance* (Jackson: University Press of Mississippi, 1996), 33.

28. "Resolutions Approved by Pleasant Porter, Swimmer, Et Al," *Sallisaw (I.T.) Star*, December 5, 1902.

29. William H. Murray, "The Constitutional Convention," *Chronicles of Oklahoma* Vol. 9, No. 2 (June 1931), 126.

30. "Indians For Statehood," *Mustang (O.T.) Mail*, April 17, 1904; Maxwell, *Sequoyah Constitutional Convention*, 35. See also Green McCurtain to Pleasant Porter, April 10, 1903, Green McCurtain Collection, Box 12, Folder 3, Western History Collections, University of Oklahoma.

31. Act for the Protection of the People of Indian Territory, June 28, 1898, *U.S. Statutes at Large*, Vol. 30, 497–98, 512.

32. Hines, *Alfalfa Bill*, 9, 13.

33. "Alfalfa Bill on Alfalfa," *Tishomingo (I.T.) Capitol-Democrat*, c. August 12, 1902.

34. William H. Murray, *Memoirs of Governor Murray and True History of Oklahoma* (Boston: Meador, 1945), 1:13.

35. W. R. Blake to William Murray, May 13, 1916, Box 3, Folder Correspondence 5-1-1916 to 5-31-1916, William H. Murray Collection, Oklahoma History Center.

36. Murray, "Constitutional Convention," 127.

37. Murray, "Constitutional Convention," 127.

38. "Election Day in the Chickasaw Nation, August 8, 1904," *Durant (I.T.) Weekly News*, August 12, 1904.

39. "Editorial on Chickasaw Schools," *South McAlester (I.T.) Capital*, October 20, 1904.

40. Elzie Ronald Caywood, "The Administration of William C. Rogers, Principal Chief of the Cherokee Nation 1903–1907," *Chronicles of Oklahoma*, Vol. 30, No. 1 (Spring 1952), 34–35.

41. "Editorial on Hulputta Micco and Mrs. A. B. Davis," *Tulsa Democrat*, March 17, 1905.

42. "Death of Hulputta Micco," *Holdenville (I.T.) Tribune*, April 20, 1905.

43. "Impeachment of Jacob Harrison," *Holdenville (I.T.) Tribune*, May 18, 1905.

44. "Indians Hold Annual Dance," *Chelsea (I.T.) Commercial*, July 21, 1905.

45. "Interview with L. C. Perryman and P. L. Berryhill," *Holdenville (I.T.) Tribune*, March 8, 1906.

46. Murray, "Constitutional Convention," 127.

47. "Idea and Hard Work Carried Haskell from 'Broke Politician to Captain of Finance,'" *Daily Oklahoman* (city of Oklahoma), March 6, 1921; Irvin Hurst, *The 46th Star: The Colorful and Authentic History of Oklahoma's Constitutional Convention and Early Statehood* (Oklahoma City: Western Heritage Books, 1980), ix.

48. Paul Nesbit, "Haskell Tells of Two Conventions, *Chronicles of Oklahoma*, Vol. 14, No. 2 (June 1936), 190, 192.

49. Francis Haskell, interview by Nancy Defore, February 1, 1975, Folder Charles Haskell/Francis, Oklahoma Territorial Museum and Carnegie Library, Guthrie, Oklahoma. See also Hurst, *The 46th Star*, 39–40.

50. Irwin Hurst, "A Day to Last a Lifetime," *Daily Oklahoman Orbit* (Oklahoma City), November 12, 1972.

51. Phillip Mellinger, "Discrimination and Statehood in Oklahoma," *Chronicles of Oklahoma*, Vol. 49, No. 3 (Autumn 1971), 353.

52. Nesbit, "Haskell Tells of Two Conventions," 196.

53. C. M. Allen, *The "Sequoyah" Movement* (Oklahoma City: Harlow Publishing Company, 1925), 23.

54. Hines, *Alfalfa Bill*, 176–177.

55. Murray, "Constitutional Convention," 127. In another version, "It was an accident, but once made, the prairie was on fire." See Allen, *"Sequoyah" Movement*, 24.

56. Oscar Fowler, *The Haskell Regime: The Intimate Life of Charles Nathaniel Haskell* (Oklahoma City: Boles, 1933), 47; Allen, *"Sequoyah" Movement*, 27.

57. Maxwell, *Sequoyah Constitutional Convention*, 47–48. Grant Foreman wrote that the convention was August 26, See Grant Foreman, "Oklahoma and Indian Territory," *Outlook*, March 10, 1906, 550.

58. Green McCurtain to Pleasant Porter, July 11, 1905, Green McCurtain Collection, Box 12, Folder 7, Western History Collections, University of Oklahoma.

59. "What Others Say About It," *Cherokee Advocate* (Tahlequah, I.T.), August 5, 1905.

60. Maxwell, *Sequoyah Constitutional Convention*, 99.

61. Maxwell, *Sequoyah Constitutional Convention*, 48.

62. "Attitude of Indians," *Tishomingo (I.T.) News*, July 19, 1905.

63. "Separate Statehood Urged by Porter at the Big Meeting," *Muskogee (I.T.) Democrat*, August 3, 1905.

64. Maxwell, *Sequoyah Constitutional Convention*, 52–53.

65. Allen, *"Sequoyah" Movement*, 90.

66. Nathaniel J. Washington, "The Historical Development of the Negro in Oklahoma" (M.A. thesis, University of Arizona, 1947), 56.

67. Maxwell, *Sequoyah Constitutional Convention*, 62–63.

68. "Muskogee Will Welcome Visitors," *Muskogee (I.T.) Daily Phoenix*, August 20, 1905.

69. Fowler, *Haskell Regime*, 57.

70. "William Hastings is Chairman: Presides Over the Deliberations of the Constitution Committee, R. L. Owen Suggests Sequoyah as Name, For Proposed State—Judge Thomas Vice Chairman—Rev. Evans Secretary," *Muskogee (I.T.) Phoenix*, August 23, 1905.

71. Haskell, interview.

72. "Editorial," *Muskogee (I.T.) Phoenix*, August 25, 1905.

73. Murray, "Constitutional Convention," 130; Foreman, "Oklahoma and Indian Territory," 550.

74. Murray, *Memoirs of Governor Murray and True History of Oklahoma*, 1:315.

75. The eleven subcommittees were (1) the Committee on Preamble, Declaration of Rights and Power of Government; (2) the Committee on County Boundaries, County Seats, and Enumeration of Population; (3) the Committee on Legislative and Executive Departments; (4) the Committee on Judicial Department; (5) the Committee on Education; (6) the Committee on Militia and Minor Administrative Departments; (7) the Committee on Corporations; (8) the Committee on Suffrage, Elections, and Preservation of Purity of Government; (9) the Committee on Finance and Revenue; (10) the Committee on Rights and Exemptions of Property; and (11) the Committee on Miscellaneous Provisions, Including Constitutional Amendments and Prohibition. See Allen, *"Sequoyah" Movement*, 36–37.

76. "Committee Adopts Map," *Daily Ardmoreite* (Ardmore, I.T.), August 31, 1905; Maxwell, *Sequoyah Constitutional Convention*, 71.

77. Foreman, "Oklahoma and Indian Territory," 550.

78. Murray, "Constitutional Convention," 129.

79. "Proposed State of Sequoyah," January 16, 1906, in *Congressional Record*, 59th Congress, 1st session, part 1 (Washington, DC: Government Printing Office, 1906), 1–4.

80. Allen, *"Sequoyah" Movement*, 32.

81. Constitution of the State of Sequoyah, October 14, 1905, Helmerich Center, Gilcrease Museum, Tulsa, Oklahoma.

82. Sarah Deer and Cecilia Knapp, "Muscogee Constitutional Jurisprudence: Vhakv Em Pvtakv (The Carpet Under the Law)," *Tulsa Law Review*, Vol. 49, No. 25 (2013), 161–162. The quotation is from Barbara Alice Mann, ed., "'A Man of Misery': Chitto Harjo and the Senate Select Committee on Oklahoma Statehood," in *Native Speakers of the Eastern Woodlands: Selected Speeches and Critical Analyses* (Santa Barbara: ABC-CLIO, 2001), 197.

83. Hines, *Alfalfa Bill*, 182; Allen, *"Sequoyah" Movement*, 41.

84. "The Muskogee convention," *Miami (I.T.) Record-Herald*, August 25, 1905; "Rename Indian Territory," *Garfield County (O.T.) Democrat*, August 31, 1905.

85. "The State of Sequoyah," *Fort Gibson (I.T.) Post*, October 15, 1904; "D. M. Hodges on Sequoyah," *Muskogee (I.T.) Phoenix*, August 31, 1905.

86. Maxwell, *Sequoyah Constitutional Convention*, 74.

87. Allen, *"Sequoyah" Movement*, 47.

88. Maxwell, *Sequoyah Constitutional Convention*, 77.

89. Allen, *"Sequoyah" Movement*, 46.

90. Murray, "Constitutional Convention," 133.

91. Maxwell, *Sequoyah Constitutional Convention*, 78; Sequoyah Convention—Inspiration, July 5, 1905, Charles Haskell Collection, Box H-26, Folder 4, Western History Collections, University of Oklahoma.

92. Maxwell, *Sequoyah Constitutional Convention*, 83.

93. Maxwell, *Sequoyah Constitutional Convention*, 87.

94. "News Item of Pleasant Porter," *Chickasaw (I.T.) Democrat*, September 21, 1902.

95. Maxwell, *Sequoyah Constitutional Convention*, 94.

96. "Challenge is Turned Down: Chairman of the Sequoyah Campaign Committee Declines Proposition of Debate on Separate or Joint Statehood," *Muskogee (I.T.) Phoenix*, September 26, 1905.

97. Sequoyah Convention—Inspiration, July 5, 1905, Charles Haskell Collection, Box H-26, Folder 4, Western History Collections, University of Oklahoma.

98. "No-Statehood Convention," *Miami (I.T.) Record-Herald*, August 25, 1905.

99. Murray, *Memoirs of Governor Murray and True History of Oklahoma*, 1:319.

100. Maxwell, *Sequoyah Constitutional Convention*, 99; Treaty with the Creeks, March 24, 1832, in Kappler, *Indian Affairs*, 341–343.

101. "The State of 'Sequoyah,'" *New York Times*, October 5, 1905.

102. Maxwell, *Sequoyah Constitutional Convention*, 96.

103. Foreman, "Oklahoma and Indian Territory," 551.

104. "Churches Are Working," ca 1906 from unknown newspaper, Green McCurtain Collection, Box 12, Folder 10 Western History Collections, University of Oklahoma. See also "Are Indian State," *Garfield County (O.T.) Democrat*, August 31, 1905.
105. Foreman, "Oklahoma and Indian Territory," 555.
106. Foreman, "Oklahoma and Indian Territory," 551; "Memorial to Sequoyans, *Muskogee (I.T.) Times Democrat*, December 2, 1905.
107. "Proposed State of Sequoyah," 1; Allen, *"Sequoyah" Movement*, 54.
108. Fowler, *Haskell Regime*, 58.
109. James R. Branch, ed., *Proceedings of the American Bankers' Association, October 16–19, 1906* (New York: Secretary American Bankers' Association, 1906), 204. A congressman told President McKinley that Porter was the greatest living Indian and the president repeated this in a speech; see John B. Meserve, "Chief Pleasant Porter," *Chronicles of Oklahoma*, Vol. 9, No. 3 (September 1931), 325.
110. "Biographical Sketch of Pleasant Porter," *St. Louis Post-Dispatch*, September 17, 1899.

Chapter 5. Becoming Oklahoma

1. Miller, *Oklahoma Populism*, 34.
2. Maxwell, *Sequoyah Constitutional Convention*, 22.
3. Edward Elmere Keso, *The Senatorial Career of Robert Lathan Owen* (Gardenvale, Quebec: Garden City Press, 1938), 15; "Table 3.—Distribution of the population of Oklahoma, Indian Territory, and of the Two Territories Combined, by Sex, by Color, and by Sex and Age: 1907, 1900, and 1890," in S. N. D. North, *Population of Oklahoma and Indian Territory 1907*, Bulletin 89 (Washington, DC: Government Printing Office, 1907), 8.
4. Letter to W. P. Boudinot, February 20, 1877, from unknown source reprinted in the *Cherokee Advocate* (Tahlequah, I.T.), March 7, 1877.
5. Miller, *Oklahoma Populism*, 37.
6. Haskell, interview.
7. Miller, *Oklahoma Populism*, 45.
8. In 1906, a national park in south-central Oklahoma would be named after the powerful senator from Connecticut for his efforts. (It is now known as Chickasaw National Recreation Area.)
9. "Table 2. Population of Oklahoma, by Counties, and of Indian Territory, by Nations: 1907 and 1900," in North, *Population of Oklahoma and Indian Territory 1907*, 7.
10. Oscar A. Kinchen, "The Abortive Territory of Cimarron," *Chronicles of Oklahoma*, Vol. 23, No. 3 (Autumn 1945), 218–231.
11. Kenneth M. Stampp, *Indiana Politics during the Civil War* (Indianapolis: Indiana Historical Bureau, 1949), 211; "Editorial," *Chicago Tribune*, July 9, 1884.

12. Morris L. Wardell, "The History of No-Man's-Land, or Old Beaver County," *Chronicles of Oklahoma*, Vol. 35, No. 3 (Spring 1957), 31–33.

13. Baird and Goble, *Story of Oklahoma*, 328.

14. Miller, *Oklahoma Populism*, 37.

15. Thomas H. Doyle, "The Supreme Court of the Territory of Oklahoma," *Chronicles of Oklahoma*, Vol. 13, No. 2 (June 1935), 214–218.

16. Miller, *Oklahoma Populism*, 48.

17. Miller, *Oklahoma Populism* 50.

18. "House Bill No. 119, Relating to Civil Rights," in *Journal of the First Session of the Legislative Assembly of Oklahoma Territory* (Guthrie, OK: Oklahoma News Publishing Company, 1890), 1016–1017.

19. "Indians Must Marry According to Law," March 12, 1897, Sec. 4, Art 2, Ch. 23, S.L. 1897, in *The Revised Laws of the State of Oklahoma* (Columbia, MO: E.W. Stephens Publishing Company, 1911), 1:1567.

20. Mellinger, "Discrimination and Statehood in Oklahoma," 353.

21. "Memorial Adopted at Statehood Convention in Oklahoma City," December 15, 1891, quoted in Luther B. Hill, *A History of the State of Oklahoma* (Chicago: Lewis Publishing Company, 1910), 1:338–339.

22. "Memorial Adopted at Statehood Convention in Oklahoma City," in Hill, *History of the State of Oklahoma*, 1:338–339.

23. Hill, *History of the State of Oklahoma*, 1:339–340.

24. Hill, *History of the State of Oklahoma*, 1:340.

25. "Report: Admission of Oklahoma," December 20, 1893, Committee on the Territories, Report No. 242, House of Representatives, 53d Congress, 2d Session, https://babel.hathitrust.org/cgi/pt?id=pur1.32754082236914&view=1up&seq=2, accessed May 12, 2022.

26. Hill, *History of the State of Oklahoma*, 1:341.

27. Okmulgee Historical Society and the Heritage Society of America, *History of Okmulgee County, Oklahoma*, 1:85.

28. Circe Sturm, "Blood Politics, Racial Classification, and Cherokee National Identity: The Trials and Tribulations of the Cherokee Freedmen," *American Indian Quarterly*, Vol. 22, Nos. 1 and 2 (Winter-Spring 1998), 236.

29. Okmulgee Historical Society and the Heritage Society of America, *History of Okmulgee County, Oklahoma*, 1:85.

30. Maxwell, *Sequoyah Constitutional Convention*, 27.

31. W. A. Jones to Cornelius N. Bless, September 26, 1897, in *Annual Report of the Commissioner of Indian Affairs 1898* (Washington, DC: Government Printing Office, 1898), 156.

32. Act for the Protection of the People of Indian Territory, June 28, 1898, *U.S. Statutes at Large*, Vol. 30, 497–98, 502.

33. Sturm, "Blood Politics, Racial Classification, and Cherokee National Identity,"36.

34. Richard Williams, "The Part-Cherokee President," *New York Times*, July 16, 1998.

35. W. A. Jones, "Indian Territory under the Curtis Act," in *Annual Report of the Commissioner of Indian Affairs 1897* (Washington, DC: Government Printing Office, 1897), 75–80,

36. Autobiography 1860–1884, Charles Curtis Collection, Box 1, Section 1, Series 1, Folder 1, Kansas Historical Society, Topeka.

37. An Act for the protection of the people of the Indian Territory [Curtis Act]," June 28, 1898, *U.S. Statutes at Large*, Vol. 30, 497–98, 592.

38. Kent Carter, *The Dawes Commission and the Allotment of the Five Civilized Tribes, 1893–1914* (Orem, UT: Ancestry.com., 1999), 35–36.

39. W. A. Jones to Cornelius N. Bless, September 26, 1898, in *Annual Report of the Commissioner of Indian Affairs 1898*, 158.

40. "Editorial on Message of Pleasant Porter," *South McAlester (I.T.) Capital*, December 14, 1899.

41. John Joseph Matthews, *Wah'Kon-Tah: The Osage and the White Man's Road* (Norman: University of Oklahoma Press, 1932), 136.

42. W. A. Jones to Ethan A. Hitchcock, October 1, 1900, in *Annual Report of the Commissioner of Indian Affairs 1900* (Washington, DC: Government Printing Office, 1900), 173.

43. "The Secretary of Interior is Hereby Authorized to Remove from the Council Any Member or Members thereof for Good Cause, to Be by Him Determined," in Osage Allotment Act, PL 59–321, June 28, 1906, Section 9, *U.S. Statutes at Large*, Vol. 34, 539; Robert M. Burrill, "The Osage Pasture Map," *Chronicles of Oklahoma*, Vol. 53, No. 2 (Summer 1975), 205.

44. Free Homes Act, PL 105, May 17, 1900, *U.S. Statutes at Large*, Vol. 31, 179.

45. Maxwell, *Sequoyah Constitutional Convention*, 29.

46. Maxwell, *Sequoyah Constitutional Convention*, 29.

47. Charles Wayne Ellinger, "The Drive for Statehood in Oklahoma, 1889–1906," *Chronicles of Oklahoma*, Vol. 41, No. 1 (Spring 1963), 25–27.

48. Hill, *History of The State of Oklahoma*, 1:344.

49. Maxwell, *Sequoyah Constitutional Convention*, 30.

50. Maxwell, *Sequoyah Constitutional Convention*, 32.

51. James A. Kehl, *Boss Rule in the Gilded Age: Matt Quay of Pennsylvania* (Pittsburgh: University of Pittsburgh Press, 1981), 59–83.

52. Maxwell, *Sequoyah Constitutional Convention*, 35.

53. Hill, *History of the State of Oklahoma*, 1:348.

54. Ellis, *History of the Constitutional Convention of the State of Oklahoma*, 13.

55. Maxwell, *Sequoyah Constitutional Convention*, 33.

56. Hill, *History of the State of Oklahoma*, 1:349.

57. Maxwell, *Sequoyah Constitutional Convention*, 36.

58. Maxwell, *Sequoyah Constitutional Convention*, 37.

59. Maxwell, *Sequoyah Constitutional Convention*, 35.

60. Maxwell, *Sequoyah Constitutional Convention*, 41.

61. Hill, *History of the State of Oklahoma*, 1:349–350.

62. The *Purcell Tribune* reported 10,000 people at Muskogee, which included 2,000 schoolchildren, See "Editorial on Reception Committee for President," *Purcell (I.T.) Tribune*, April 7, 1905.

63. Maxwell, *Sequoyah Constitutional Convention*, 45.

64. Allen, *"Sequoyah" Movement*, 20.

65. Maxwell, *Sequoyah Constitutional Convention*, 50.

66. Hill, *History of the State of Oklahoma*, 1:350.

67. "Sequoyah Convention and Letter Signed by Pleasant Porter," *South McAlester (I.T.) Capital*, October 12, 1905.

68. Hannibal B. Johnson, *Acres of Aspiration: The All-Black Towns in Oklahoma* (Austin: Eakin Press, 2007), 61.

69. In 1890 the militia of the territory of Oklahoma was created as the forerunner of the Oklahoma National Guard. See Art T. Burton, *Black Gun, Silver Star: The Life and Legend of Frontier Marshal Bass Reeves* (Lincoln: University of Nebraska Press, 2006), 141.

70. Johnson, *Acres of Aspiration*, 61.

71. Roberts, *I've Been Here All the While*, 101.

72. "Fred Parkinson Returns Home," *Muskogee Phoenix*, November 23, 1905.

73. Hines, *Alfalfa Bill*, 185.

74. "The Statehood Bill," H.R. 12707, March 5, 1906, in *Congressional Record-Senate*, 3330–3332, https://www.govinfo.gov/content/pkg/GPO-CRECB-1906-pt4-v40/pdf/GPO-CRECB-1906-pt4-v40-6.pdf, accessed June 17, 2020.

75. "Senate Passes Statehood Measure Amended," *Daily Oklahoman* (city of Oklahoma), March 9, 1906.

76. An Act to Enable the People of Oklahoma and of the Indian Territory to form a Constitution and State Government and be Admitted into the Union on an Equal Footing with the Original States; and to Enable the People of New Mexico and of Arizona to form a Constitution and State Government and be Admitted into the Union on an Equal Footing with the Original States, PL 59–234, June 16, 1906, *U.S. Statutes at Large*, Vol. 34, 267.

77. Hurst, *46th Star*, xiii.

78. E. E. Hull, "Snake Indians Care But Little About Statehood," *Vinita (I.T.) Daily Chieftain*, June 3, 1906.

79. Okmulgee Historical Society and the Heritage Society of America, *History of Okmulgee County, Oklahoma*, 1:98.

80. Baird and Goble, *Story of Oklahoma*, 332.

81. Blue Clark, "Delegates to the Constitution Convention," *Chronicles of Oklahoma*, Vol. 48, No. 4 (Winter 1970–1971), 408.

82. Hurst, *46th Star*, 6.

83. Hurst, *46th Star*, 10.

84. Keso, *Senatorial Career of Robert Lathan Owen*, 18.

85. Hurst, *46th Star*, 46.

86. Proclamation to adjourn Oklahoma Constitutional Convention by William H. Murray, November 16, 1907, Box 13, Folder William H. Murray Adjournment of Constitutional Convention, November 16, 1907, William H. Murray Collection, Oklahoma History Center.

87. Hurst, *46th Star*, x.

88. Baird and Goble, *Story of Oklahoma*, 334.

89. Monroe Lee Billington, *Thomas P. Gore: The Blind Senator from Oklahoma* (Lawrence: University of Kansas Press, 1967), 4.

90. Keso, *Senatorial Career of Robert Lathan Owen*, 13–14.

91. Billington, *Thomas P. Gore*, 4.

92. Billington, *Thomas P. Gore*, 20.

93. Baird and Goble, *Story of Oklahoma*, 336.

94. Muriel Wright, "The Wedding of Oklahoma and Miss Indian Territory," *Chronicles of Oklahoma*, Vol. 35, No. 3 (Fall 1957), 255.

95. Wright, "Wedding of Oklahoma and Miss Indian Territory," 257, 258.

96. "Oklahoma Becomes a State," November 17, 1907, *Oklahoma State Capital* (Guthrie, O.T.); Wright, "Wedding of Oklahoma and Miss Indian Territory," 258.

97. Haskell, interview.

98. Hurst, *46th Star*, 32.

99. "Papers Relating to the Foreign Relations of the United States with the Annual Message of the President Transmitted to Congress December 3, 1907," Document No. 1, in *House of Representatives*, 60th Congress, 1st Session (Washington, DC: Government Printing Office, 1910), 43.

100. Chang, *Color of the Land*, 138.

101. The text of "Ranch Life in the West," speech Roosevelt delivered in New York City in January 1886 cannot be found, although secondary sources have cited it. See Herman Hagedorn, *Roosevelt in the Badlands* (Boston: Houghton Mifflin Company, 1921), 355. However, this particular quotation appears in "Roosevelt on Cow Boys and Indians," *Bismarck (ND) Weekly Tribune*, January 22, 1886.

102. Thomas G. Dyer, *Theodore Roosevelt and the Idea of Race* (Baton Rouge: Louisiana State University Press, 1980), 70–71.

103. Dyer, *Theodore Roosevelt and the Idea of Race*, 83.

104. Dyer, *Theodore Roosevelt and the Idea of Race*, 88.

Chapter 6. Dream of a Black State and the Rise of Indian Nationalism

1. Crockett, *Black Towns*, 16.

2. Crockett, *Black Towns*, 16.

3. Jere W. Roberson, "Edward P. McCabe and the Langston Experiment," *Chronicles of Oklahoma*, Vol. 51, No. 3 (Fall 1973), 343–355.

4. Walt Wilson, "Freedmen in Indian Territory During Reconstruction," *Chronicles of Oklahoma*, Vol. 49, No. 2 (Summer 1971), 234–235.

5. Roberts, *I've Been Here All the While*, 69.

6. Wilson, "Freedmen in Indian Territory During Reconstruction,"238–244.

7. Randy Krehbiel, "1867 Vision for What's Now Oklahoma was an all-Black Territory of Lincoln," *Tulsa World*, November 27, 2020.

8. Crockett, *Black Towns*, 39.

9. Painter, *Exodusters*, 184–201.

10. "The Oklahoma Lands," *Leavenworth (Kansas) Advocate*, March 23, 1889.

11. Cyrus Leondus Blackburn, "The Jubilee in Sight," *Indian Chieftain* (Vinita, I.T.), January 26, 1888.

12. Jimmie Lewis Franklin, *Journey Toward Hope: A History of Blacks in Oklahoma* (Norman: University of Oklahoma Press, 1982), 13.

13. Painter, *Exodusters*, 184–201.

14. "A New Oklahoma Town," *Evening Gazette* (City of Oklahoma, O.T.), August 11, 1889.

15. Martin Dann, "From Sodom to the Promised Land: E. P. McCabe and the Movement for Oklahoma Colonization," *Kansas History*, Vol. 40, No. 3 (Autumn 1974), 370–378.

16. Williams, "Oklahoma: Genesis and Tradition of the Black Press," 268–269.

17. Roberson, "Edward P. McCabe and the Langston Experiment," 344–345.

18. Dann, "From Sodom to the Promised Land," 377, 370–378.

19. Roberts, *I've Been Here All the While*, 84.

20. Franklin, *Journey Toward Hope*, 14; Crockett, *Black Towns*, 124.

21. "To Make A Negro State," *New York Times*, February 28, 1890.

22. "The Gazette Raves," *Oklahoma State Capitol* (Guthrie, O.T.), June 14, 1890.

23. Franklin, *Journey Toward Hope*, 11; Melissa Nicole Stuckey, "All Men Up: Race, Rights, and Power in the All-Black Town of Boley, Oklahoma, 1903–1939" (Ph.D. diss., Yale University, 2009), 13.

24. Crockett, *Black Towns*, 56.

25. Stuckey, "All Men Up," 10.

26. "Convention For Separate Statehood for Indian Territory," *Oklahoma State Register* (Guthrie, O.T.), August 24, 1905.

27. Sequoyah Convention—Inspiration, July 5, 1905, Charles Haskell Collection, Box H-26, Folder 4, Western History Collections, University of Oklahoma.

28. "Double Statehood vs Negro's Interest," *Muskogee Cimeter*, August 17, 1905. See also, "The Statehood convention," *Muskogee Cimeter*, August 3, 1905.

29. "White Man's Principle," *Alva (I.T.) Weekly Pioneer*, November 2, 1906.

30. "Lynching," *Muskogee Cimeter*, January 3, 1908.

31. Williams, "Oklahoma: Genesis and Tradition of the Black Press," 283.

32. Williams, "Oklahoma: Genesis and Tradition of the Black Press," 283.

33. Williams, "Oklahoma: Genesis and Tradition of the Black Press," 283.

34. Fowler, *Haskell Regime*, 59.

35. "Proposed State of Sequoyah," 1.

36. Act of Congress approved April 30, 1908 (35 Stats. L. 71), Relating to Certain Lands and Other Property of the Seminole Indians of Oklahoma, January 28, 1932, p. 47, House of Representatives, Sub-Committee of the Committee on Indian Affairs, Seminole Nation Collection, Box 1, Folder 8, Western History Collections, Western History Collections, University of Oklahoma.

37. Maxwell, *State of Sequoyah Constitutional Convention*, 143.

38. Keso, *The Senatorial Career of Robert Lathan Owen*, 51; Baron Creager, "The Lost Trail of Sequoyah," *Tulsa World*, February 9, 1947.

39. Orpha B. Russell, "Sequoyah—Cadmus of the Cherokees," *Tulsa World*, February 9, 1947.

40. "Keetoowah's Sacred Ceremony of White Chicken Photographed First Time," *Muskogee Times Democrat*, July 20, 1931.

41. Thomas Cook, "Mystic Keetoowah Nighthawks, 2000 Strong, Dance Once More at Stomp Grounds Near Gore," *Muskogee Daily Phoenix*, July 20, 1931.

42. Muriel H. Wright to Cecilia D. Monahan, January 2, 1951, Box 7a, Folder 16, Muriel Wright Papers, Oklahoma History Center, Oklahoma City.

43. Thomas A. Britten, *American Indians in World War I: At War and at Home* (Albuquerque: University of New Mexico Press, 1997), 74–75.

44. U.S. Citizenship for Indian Veterans of World War I Act, November 6, 1919, *U.S. Statutes at Large*, Vol. 41, 350.

45. "Murray At the Grave of Haskell," *Muskogee Phoenix*, July 7, 1933. See also, Hines, *Alfalfa Bill*.

46. Lewis Meriam, et al., *The Problem of Indian Administration* (Baltimore: Johns Hopkins Press, 1928), 21–22, 86–89.

47. Graham D. Taylor, *The New Deal and American Indian Tribalism: The Administration of the Indian Reorganization Act, 1934–45* (Lincoln: University of Nebraska Press, 1980), 35.

48. Oklahoma Indian Welfare Act, PL 107–63, June 26, 1936, *U.S. Statutes at Large*, Vol. 49, 1967–1968.

49. Taylor, *New Deal and American Indian Tribalism*, 36.

50. "Recognition of Keetoowah Indians Act," PL 715, August 13, 1936, *U.S. Statutes at Large*, Vol. 60, pt. 1, 976.

51. Memorandum to Members of the Inter-Tribal Council of the Five Civilized Tribes from Area Director Paul L. Fickinger, March 9, 1955, Grant Foreman Collection, Box 22, Folder 3, Oklahoma History Center, Oklahoma City.

52. File 220b, Cherokee Miscellaneous 1965, W. W. Keeler Collection, Cherokee Nation Historical Society, Tahlequah, Oklahoma.

53. To Authorize Each of the Five Civilized Tribes of Oklahoma to Popularly Select Their Principal Officer, and for other purposes, PL 91–495, October 22, 1970, *U.S. Statutes at Large*, Vol. 84, 1091.

54. Indian Self-Determination and Education Assistance Act, PL 93–638, *U.S. Statutes at Large*, Vol. 88, 2203–2217.

55. Donald Fixico, "The Muscogee Creeks: A Nativistic People," in *Between Two Worlds: The Survival of Twentieth-Century Indians*, ed. Arrell Morgan Gibson (Oklahoma City: Oklahoma Historical Society, 1986), 30–43.

56. Walter J. Heshel to President Spiro T. Agnew, May 20, 1970, Mss 12, Folder 1, Box 2, Charles Cobb Victory Papers, Cherokee Nation Historical Society, Tahlequah, Oklahoma.

57. Jerry Fink, "Bingo Ushers in New Economic Era for Cherokee Nation," *Tulsa World*, November 16, 1990.

58. Inter-Tribal Council of the Five Civilized Tribes, https://www.fivecivilizedtribes.org, accessed July 17, 2023.

59. Crockett, *Black Towns*, 168.

60. Crockett, *Black Towns*, 215.

Epilogue

1. For more on the depth of historical consciousness, see John Lukacs, *Historical Consciousness: The Remembered Past*, 7th ed. (New Brunswick, NJ: Transaction, 1994), 128–167.

2. Allen, *"Sequoyah" Movement*, 1; Annie Abel, "Proposals for an Indian State," in *Annual Report of the American Historical Association for the Year 1907* (Washington, DC: Government Printing Office, 1907), 1:87–108.

3. Treaty with the Delawares, September 17, 1778, in Kappler, *Indian Affairs*, 2–5.

4. *Worcester v. Georgia*, March 23, 1832, 31 U.S. 6 Pet. 515 (1832).

5. Allen, *"Sequoyah" Movement*, 4–5.

6. Allen, *"Sequoyah" Movement*, 60.

7. Arrell Morgan Gibson, "Oklahoma: Land of the Drifter Deterrents to Sense of Place," *Chronicles of Oklahoma*, Vol. 64, No. 2 (Summer 1986), 7–10.

8. "Act for the Protection of the People of Indian Territory," June 28, 1898, *U.S. Statutes at Large*, Vol. 30, 497–98, 512.

9. Maxwell, *Sequoyah Constitutional Convention*, 27.

10. Maxwell, *Sequoyah Constitutional Convention*, 33.

11. Caywood, "The Administration of William C. Rogers," *Chronicles of Oklahoma*, Vol. 30, No. 1 (Spring 1952), 34–35.

12. "Indian Self-Determination and Education Assistance Act," P.L. 93-638, *U.S. Statutes at Large*, Vol. 88, 2203–2217.

13. *Harjo v. Kleppe*, 420 F. Supp. 1110 (D.D.C. 1976)

14. *United States v. Martinez*, 540 F.2d 1039 (10th Cir. 1976).

15. Major Crimes Act, March 3, 1885, *U.S. Statutes at Large*, Vol. 23, 385.

16. Adam Goodrum, "Meeting the *McGirt* Moment: The Five Tribes, Sovereignty & Criminal Jurisdiction in Oklahoma's New Indian Country," *American Indian Law*

Review, Vol. 46, No. 1 (2021–2022), 205; Robert J. Miller and Torey Dolan, "The Indian Law Bombshell: *McGirt v. Oklahoma*," *Boston University Law Review*, Vol. 101, No. 6 (2021), 2073.

17. Goodrum, "Meeting the *McGirt* Moment," 205–206.
18. Goodrum, "Meeting the *McGirt* Moment," 211.
19. Claire Blumental, "'We Hold the Government to Its Word': How *McGirt v. Oklahoma* Revives Aboriginal Title," *Yale Law Journal*, Vol. 131, No. 7 (May 2022), 2331.
20. Blumental, "'We Hold the Government to Its Word,'" 2338.
21. Robert J. Miller and Robbie Ethridge, *A Promise Kept: The Muscogee (Creek) Nation and McGirt v. Oklahoma* (Norman: University of Oklahoma Press, 2023), 135, 139.
22. *Lone Wolf v. Hitchcock*, 187 U.S. 553 (1903).
23. See Miller and Ethridge, *A Promise Kept*.

Bibliography

Primary Sources

Manuscript Collections

American Philosophical Society, Philadelphia, Pennsylvania
    Charles B. Davenport Papers
Cherokee Nation Historical Society, Tahlequah, Oklahoma
    W. W. Keeler Collection
    Charles Cobb Victory Papers
Gerald Ford Presidential Library, Ann Arbor, Michigan
    Theodore Marrs Collection
    Bradley Patterson Collection
Helmerich Center for American Research, Gilcrease Museum, Tulsa, Oklahoma
    Civil War Papers
John Vaughan Library, Northeastern State University, Tahlequah, Oklahoma
    Thomas L. Ballenger Collection
Kansas Historical Society, Topeka, Kansas
    Charles Curtis Collection
    Howel Jones and Ross Burns Collection
Oklahoma Historical Society, Oklahoma City, Oklahoma
    Berlin B. Chapman Collection
    William H. Murray Collection
    Muriel Wright Papers
Oklahoma Territorial Museum and the Carnegie Library, Guthrie, Oklahoma
Special Collections and University Archives, McFarlin Library, University of Tulsa,
    Tulsa, Oklahoma
    DeWitt Clinton Lipe—Cherokee Strip Papers, 1870–1913
Western History Collections, University of Oklahoma Libraries, Norman, Oklahoma
    H. O. Boggs Collection

Frank J. Boudinot Collection
W. P. Boudinot Collection
John F. Brown Collection
B. C. Burney Collection
Dennis Wolf Bushyhead Papers
William L. Byrd Collection
Frank M. Canton Papers
Roscoe Simmons Cate Papers
Berlin Basil Chapman Papers
Chickasaw Nation Collection Papers
Choctaw Nation Collection
John Chupco Collection
Coleman Cole Collection
Henry Vernon Foster Papers
Grayson Family Collection
G. W. Grayson Papers
Jacob Harrison Collection
Indian-Pioneer Papers
Lochar Harjo Collection
Charles Nathan Haskell Collection
Green McCurtain Collection
Roley McIntosh Collection
Hulbutta Micco Collection
Muskogee, Oklahoma, Indian Centennial Collection
Daniel O'Dell Papers
David Payne Collection
L. C. Perryman Collection
Pleasant Porter Collection
Seminole Nation Collection
Moty Tiger Collection
Allen Wright Collection

Government Documents

Act Creates the Commissioner of Indian Affairs, July 9, 1832, *U.S. Statutes at Large*, 4:564.

Act for the Protection of the People of Indian Territory, June 28, 1898, *U.S. Statutes at Large*, 30:497–98, 502.

Act Making Appropriations for the Current and Contingent Expenses of the Indian Department, March 2, 1889, *U.S. Statutes at Large*, 14:1005.

An Act making Appropriations for the current and contingencies of the Indian Department, February 27, 1851, *U.S. Statutes at Large*, 9:574.

Act of Congress Approved April 30, 1908 (35 Stats. L. 71), Relating to Certain Lands and Other Property of the Seminole Indians of Oklahoma, January 28, 1932, House of Representatives, Sub-Committee of the Committee on Indian Affairs, Washington, DC.

Act to Enable the people of Oklahoma and of the Indian Territory to Form a Constitution and State Government and Be Admitted into the Union on an Equal Footing with the Original States; and to Enable the People of New Mexico and of Arizona to Form a Constitution and State Government and Be Admitted into the Union on an Equal Footing with the Original States, P.L. 59-234, June 16, 1906, *U.S. Statutes at Large,* 34:267.

Act to Provide a Temporary Government for the Territory of Oklahoma, P.L 51–182, May 2, 1890, *U.S. Statutes at Large,* 26:81.

Act to Secure Homesteads to Actual Settlers on the Public Domain, P.L. 37-64, May 20, 1862, *U.S. Statutes at Large,* 12:392.

Agreement between the Commission to the Five Civilized Tribes and the Seminole Commission, Seminole Nation Collection, Box 1, Folder 6, Western History Collections, Western History Collections, University of Oklahoma.

Annual Report of the Commissioner of Indian Affairs 1879. Washington, DC: Government Printing Office, 1879.

Annual Report of the Commissioner of Indian Affairs 1880. Washington, DC: Government Printing Office, 1880.

Annual Report of the Commissioner of Indian Affairs 1881. Washington. DC: Government Printing Office, 1881.

Annual Report of the Commissioner of Indian Affairs 1882. Washington, DC: Government Printing Office, 1882.

Annual Report of the Commissioner of Indian Affairs 1886. Washington, DC: Government Printing Office, 1886.

Annual Report of the Commissioner of Indian Affairs 1898. Washington, DC: Government Printing Office, 1898.

Annual Report of the Commissioner of Indian Affairs 1900. Washington, DC: Government Printing Office, 1900.

Cherokee Nation v. Georgia, 30 U.S. 5 Pet. 1 (1831).

Free Homes Act, P.L. 105, May 17, 1900, *U.S. Statutes at Large,* 31:179.

Harjo v. Kleppe, 420 F. Supp. 1110 (D. D.C. 1976)

House Bill No. 119, Relating to Civil Rights, December 22, 1890. In *Journal of the First Session of the Legislative Assembly of Oklahoma Territory,* 1016–1017. Guthrie, OK: Oklahoma News Publishing Company, 1890.

HR 10701, amendment, March 3, 1901, *U.S. Statutes At Large,* 31:1447.

Indians Must Marry According to Law, March 12, 1897. In *The Revised Laws of the State of Oklahoma,* 1:1567. Columbia, MO: E.W. Stephens Publishing Company, 1911.

Indian Removal Act, May 28, 1830, *U.S. Statutes At Large,* 4:411.

Indian Reorganization Act, P.L. 73-383, June 18, 1934, *U.S. Statutes At Large,* 48:984–988.

Indian Self-Determination and Education Assistance Act, P.L. 93-638, August 23, 1996, *U.S. Statutes At Large*, 88:2203–2217.

Joint Resolution for Annexing Texas to the United States, H.R. 46, January 27, 1845, *U.S. Statutes At Large*, 5:797–798.

Lone Wolf v. Hitchcock, January 5, 1903, 187 U.S. 553 (1903).

Major Crimes Act, March 3, 1885, *U.S. Statutes At Large*, 23:385.

Marriages between Negroes and Whites Prohibited, May 22, 1908. In *Revised Laws of the State of Oklahoma*, 1:1565.

McGirt v. Oklahoma, July 9, 2020, 140 S. Ct. 2452 (2020).

Meriam, Lewis, Ray A. Brown, Henry Roe Cloud, Edward Everett Dale, Emma Duke, Herbert R. Edwards, Fayette Avery McKenzie, Mary Louise Mark, W. Carson Ryan Jr., and William J. Spillman. *The Problem of Indian Administration*. Baltimore: Johns Hopkins Press, 1928.

Oklahoma Indian Welfare Act, P.L. 107-63, June 26, 1946, *U.S. Statutes At Large*, 49:1967–1968.

Osage Allotment Act, P.L. 59-321, June 28, 1906, *U.S. Statutes At Large*, 34:539.

Papers Relating to the Foreign Relations of the United States with the Annual Message of the President Transmitted to Congress December 3, 1907, part 1. Washington, DC: Government Printing Office, 1910.

Proclamation by the President of the United States of America, No. 2, March 23, 1889, *U.S. Statutes At Large*, 25:1546.

Proposed State of Sequoyah, January 16, 1906, Document No. 143. In *Journal of the Senate of the United States of America, Being the First Session of the Fifty-Ninth Congress, Begun and Held at the City of Washington, December 4, 1905*, 1–7. Washington, DC: Government Printing Office, 1906.

Recognition of Keetoowah Indians Act, P.L. 715, August 13, 1946, *U.S. Statutes At Large*, 60:976.

Report from the Committee on Territories, Report No. 75, January 23, 1889. In *Journal of the Senate of the United States of America, Being the Second Session of the Fiftieth Congress, Begun and Held at the City of Washington December 3, 1888*, 41. Washington, DC: Government Printing Office, 1889.

Report No. 2579, May 25, 1886. In *Journal of the House of Representatives of the United States, First Session of the Forty-Ninth Congress*, vol. 2, 1706. Washington, DC: Government Printing Office, 1886).

"Table 2.—Population of Oklahoma, by Counties, and of Indian Territory, by Nations: 1907 and 1900." On S. N. D. North, *Population of Oklahoma and Indian Territory 1907*, Bulletin 89, 7. Washington, DC: Government Printing Office, 1907.

"Table 3.—Distribution of the Population of Oklahoma, Indian Territory, and of the Two Territories Combined, by Sex, by Color, and by Sex and Age: 1907, 1900, and 1890." In North, *Population of Oklahoma and Indian Territory 1907*, 9.

To Authorize Each of the Five Civilized Tribes of Oklahoma to Popularly Select their Principal Officer, and for Other Purposes, P.L. 91-495, October 22, 1970, *U.S. Statutes At Large*, 84:1091.

To Provide for the Union of Oklahoma Territory and the Indian Territory as One State, and to enable the people thereof to form a constitution and State government . . . , HR 10010 introduced by Congressman James M. Robinson, January 14, 1904, 2nd Session, 58th Congress, https://www.govinfo.gov/content/pkg/GPO-CRECB -1905-pt1-v39/pdf/GPO-CRECB-1905-pt1-v39-15-1.pdf.

Treaty with the Cherokees, July 8, 1817. In Charles J. Kappler, ed., *Indian Affairs, 1778–1883*, 140–144. New York: Interland, 1972.

Treaty with the Cherokees, February 27, 1819. In Kappler, *Indian Affairs*, 177–181.

Treaty with the Cherokees, July 19, 1866. In Kappler, *Indian Affairs*, 942–950.

Treaty with the Chickasaws, October 20, 1832. In Kappler, *Indian Affairs*, 356–362.

Treaty with the Chickasaws, October 22, 1832. In Kappler, *Indian Affairs*, 362–364.

Treaty with the Choctaws, September 27, 1830. In Kappler, *Indian Affairs*, 310–319.

Treaty with the Choctaws and Chickasaws, July 12, 1861. In Vine Deloria, Jr. and Raymond J. DeMallie, eds., *Documents of American Indian Diplomacy: Treaties, Agreements, and Conventions, 1775–1979*, 603–618. Norman: University of Oklahoma Press, 1999.

Treaty with the Choctaws and Chickasaws, April 28, 1866. In Kappler, *Indian Affairs*, 918–931.

Treaty with the Creeks, January 8, 1821. In Kappler, *Indian Affairs*, 197–198.

Treaty with the Creeks, March 24, 1832. In Kappler, *Indian Affairs*, 341–343.

Treaty with the Creeks, July 10, 1861. In Deloria and DeMallie, *Documents of American Indian Diplomacy*, 588–603.

Treaty with the Creeks, June 14, 1866. In Kappler, *Indian Affairs*, 931–937.

Treaty with the Delawares, September 17, 1778. In Kappler, *Indian Affairs*, 2–5.

Treaty with the Seminoles, May 9, 1832. In Kappler, *Indian Affairs*, 344–345.

Treaty with the Seminoles, March 21, 1866. In Kappler, *Indian Affairs*, 910–915.

Treaty with the Western Cherokees, May 6, 1828. In Kappler, *Indian Affairs*, 288–292.

Worcester v. Georgia, March 23, 1832, 31 U.S. (6 Pet.) 515 (1832).

United States v. Martinez, August 16, 1976, 540 F.2d 1039 10th Cir. (1976).

United States v. Payne, November 11, 1884. In Frank Dale, *Reports of Cases Argued and Determined in the Supreme Court of the Territory of Oklahoma*, vol. 4, 424. Guthrie, O.T.: Union Label, 1897.

US Citizenship for Indian Veterans of World War I Act, November 6, 1919, *U.S. Statutes At Large*, 41:350.

US Constitution, Amendment XI, Article 3, Section 2.

Published Primary Sources

Abel, Annie. "Proposals for an Indian State." In *Annual Report of the American Historical Association for the Year 1907*, vol. 1, 87–108. Washington, DC: Government Printing Office, 1907.

Adair, James. *The History of American Indians*. London. n.p., 1775.

Addresses and Arguments by Prominent Men in Favor of Separate Statehood for Indian Territory. Kinta, I.T.: Kinta Separate Statehood Club, 1905.

Anonymous. Sketch of Joseph Benson Foraker, 1883. Dayton, OH: Press of U.B., 1885.

Barrows, Isabel C. ed. Proceedings of the Twentieth Annual Meeting of the Lake Mohonk Conference of Friends of the Indian 1902. Lake Mohonk, NY: The Lake Mohonk Conference, 1903.

Basler, Roy P., ed. Collected Works of Abraham Lincoln, 1809–1865. Vol. 4. New Brunswick, NJ: Rutgers University Press, 1953.

Branch, James R. Proceedings of the American Bankers' Association, October 16–19, 1906. New York: Secretary American Bankers' Association, 1906.

Darwin, Charles. The Origin of Species. 1859. Reprint, New York: Signet, 2003.

Delegates of the Antlers' Convention, Before the Dawes Commission, Fort Smith, Arkansas, December 9th, 1896. N.P.: Choctaw Herald Print, 1896.

Duncan, Walter A. Letter to the President, Touching Statehood for Indian Territory. Washington, DC: Gibson Bros., 1894.

Dunn, J. E. Indian Territory: a Pre Commonwealth. Indianapolis: Press of American Printing Company, Inc., 1904.

Five Civilized Tribes Protest against Congressional Legislation Contemplating Annexation of Indian Territory to Oklahoma or Territorial Form of Government Prior to March 4th, 1906. N.P., 1906.

Moulton, Gary E. ed., The Papers of John Ross, 1807–1839. Vol. 1. Norman: University of Oklahoma Press, 1985.

Murray, William H. Memoirs of Governor Murray and True History of Oklahoma. Vol. 1. Boston: Meador, 1945.

———. Rights of Americans Under the Constitution of the Federal Republic. Boston: Meador, 1937.

Posey, Alexander. The Fus Fixico Letters: A Creek Humorist in Early Oklahoma. Edited by Daniel Littlefield and Carol A. Petty Hunter. Norman: University of Oklahoma Press, 2002.

Report of the Commissioner of Indian Affairs 1872. Washington, DC: Government Printing Office, 1873.

Scott, Nancy N. ed., A Memoir of Hugh Lawson White: Judge of the Supreme Court of Tennessee, Member of the Senate of the United States, Etc., Etc. Philadelphia: J. B. Lippincott & Company, 1856.

Wilber, Charles Dana. The Great Valleys and Prairies of Nebraska and the Northwest. Omaha: Daily Republican, 1881.

Newspapers

Alva (I.T.) Weekly Pioneer

Atlanta Constitution

Atoka (I.T.) Independent

Atoka (I.T.) Vindicator
Bismarck (ND) Weekly Tribune
Bixby (I.T.) Bulletin
Chelsea (I.T.) Commercial
Chelsea (I.T.) Reporter
Cherokee Advocate (Tahlequah, I.T.)
Cherokee Telephone (Tahlequah, I.T.)
Chicago Tribune
Chickasaw Democrat (Chickasha, I.T.)
Claremore (I.T.) Messenger
Claremore (I.T.) Progress
Collinsville (I.T.) News
Daily Ardmoreite (Ardmore, I.T.)
Daily Oklahoman (Oklahoma City)
Detroit Free Press
Durant (I.T.) Weekly News
Eastern Times-Register (Vian, OK)
Edmond (O.T.) Sun-Democrat
Oklahoma City Evening Gazette
Fort Gibson (I.T.) Post
Fort Smith Elevator
Fort Smith Times Record
Francis Banner (Newton, I.T.)
Garfield County Democrat (Enid, O.T.)
Geuda Springs (KS) News
Guthrie (O.T.) Daily Leader
Hartford Courant
Hartshorne (I.T.) Sun
Holdenville (I.T.) Tribune
Indian Chieftain (Vinita, I.T.)
Indian Citizen (Atoka, I.T.)
Indian Journal (Eufaula, I.T.)
Kansas City (MO) Times
Leavenworth (KS) Advocate
Los Angeles Times
Marietta (I.T.) Monitor
Miami (I.T.) Record-Herald
Minco (O.T.) Minstrel
Muscogee Nation News (Okmulgee, OK)
Muskogee Cimeter
Muskogee Daily Phoenix
Muskogee Democrat
Muskogee Evening Times

Muskogee New-State Tribune
Muskogee Phoenix
Muskogee Times Democrat
Mustang (O.T.) Mail
New York Times
New York Tribune
Niles' Weekly Register
Nowata (I.T.) Weekly Star
Okemah (I.T.) Independent
Oklahoma City Journal Record
Oklahoma Democrat (El Reno, O.T.)
Oklahoma State Capitol (Guthrie, O.T.)
Oklahoma State Register (Guthrie, O.T.)
Oklahoma Times (Oklahoma City)
Oklahoma War Chief (Wichita)
Poteau (I.T.) Journal
Purcell (O.T.) Register
Purcell (O.T.) Tribune
Sallisaw (I.T.) Star
South McAlester (I.T.) Capital
St. Louis Post-Dispatch
Sumner County Standard (Wellington, KS)
Terre Haute Daily Express
Tillman County Chronicles (Frederick, OK)
Tishomingo (I.T.) Capitol-Democrat
Tishomingo (I.T.) News
Tulsa Daily World
Tulsa Democrat
Tulsa Tribune
Tulsa World
Vinita (I.T.) Daily Chieftain
Wagoner (I.T.) Record
Washington Post
Weleetka (I.T.) American
Wichita Beacon
Wichita Eagle

Oral History Interviews

Barnett, Nancy Grayson. Interview by Grace Kelley, November 11, 1937. Interview 12128, 395. Bryant, Oklahoma. Indian-Pioneer History Project for Oklahoma, Western History Collections, University of Oklahoma Libraries, Norman.

Conrad, George. Interview, n.d. In Kaye M. Teall, *Black History in Oklahoma: A Resource Book*, 114. Oklahoma City: Oklahoma City Public Schools, 1971.

Guess, George. Interview by Jeremiah Evarts, 1828. In *Missionary Herald* 24 (April 1828), 133–134.

Haskell, Francis. Interview by Nancy Defore, February 1, 1975, Oklahoma City, Oklahoma, Folder Charles Haskell/Francis, Oklahoma Territorial Museum and the Carnegie Library, Guthrie.

Haynes, Sam J. Interview by Effie S. Jackson, February 18, 1938, Interview 12992, 329, Okmulgee, Oklahoma, Indian-Pioneer Papers, Western History Collections, University of Oklahoma Libraries, Norman.

Secondary Sources

Books

Agnew, Brad. *Fort Gibson: Terminal on the Trail of Tears*. Norman: University of Oklahoma ress, 1980.

Allen, C. M. *The Sequoyah Convention*. Oklahoma City: Harlow Publishing Company, 1925.

Armstrong, J. A. *Nations Before Nationalism*. Chapel Hill: University of North Carolina Press, 1982.

Awiakta, Marilou. *Selu: Seeking the Corn-Mother's Wisdom*. Golden, CO: Fulcrum, 1993.

Baird, W. David, and Danney Goble. *The Story of Oklahoma*. Norman: University of Oklahoma Press, 1994.

Bass, Althea. *Cherokee Messenger*. Norman: University of Oklahoma Press, 1936.

Bealey, Frank. *The Blackwell Dictionary of Political Science*. Malden, MA: Blackwell, 1999.

Billington, Monroe Lee. *Thomas P. Gore: The Blind Senator from Oklahoma*. Lawrence: University of Kansas Press, 1967.

Blackman, Jon S. *Oklahoma's Indian New Deal*. Norman: University of Oklahoma Press, 2013.

Britten, Thomas A. *American Indians in World War I: At War and at Home*. Albuquerque: University of New Mexico Press, 1997.

Brown, Walter Lee. *A Life of Albert Pike*. Fayetteville: University of Arkansas Press, 1997.

Burton, Art T. *Black Gun, Silver Star: The Life and Legend of Frontier Marshal Bass Reeves*. Lincoln: University of Nebraska Press, 2006.

Burton, Jeffrey. *Indian Territory and the United States, 1866–1906: Courts, Government, and the Movement for Oklahoma Statehood*. Norman: University of Oklahoma Press, 1995.

Calloway, Colin G. *The Indian World of George Washington: The First President, the First Americans, and the Birth of the Nation*. New York: Oxford University Press, 2018.

Carleton, W. A. *Not Yours, but You.* Berkeley, CA: privately printed, c. 1954.

Carson, James Taylor. *Searching for the Bright Path: The Mississippi Choctaws from Prehistory to Removal.* Lincoln: University of Nebraska Press, 1999.

Carter, Kent. *The Dawes Commission and the Allotment of the Five Civilized Tribes, 1893–1914.* Orem, UT: Ancestry.com, 1999.

Carter, L. Edward. *The Story of Oklahoma Newspapers, 1844–1984.* Oklahoma City: Oklahoma Heritage Association, 1984.

Cassity, Michael, and Danney Goble. *Divided Hearts: The Presbyterian Journey through Oklahoma History.* Norman: University of Oklahoma Press, 2009.

Cave, Alfred A. *Sharp Knife: Andrew Jackson and the American Indians.* Santa Barbara: ABC-CLIO, 2017.

Chang, David A. *The Color of the Land: Race, Nation, and the Politics of Landownership in Oklahoma, 1832–1929.* Chapel Hill: University of North Carolina Press, 2010.

Chaudhuri, Jean, and Joyotpaul Chaudhuri, *A Sacred Path: The Way of the Muscogee Creeks.* Los Angeles: UCLA American Indian Studies Center, 2001.

Conley, Robert J. *The Cherokee Nation: A History.* Albuquerque: University of New Mexico Press, 2005.

Crockett, Norman. *The Black Towns.* Lawrence: Regents Press of Kansas, 1979.

D'Entreves, A. P. *The Notion of the State.* Oxford: Clarendon, 1967.

Drago, Harry. *Great American Cattle Trails: The Story of the Old Cow Paths of the East and the Longhorn Highways of the Plains.* New York: Dodd, Mead, 1965.

Debo, Angie. *The Rise and Fall of the Choctaw Republic.* Norman: University of Oklahoma Press, 1934.

Debo, Angie. *The Road to Disappearance: A History of the Creek Indians.* 1941. Reprint, Norman. University of Oklahoma Press, 1979.

Dunleavy, P., and B. O'Leary, *Theories of the State.* London. Macmillan, 1987.

Dyer, Thomas G. *Theodore Roosevelt and the Idea of Race.* Baton Rouge: Louisiana State University Press, 1980.

Ellis, Albert H. *A History of the Constitutional Convention of the State of Oklahoma.* Muskogee, OK: Economy Printing Company, 1923.

Ellisor, John T. *The Second Creek War: Interethnic Conflict and Collusion on a Collapsing Frontier.* Lincoln: University of Nebraska Press, 2010.

Fixico, Donald L. *Termination and Relocation: Federal Indian Policy, 1945–1960.* Albuquerque: University of New Mexico Press, 1986.

———. *The Invasion of Indian Country in the Twentieth Century: American Capitalism and Tribal Natural Resources.* Niwot: University Press of Colorado, 1998.

Fixico, Donald L., ed. *Indian Treaties in the United States: An Encyclopedia and Documents Collection.* Santa Barbara and Denver: ABC-CLIO, 2018.

Foreman, Grant. *Sequoyah.* Norman: University of Oklahoma Press, 1938.

Fowler, Oscar. *The Haskell Regime: The Intimate Life of Charles Nathaniel Haskell.* Oklahoma City: Boles, 1933.

Franklin, Jimmie Lewis. *Journey Toward Hope: A History of Blacks in Oklahoma*. Norman: University of Oklahoma Press, 1982.

Garrison, Tim Alan. *The Legal Ideology of Removal: The Southern Judiciary and the Sovereignty of Native American Nations*. Athens: University of Georgia Press, 2002.

Gillham, Nicholas Wright. *A Life of Sir Francis Galton: From African Exploration to the Birth of Eugenics*. Oxford: Oxford University Press, 2001.

Gittinger, Roy. *The Formation of the State of Oklahoma 1803–1906*. Norman: University of Oklahoma Press, 1939.

Glasrud, Bruce A., and Michael N. Searles. eds. *Buffalo Soldiers in the West: A Black Soldiers Anthology*. College Station: Texas A&M University Press, 2007.

Hagan, William T. *Taking Indian Lands: The Cherokee (Jerome) Commission 1889–1893*. Norman: University of Oklahoma Press, 2003.

Hagedorn, Herman. *Roosevelt in the Badlands*. Boston: Houghton Mifflin Company, 1921.

Harmon, S. W. *Hell on the Border: He Hanged Eighty-Eight Men*. Lincoln: University of Nebraska Press, 1992.

Herrick, James A. *The History and Theory of Rhetoric: An Introduction*. Boston: Pearson, 2009.

Hightower, Michael J. *1889: The Boomer Movement, the Land Run, and Early Oklahoma City*. Norman: University of Oklahoma Press, 2018.

Hill, Luther B. *A History of the State of Oklahoma*. Vol.1. Chicago: Lewis, 1910.

Hines, Gordon. *Alfalfa Bill: An Intimate Biography*. Oklahoma City: Oklahoma Press, 1931.

Hoig, Stan. *David L. Payne: The Oklahoma Boomer*. Oklahoma City: Western Heritage Books, 1980.

———. *The Oklahoma Land Rush of 1889*. Oklahoma City: Oklahoma Historical Society, 1984.

Horsman, Reginald. *Race and Manifest Destiny: The Origins of American Racial Anglo-Saxonism*. Cambridge, MA: Harvard University Press, 1981.

Hurst, Irvin. *The 46th Star: A History of Oklahoma's Constitutional Convention and Early Statehood*. Oklahoma City: Western Heritage Books, 1980.

Johnson, Hannibal B. *Acres of Aspiration: The All-Black Towns in Oklahoma*. Austin, TX: Eakin Press, 2007.

Johnson, Larry G. *Tar Creek: A History of the Quapaw Indians, the World's Largest Lead and Zinc Discovery, and the Tar Creek Superfund Site*. Mustang, OK: Tate, 2008.

Kehl, James A. *Boss Rule in the Gilded Age: Matt Quay of Pennsylvania*. Pittsburgh: University of Pittsburgh Press, 1981.

Keso, Edward Elmere. *The Senatorial Career of Robert Lathan Owen*. Gardenvale, Quebec: Garden City Press, 1938.

Krohn, William. *Alfalfa Bill Murray: Governor of Oklahoma*. Ardmore, OK: Krohn Oil Review, 1931.

Leckie, William H. *The Buffalo Soldiers: A Narrative of the Negro Cavalry in the West.* Norman: University of Oklahoma Press, 1967.

Littlefield, Daniel F., Jr.. *Africans and Creeks: From the Colonial Period to the Civil War.* Westport, CT: Greenwood Press, 1979.

———. *Seminole Burning: A Story of Racial Vengeance.* Jackson: University Press of Mississippi, 1996.

Lukacs, John. *Historical Consciousness: The Remembered Past.* 7th ed. New Brunswick, NJ: Transaction, 1994.

Lund, Brian. *Housing Politics in the United Kingdom.* Bristol: Bristol University Press, 2016.

Lynn-Sherow, Bonnie. *Red Earth: Race and Agriculture in Oklahoma Territory.* Lawrence: University Press of Kansas, 2004.

McBride, Lela J. *Opothleyahola and the Loyal Muskogee: Their Flight to Kansas in the Civil War.* Jefferson, NC: McFarland, 2000.

McReynolds, Edwin. *Oklahoma: A History of the Sooner State.* Norman: University of Oklahoma Press, 1954.

Mahon, John K. *History of the Second Seminole War.* Gainesville: University of Florida Press, 1967.

Mann, Barbara Alice, ed. *Native Speakers of the Eastern Woodlands: Selected Speeches and Critical Analyses.* Santa Barbara: ABC-CLIO, 2001.

Matthews, John Joseph. *Wah'Kon-Tah: The Osage and the White Man's Road.* Norman: University of Oklahoma Press, 1932.

Maxwell, Amos D. *The Sequoyah Constitutional Convention.* Boston: Meador, 1953.

Miles, Tyia. *Ties That Bind: The Story of an Afro-Cherokee Family in Slavery and Freedom.* Berkeley: University of California Press, 2006.

Miller, Robert J., and Robbie Ethridge. *A Promise Kept: The Muscogee (Creek) Nation and McGirt v. Oklahoma.* Norman: University of Oklahoma Press, 2023.

Miller, Worth Robert. *Oklahoma Populism: A History of the People's Party in the Oklahoma Territory.* Norman: University of Oklahoma Press, 1987.

Mooney, James. *Historical Sketch of the Cherokee.* Chicago: Aldine, 1975.

Moulton, Gary. *John Ross: Cherokee Chief.* Athens: University of Georgia Press, 1978.

Mulroy, Kevin. *The Seminole Freedmen: A History.* Norman: University of Oklahoma Press, 2007.

O'Beirne, H. F. *Leaders and Leading Men of the Indian Territory: With Interesting Biographical Sketches.* Chicago: American Publishers' Association, 1891.

Okmulgee Historical Society and the Heritage Society of America, eds. *History of Okmulgee County, Oklahoma.* Vol. 1. Tulsa: Historical Enterprises, 1985.

Patton, Fred J. *History of Fort Smith, Arkansas 1817–2003.* Hampton, VA: Prestige Press, 2003.

Painter, Nell Irvin. *Exodusters: Black Migration to Kansas After Reconstruction.* New York: Alfred A. Knopf, 1977. Reprint, New York: W. W. Norton, 1992.

Parins, James W. *Elias Cornelius Boudinot: A Life on the Cherokee Border.* Lincoln: University of Nebraska Press, 2006.

Pascoe, Peggy. *What Comes Naturally: Miscegenation Law and the Making of Race in America.* New York: Oxford University Press, 2009.

Pettigrew, Richard F. *The Course of Empire: An Official Record.* New York: Boni and Liveright, 1920.

———. *Triumphant Plutocracy: The Story of American Public Life from 1870 to 1920.* New York: Academy Press, 1922.

Rister, Carl Coke. *Land Hunger: David L. Payne and the Oklahoma Boomers.* Norman: University of Oklahoma Press, 1942.

Ritter, Harry. *Alaska's History: The People, Land, and Events of the North Country.* Berkeley: West Margin Press, 2020.

Roberts, Alaina E. *I've Been Here All the While: Black Freedom on Native Land.* Philadelphia: University of Pennsylvania Press, 2021.

Ross, Bob L. *Campbellism: Its History and Heresies.* Pasadena, TX: Pilgrim, 1976.

St. Jean, Wendy. *Remaining Chickasaw in Indian Territory, 1830s–1907.* Tuscaloosa: University of Alabama Press, 2011.

Schubert, Frank N. *Voices of the Buffalo Soldier: Records, Reports, and Recollections of the Military Life and Service in the West.* Albuquerque: University of New Mexico Press, 2003.

Schultz, George A. *An Indian Canaan: Isaac McCoy and the Vision of an Indian State.* Norman: University of Oklahoma Press, 1972.

Schultz, Jack M. *The Seminole Baptist Churches of Oklahoma: Maintaining a Traditional Community.* Norman: University of Oklahoma Press, 1999.

Smith, Tash. *Capture These Indians for the Lord: Indians, Methodists, and Oklahomans, 1844–1939.* 2nd ed. Tucson: University of Arizona Press, 2014.

Stampp, Kenneth M. *Indiana Politics During the Civil War.* Indianapolis: Indiana Historical Bureau, 1949.

Strickland, Rennard. *Fire and the Spirits: Cherokee Law from Clan to Court.* Norman: University of Oklahoma Press, 1975.

Tabrah, Ruth. *Hawaii: A History.* New York. W. W. Norton, 1984.

Taylor, Graham D. *The New Deal and American Indian Tribalism: The Administration of the Indian Reorganization Act, 1934–45.* Lincoln: University of Nebraska Press, 1980.

Thoburn, Joseph Bradfield, and Isaac Mason Holcomb, *A History of Oklahoma.* San Francisco: Doub & Company, 1908.

Thorne, Tanis C. *The World's' Richest Indian: The Scandal over Jackson Barnett's Oil Fortune.* New York: Oxford University Press, 2003.

Tuller, Roger H. *"Let No Guilty Man Escape": A Judicial Biography of "Hanging Judge" Isaac C. Parker.* Norman: University of Oklahoma Press, 2001.

Unrau, William E. *The Rise and Fall of Indian Country, 1825–1855.* Lawrence: University Press of Kansas, 2007.

Veracini, Lorenzo. *Settler Colonialism: A Theoretical Overview.* London: Palgrave, 2010.

Wallace, Anthony F. C. *Jefferson and the Indians: The Tragic Fate of the First Americans.* Cambridge, MA: Belknap Press of Harvard University Press, 1999.

Warde, Mary Jane. *George Washington Grayson and the Creek Nation, 1843–1920.* Norman: University of Oklahoma Press, 1999.

Wardell, Morris L. *A Political History of the Cherokee Nation, 1838–1907.* 1938. Reprint, Norman: University of Oklahoma Press, 1977.

Weeks, W. Dale. *Cherokee Civil Warrior: Chief John Ross and the Struggle for Tribal Sovereignty.* Norman: University of Oklahoma Press, 2023.

Williams, David. *Georgia Gold Rush: Twenty-Niners, Cherokees, and Gold Fever.* Columbia, SC: University of South Carolina Press, 1993.

Williams, John Alexander. *West Virginia: A History.* New York: W. W. Norton, 1976.

Williams, Samuel Cole., ed. *Adair's History of the American Indians.* New York: Promontory Press, 1930.

Wolfe, Patrick. *Settler Colonialism and the Transformation of Anthropology: The Politics and Poetics of an Ethnographic Event.* London: Cassell, 1999.

Woodward, Grace Steele. *The Cherokees.* Norman: University of Oklahoma Press, 1963.

Yarbrough, Fay A. *Race and the Cherokee Nation: Sovereignty in the Nineteenth Century.* Philadelphia: University of Pennsylvania Press, 2008.

Articles and Book Chapters

Applen, A. G. "An Attempted Indian State Government: The Okmulgee Constitution in Indian Territory, 1870–1876." *Kansas Quarterly* 3 (Fall 1971): 89–99.

Balyeat, Frank A. "Joseph Samuel Murrow, Apostle to the Indians." *Chronicles of Oklahoma* 35, no. 3 (Autumn 1957): 298–299.

Baird, W. David. "William A. Jones 1897–1904." In *The Commissioners of Indian Affairs, 1824–1977,* edited by Robert M. Kvasnicka and Herman J. Viola, 211–220. Lincoln: University of Nebraska Press, 1979.

Berthrong, Donald J. "Legacies of the Dawes Act: Bureaucrats and Land Thieves at the Cheyenne-Arapaho Agencies of Oklahoma." *Arizona and the West* 21, no. 4 (Winter 1979): 335–354.

Blumental, Claire. "'We Hold the Government to Its Word': How *McGirt v. Oklahoma* Revives Aboriginal Title." *Yale Law Journal* 131, no. 7 (May 2022): 2326–2386.

Blochowiak, Mary Ann. "'Justice is our Battle Cry': The Territorial Free Home League." *Chronicles of Oklahoma* 62, No. 1 (Spring 1984): 38–55.

Boudinot, E. C. "The Indian Territory and Its Inhabitants," *Journal of the American Geographical Society of New York* 5 (1874): 222–223.

Brightman, Robert A. and Pamela S. Wallace, "Chickasaw." In *Southeast,* 478–498. Vol. 14 of *Handbook of the North American Indians,* edited by Raymond Fogleson. Washington, DC: Smithsonian Institution, 2004.

Buck, Solon J. "The Settlement of Oklahoma." In *Transactions of the Wisconsin Academy of Sciences, Arts and Letters,* ed. Secretary, 325–380. Vol. 15, part 2. Madison. Democrat Printing Company, 1907.

Bullard, Clara Williamson Warren. "Pioneer Days in the Cherokee Strip." *Chronicles of Oklahoma* 36, no. 3 (Autumn 1958): 258–269.

Burrill, Robert M. "The Osage Pasture Map." *Chronicles of Oklahoma* 53, no. 2 (Summer 1975): 204–211.

Caywood, Elzie Ronald. "The Administration of William C. Rogers, Principal Chief of the Cherokee Nation 1903–1907." *Chronicles of Oklahoma* 30, no. 1 (Spring 1952): 29–37.

Clark, Blue. "Delegates to the Constitution Convention." *Chronicles of Oklahoma* 48, no. 4 (Winter 1970–71): 400–415.

———. "Opothleyahola and the Creeks During the Civil War." In *Indian Leaders: Oklahoma's First Statesmen,* edited by H. Glenn Jordan and Thomas M. Holm, 49–63. Oklahoma City: Oklahoma Historical Society, 1979.

Chapman, Berlin B. "Freedmen and the Oklahoma Lands." *Southwestern Social Science Quarterly* 29, no. 2 (September 1948): 150–159.

———. "The Land Run of 1893 as Seen at Kiowa." *Kansas Historical Quarterly* 31, no. 1 (Summer 1965): 67–75.

———. "Opening of the Cherokee Outlet: An Archival Study, Part I." *Chronicles of Oklahoma* 40, no. 2 (Summer 1962): 158–181.

———. "The Legal Sooners of 1889." *Chronicles of Oklahoma* 35, no. 4 (Winter 1957–58): 382–415.

Colbert, Thomas Burnell. "James B. Weaver, Kansas, and the Oklahoma Lands, 1884–1890." *Kansas History* 31, no. 3 (Autumn 2008): 176–193.

Dann, Martin. "From Sodom to the Promised Land: E. P. McCabe and the Movement for Oklahoma Colonization." *Kansas History* 40, no. 3 (Autumn 1974): 370–378.

Davis, John B. "The Life and Work of Sequoyah." *Chronicles of Oklahoma* 8, no. 2 (June 1930): 149–180.

Deer, Sarah, and Cecilia Knapp. "Muscogee Constitutional Jurisprudence: Vhakv Em Pvtakv (The Carpet Under the Law)." *Tulsa Law Review* 49, no. 1 (2013): 125–181.

Doran, Michael F. "Population Statistics of Nineteenth-Century Indian Territory," *Chronicles of Oklahoma* 53, no. 4 (Winter 1975–76): 492–515.

Doyle, Thomas H. "The Supreme Court of the Territory of Oklahoma," *Chronicles of Oklahoma* 13, no. 2 (June 1935): 214–218.

DuChateau, Andre Paul. "Creek Nation on the Eve of the Civil War." *Chronicles of Oklahoma* 52, no. 3 (Fall 1974): 290–315.

Durham, A. W. "Oklahoma City Before the Run of 1889," *Chronicles of Oklahoma* 36, no. 1 (Spring, 1958): 72–78.

Ellinger, Charles Wayne. "The Drive for Statehood in Oklahoma, 1889–1906." *Chronicles of Oklahoma* 41, no. 1 (Spring 1963): 15–37.

Fisher, LeRoy H. "Oklahoma Territory, 1899–1907," *Chronicles of Oklahoma* 53, no. 1 (Spring 1975): 3–8.

Fixico, Donald. "The Muscogee Creeks: A Nativistic People." In *Between Two Worlds: The Survival of Twentieth-Century Indians*, edited by Arrell Morgan Gibson, 30–43. Oklahoma City: Oklahoma Historical Society, 1986.

Foreman, Grant. "Oklahoma and Indian Territory," *The Outlook* 82, no. 10 (1906): 550–552.

Frank, Andrew K. "The Rise and Fall of William McIntosh: Authority and Identity on the Early American Frontier." *Georgia Historical Quarterly* 86, no. 1 (Spring 2002): 18–48.

Franks, Kenny A. "An Analysis of the Confederate Treaties with the Five Civilized Tribes." *Chronicles of Oklahoma* 51, no. 4 (Winter 1972): 458–473.

———. "The Implementation of the Confederate Treaties with the Five Civilized Tribes." *Chronicles of Oklahoma* 51, no. 1 (Spring 1973): 21–33.

Freeman, Charles R. "The Battle of Honey Springs." *Chronicles of Oklahoma* 13, no. 2 (June 1935): 154–168.

Galloway, Patricia and, Clara Sue Kidwell. "Choctaw in the East." In Fogleson, *Handbook of the North American Indians*, 14: 499–519. Washington: Smithsonian Institution, 2004.

George, Preston and Sylvan R. Wood. "The Railroads of Oklahoma." *Railway and Locomotive Historical Society Bulletin* 60 (January 1943): 7.

Gibson, Arrell Morgan. "Oklahoma: Land of the Drifter Deterrents to Sense of Place." *Chronicles of Oklahoma* 64, no. 2 (Summer 1986): 5–13.

Giezentanner, Veda. "In Dugouts and Sod Houses." *Chronicles of Oklahoma* 39, no. 2 (Summer 1961): 140–149.

Goodrum, Adam. "Meeting the *McGirt* Moment: The Five Tribes, Sovereignty & Criminal Jurisdiction in Oklahoma's New Indian Country." *American Indian Law Review* 46, no. 1 (2021–22): 201–237.

Hastings, James K. "The Opening of Oklahoma." *Chronicles of Oklahoma* 27, no. 1 (Spring, 1949): 70–88.

Hayostek, Cindy. "Douglas Delegates to the 1910 Constitution Convention and Arizona's Progressive Heritage." *Journal of Arizona History* 47, no. 4 (2006): 347–366.

Hoig, Stan. "Carpenter, Charles C." In *The Encyclopedia of Oklahoma History and Culture*, edited by Dianna Everett, 223–224. Vol. 1. Oklahoma City: Oklahoma Historical Society, 2009.

Jordan, Pamela G. "Edward W. Sweeney, '89er: 'A Legend in His Time.'" *Chronicles of Oklahoma* 76, no. 3 (Fall 1998): 318–335.

Kinchen, Oscar A. "The Abortive Territory of Cimarron." *Chronicles of Oklahoma* 23, no. 3 (Autumn 1945): 218–231.

LoConto, David G. "Discrimination Against and Adaptation of Italians in the Coal Counties of Oklahoma." *Great Plains Quarterly* 24, no. 4 (Fall 2004): 249–261.

Logsdon, Guy. "Oklahoma's First Book: Istutsi in Naktsoku." *Chronicles of Oklahoma* 54, no. 2 (Summer 1976): 179–191.

McNeil, Kinneth. "Confederate Treaties with the Tribes of Indian Territory." *Chronicles of Oklahoma* 42, no. 4 (Winter 1964–65): 408–420.

Marble, A. D. "Oklahoma Boomers' Trials and Troubles," *Sturm's Oklahoma Magazine,* July 1908.

Marsh, Ralph. "Crazy Snake's Rebellion: How Chitto Harjo, Lived, and Died, By a Treaty's Promise." *Oklahoma Today,* May–June 1992: 31.

Maxwell, Amos D. "The Sequoyah Convention." *Chronicles of Oklahoma* 28, no. 2 (Summer 1950): 161–192.

Mellinger, Phillip. "Discrimination and Statehood in Oklahoma." *Chronicles of Oklahoma* 49, no. 3 (Autumn 1971): 340–378.

Meserve, John B. "Chief Pleasant Porter." *Chronicles of Oklahoma* 9, no. 3 (September 1931): 316–334.

Meyer, Roy W. "Ezra A. Hayt, 1877–80." In Kvasnicka and Viola, *Commissioners of Indian Affairs,* 155–166.

Miller, Robert J., and Torey Dolan, "The Indian Law Bombshell: *McGirt v. Oklahoma." Boston University Law Review* 101, no. 6 (2021): 2049–2104.

Morris, A. Suman. "Captain David L. Payne: The Cimarron Scout," *Chronicles of Oklahoma* 42, no. 1 (Spring 1964): 7–26.

Morrison, James D. "The Union Pacific, Southern Branch." *Chronicles of Oklahoma* 14, no. 2 (June 1936): 173–187.

Murray, William H. "The Constitutional Convention." *Chronicles of Oklahoma* 9, no. 2 (June 1931): 126–138.

Nesbit, Paul. "Haskell Tells of Two Conventions." *Chronicles of Oklahoma* 14, no. 2 (June 1936): 189–217.

Nolen, C. L. "The Okmulgee Constitution: A Step Towards Indian Self-Determination." *Chronicles of Oklahoma* 58, no. 3 (Fall 1980): 264–281.

"Okmulgee Constitution." *Chronicles of Oklahoma* 3, no. 3 (September 1925): 216–228.

Peery, Dan W. "Colonel Crocker and the Boomer Movement." *Chronicles of Oklahoma* 13, no. 3 (September 1935): 273–296.

Rister, Carl Coke. "Free Land Hunters of the Southern Plains." *Chronicles of Oklahoma* 22, no. 4 (Winter 1944–45): 392–401.

Roberson, Jere W. "Edward P. McCabe and the Langston Experiment." *Chronicles of Oklahoma* 51, no. 3 (Fall 1973): 343–355.

Ross, Allen. "The Murder of Elias Boudinot." Edited by Grant Foreman. *Chronicles of Oklahoma* 12, no. 1 (March 1934): 19–25.

St. Jean, Wendy St. "'You Have the Land, I Have the Cattle': Intermarried Whites and the Chickasaw Range Lands." *Chronicles of Oklahoma* 78, no. 2 (Summer 2000): 182–195.

Shirk, George H. "First Post Offices within the Boundaries of Oklahoma." *Chronicles of Oklahoma* 30, no. 1 (Spring 1952): 38–104.

Shoemaker, Arthur. "The Battle of Chustenahlah." *Chronicles of Oklahoma* 38, no. 2 (Summer 1960): 180–184.

Smallwood, James M. "Segregation," In Everett, *Encyclopedia of Oklahoma History and Culture,* 2: 1344–1346.

Steacy, Stephen. "The Chickasaw Nation on the Eve of the Civil War." *Chronicles of Oklahoma* 49, no. 1 (Spring 1971): 51–74.

Stiles, George W. "Early Days in the Sac and Fox Country." *Chronicles of Oklahoma* 33, no. 3 (Autumn 1955): 316–338.

Sturm, Circe. "Blood Politics, Racial Classification, and Cherokee National Identity: The Trials and Tribulations of the Cherokee Freedmen." *American Indian Quarterly* 22, nos. 1 and 2 (Winter–Spring 1998): 230–258.

Sturtevant, William C. and Jessica. R. Cattlelino, "Florida Seminole and Miccosukee." In Fogleson, *Handbook of the North American Indians,* 14:429–449.

Swartz, Orvoe. "A Pioneer's Sod House Memories." *Chronicles of Oklahoma* 41, no. 4 (Winter 1963–64): 408–424.

Trickett, Dean. "The Civil War in Indian Territory 1862 (Continued)." *Chronicles of Oklahoma* 19, no. 4 (December 1941): 381–396.

Unrau, William E. "Charles Curtis/Kaw." In *The New Warriors: Native American Leaders since 1900,* edited by R. David Edmunds, 17–34. Lincoln: University of Nebraska Press, 2004.

Warde, Mary Jane. "Fight for Survival: The Indian Response to the Boomer Movement." *Chronicles of Oklahoma* 67, no. 1 (Spring 1989): 30–51.

Wardell, Morris L. "The History of No-Man's-Land, or Old Beaver County." *Chronicles of Oklahoma* 35, no. 3 (Spring 1957): 11–34.

Westmoreland, Ingrid P. "Inter-Tribal Council of the Five Civilized Tribes." In Everett, *Encyclopedia of Oklahoma History and Culture,* 1:741–742.

Williams, Nudie Eugene. "Oklahoma: Genesis and Tradition of the Black Press, 1889–1980." In *The Black Press in the Middle West, 1865–1985,* edited by Henry Lewis Suggs, 267–295. Westport, CT: Greenwood Press, 1996.

Wilson, T. Paul. "Confederate Delegates of the Five Civilized Tribes." *Chronicles of Oklahoma* 53, no. 3 (Fall 1975): 354–356.

Wilson, Walt. "Freedmen in Indian Territory During Reconstruction." *Chronicles of Oklahoma* 49, no. 2 (Summer 1971): 234–235.

Wolfe, Patrick. "Settler Colonialism and the Elimination of the Native." *Journal of Genocidal Research,* 8, no. 4 (2006): 387–409.

Wright, Muriel H. "General Douglas H. Cooper, C.S.A." *Chronicles of Oklahoma* 32, no. 2 (Summer 1954): 142–184.

Wright, Muriel H. "The Wedding of Oklahoma and Miss Indian Territory." *Chronicles of Oklahoma* 35, no. 3 (Fall 1957): 255–264.

Dissertations and Theses

Hurt, Douglas A. "The Shaping of a Creek (Muscogee) Homeland in Indian Territory, 1828–1907." PhD diss., University of Oklahoma, 2000.
Stuckey, Melissa Nicole. "All Men Up: Race, Rights, and Power in the All-Black Town of Boley, Oklahoma, 1903–1939." PhD diss., Yale University, 2009.
Washington, Nathaniel J. "The Historical Development of the Negro in Oklahoma." Master's thesis, University of Arizona, 1947.
White, Jerran Burris. "The Missionary Work of Samuel A. Worcester Among the Cherokee: 1825–1840." Master's thesis, North Texas State University, 1970.

Online Sources

"About Us." *Cherokee Phoenix*, https://www.cherokeephoenix.org/site/about.html, accessed April 28, 2022.
Arthur, Chester A. "July 1, 1884: Message Regarding Settlement on Indian Territory." Transcript. University of Virginia Miller Center, https://millercenter.org/the -presidency/presidential-speeches/july-1-1884-message-regarding-settlement-indian -territory, accessed June 12, 2020.
Candell, Harry B. "A Brief Refuge History." Wichita Mountains Wildlife Refuge, US Fish and Wildlife Service, https://www.fws.gov/refuge/Wichita_Mountains/about /history.html, accessed June 11, 2020.
Cook, Kevin L. "Oklahoma's Land Lottery: The Last Great Opening." *HistoryNet*, https://www.historynet.com/oklahomas-land-lottery-last-great-opening.htm, accessed December 24, 2019.
"Inter-Tribal Council of the Five Civilized Tribes," https://www.fivecivilizedtribes.org, accessed July 17, 2023.
Simpson, Linda. "Seminole Light Horse Police." August 2, 2015. *Seminole Nation, I.T.*, http://www.seminolenation-indianterritory.org/lighthorse.htm, accessed April 19, 2022.

Index